This journal belongs to

....

Date

....

A Promise of Peace

I will listen to what God the LORD says; he promises peace to his people, his faithful servants—but let them not turn to folly.

PSALM 85:8 NIV

Whenever I am full of unrest, feeling anxious and chaotic, I am almost certain I'm failing to listen to God. Why? Because He "promises peace to His people."

Even when we read about God judging wickedness in the Bible, we recognize that He is a God of peace. In Romans 16:20 (NIV) we read, "The God of peace will soon crush Satan under your feet." At first glance that seems like a dichotomy. How can He be a God of peace while He is crushing Satan? But if He is indeed a God of peace, then of course He would crush the one whose goal it is to shatter peace on earth (and in you). So, my job is to actually believe what He says—that He wants me to have peace.

That means that if I am feeling anxious about my circumstances, then my anxiety is not from God. It is either from my own circular thinking or from the pit of hell.

No matter what happens today, know that God is with you and that He intends good for you.

Father, fill me with Your peace that I can only comprehend with Your help.

January 2

Let There Be Light

Then God said, "Let there be light"; and there was light.

Genesis 1:3 NASB

Photosynthesis is a combination of two Greek words: *photo*, "light," and *synthesis*, "putting together, composition." It is the process by which plants use light and water to produce their own food and energy. This "cellular respiration" is a matter of survival not only for plants but also for all the organisms that breathe the oxygen they create—and it's sunlight that triggers this process. The process of photosynthesis is so essential to life on this planet that the presence of light is indeed a matter of survival.

Yet light itself remains something of a mystery. Is light a wave? Is light comprised of particles? Scientists aren't in agreement, but the very existence of mysterious light argues convincingly for the existence of an omnipotent creative power with astonishing wisdom and forethought. Specifically, all life on earth depends on the power of light that burst forth from the imagination of God.

The God of wonders spoke into existence what had never before been: glorious light. And His eternal design requires all creation to need this brilliant, life-giving light even as its mysterious existence invites human beings to see the Creator of that light. The world around us truly reflects God's amazing power and sings the glory of His name.

Dear God, all creation extols Your majesty, Your power, and Your glory.

The Supreme God

I am God, the only God there is. I form light and create darkness, I make harmonies and create discords. I, God, do all these things.

Isaiah 45:7 MSG

Light and darkness were recurring themes in ancient empires, especially during Isaiah's ministry when Cyrus the Great ruled a vast, two-thousand-mile empire and the Magian religion prevailed. The Persian Magi deemed Light and Darkness to be two, co-eternal but independent supreme beings that always acted in opposition to each other. When Light was in charge, men were happy and good. When Darkness got the upper hand, then all was misery and evil.

During Cyrus's thirty-year reign, Isaiah rose up and declared the Lord God to be sovereign, counter to the prevailing notions of the time. Through His prophet, God said, "*I* am the Lord. *I* form the light. *I* make darkness." This was a bold proclamation, and Cyrus didn't even try and silence it. He went so far as to permit Jerusalem to be rebuilt in God's name.

The Lord still declares His sovereignty over darkness with light—His light of truth, the light of grace, the light of guidance, the light of joy and comfort, the light of eternal glory and happiness. All of it from the supreme and omnipotent God, who *is* light.

Father of Lights, thank You for dispelling our darkness.

The Grand Tour

God's glory is on tour in the skies, God-craft on exhibit across the horizon. Madame Day holds classes every morning, Professor Night lectures each evening.

Psalm 19:1–2 MSG

The experience was known as the Grand Tour. Although it began in the sixteenth century, it was most popular in the seventeenth and eighteenth centuries. The young British elites of the day would spend two or three years traveling around Europe, broadening their cultural horizons. The purpose was to learn about language, architecture, geography, and art. The glory of the humanities was on display throughout Europe for the privileged to enjoy and absorb.

An even grander tour is available for everyone, regardless of class or status or era: it's the Grand Tour of God's awe-inspiring creation. As Psalm 19 proclaims, we can learn much by being students of God's amazing handiwork by considering the galactic proportions of His crafting, His attention to microscopic detail, and everything in between. His wonders are on breathtaking display. When was the last time you stopped to notice?

The wonders of creation shout Your glory, O God. Help me to do the same.

January 5

Father Knows Best

He makes grass grow for the cattle, and plants for people to cultivate—
bringing forth food from the earth.
Psalm 104:14 NIV

Even city slickers may not be surprised to read that cows are happiest and healthiest when they are grazing. The reason is quite simple: the roughage provided by the grass they eat increases the production of saliva, which helps neutralize the acids that exist naturally in their digestive systems. A grass-munching cow is a happy cow. And that is by design. God's design.

God's intricate design for life—a design that includes ecosystems and food chains and weather and the orbit of planets and the miracle of a baby—is absolutely perfect. There is nothing random about it. The Master Designer and Creator has left nothing to chance in creation: He sustains the creation He delights in—and when we, as His appointed caretakers on this planet, allow His design to operate as He intended, it is for the betterment of all His creatures.

The Lord of all Creation has left no detail untended. He is the Architect of all creation, and He—our heavenly Father—always knows best.

Father, You know best. Your marvelous designs cannot be improved upon.

Ain't No Mountain High Enough

Every valley shall be raised up, every mountain and hill made low; the rough ground shall become level, the rugged places a plain. And the glory of the Lord will be revealed, and all people will see it together. For the mouth of the Lord has spoken.

Isaiah 40:4–5 NIV

When a king in the ancient world was to make a royal visit to another city, road workers were sent in advance of his visit. That the king travel on level, straight roads was required, so potholes would have been filled. Rough surfaces would have been smoothed. His way would have been prepared by the removal of any obstacles.

The design of creation is to bring God and His people into close relationship. There are all sorts of obstacles that can hinder the unity that God desires to have with each of us, but the original hindrance is our sin. And yet, God's love is a love in action. It's a love that will not be denied.

He was willing to prepare the way by sending His Son, Jesus, into the world—and now there is nothing that can keep us from the wonder and power of God's love except unbelief. Every mountain that blocks and every valley that is too deep will be turned into a smooth plain, and His glory will be made obvious—the glory of a God who is powerful enough to remove every obstacle between us and Him.

You have spoken it, powerful Lord. Thank You for making the way clear between You and me.

Master Potter

Yet, O Lord, you are our Father. We are the clay, you are the potter;
we are all the work of your hand.

Isaiah 64:8 niv

When God created Adam, He shaped a human form from the clay of the earth. In the original Hebrew the word "clay" means "to boil up, to be fervent, to glow." God wasn't working with some dead lump of earth. Instead, it held the potential for life and was ready to be fashioned into something expectant and keen to be alive. It just needed the touch of the Master Potter.

All of creation reflects the fingerprints of God and exudes the divine energy of this amazing Creator. God made something—God made *everything*—from nothing and breathed life into it: He is responsible for Creation's very existence, from its light-from-darkness beginning until the end of time.

Moses recognized this truth, as evidenced in his wonderful song at the end of his life: "Is he not your Father, your Creator, who made you and formed you?" Like Isaiah, Moses directs our attention to the Creator, our Source, our Originator.

Should we ever think the world revolves around us, these words draw our focus back to our Father, the Master Designer of the universe.

O Lord. we marvel at the work of Your hands and submit our lives to You.

The Weight of Glory

I am the L*ORD; that is my name! I will not give my glory to anyone else, nor share my praise with carved idols.*

ISAIAH 42:8 NLT

The Old Testament speaks of God's glory approximately two hundred times. This word has always communicated beauty, majesty, and high standing. *Kabod*, the Hebrew word for "glory," carries with it the idea of being heavy or weighty. Remember the story of Phinehas' wife in the Old Testament? She was in despair and named her child Ichabod, that is, "no glory."

Our King of kings will not share His glory. In the first place, nothing can bear the weight of His majesty, beauty, and reputation. He is the only one who can do what He does. He is the Lord! And He wants us to know this. Why? Because putting our hope in anything or anyone other than Him would lead us to despair. Hoping in anything other than God is hoping in less than God—and only He can do what needs to be done in the lives and hearts of His people.

So God makes it known with crystal clarity: He is the Lord, and He alone carries the weight of His glory. Consider all that God holds together by His mighty hand. Be amazed at His glory, and grateful that He doesn't share that glory with something that would fail us.

You alone deserve my praise. You are the LORD of all!

He Said So

The nations around you that are still in existence will realize that I, God, rebuild ruins and replant empty waste places. I, God, said so, and I'll do it.

Ezekiel 36:36 msg

Most parents swear they'll never say it, but given the right amount of stress coupled with a young child asking why for the fifteenth time in as many seconds, and parents will fall back on a line they heard as a child: "Because I said so." At that point, the time for dialogue and explanation is over. It's time for the child to behave according to Mom's or Dad's wishes.

The situation is a little different in Ezekiel 36. God is not asking anyone to do anything. Rather, it is God who does something; He rebuilds and replants wastelands. And why does He do it? Because He said so. Whatever He says He will do, He does.

God fulfills His promises. No matter how enormous the task or unimaginable the goal, no matter what circumstances arise or obstacles may seem to stand in the way, God will make things happen. Whenever God gives His word, the deed is as good as done.

You can almost hear the exchange as one of the faithful asks, "Why are You doing this, Lord?" His response is unmistakable: "Because I said so. That's why."

Your commitment to Your promises is my strength. Thank You for upholding Your word.

The Big and the Small

Bless our God, O peoples, and sound His praise abroad, who keeps us in life and does not allow our feet to slip.

Psalm 66:8–9 NASB

Thomas à Kempis said, "If you remember the dignity of the Giver, no gift will seem small or mean, for nothing can be valueless that is given by the most high God." These "small" gifts are much more frequent than the obvious miracles in our lives, but every bit as miraculous.

When God comes through in a big way, it's easy to recognize it and give Him praise. The miraculous moments in life grab our attention and bring us to a place of gratitude and worship.

But lost in the great miracles sometimes are the smaller wonders. Think about it: the writer of Psalm 66 had earlier praised God for parting the waters of the Red Sea, and then he praised God for keeping the people's feet from slipping. Both were the Lord's wonderful work.

It's easy for us to thank God for the big miracles. But what about those smaller things? Stop and pay attention to the details of your life today. Our amazing God is to be praised for *all* His perfect gifts!

I don't want to forget to say thank You for every blessing—open my eyes to the praiseworthy things I have overlooked.

King of the Kings

The next morning King Darius got up at dawn and hurried to the lions' den. As he came near the den, he was worried. He called out to Daniel, "Daniel, servant of the living God! Has your God that you always worship been able to save you from the lions?" Daniel answered, "O king, live forever! My God sent his angel to close the lions' mouths. They have not hurt me, because my God knows I am innocent. I never did anything wrong to you, O king."

DANIEL 6:19–22 NCV

Throughout human history, the undisputed king of the jungle has been the lion. This great cat's strenth, weight, and length make it a beast that lives largely unchallenged. It was into a den of such power that Daniel was thrown. And it was in exactly such a den that the power of the King of the king of the jungle was on display for all to see.

God's saving power kept Daniel from certain death; in fact, the faithful servant wasn't even harmed. Furthermore, King Darius learned that day of the One greater than any earthly king, including himself. Our God—the King of *all* the kings—is mighty to save.

What a blessing to know You are mighty to save!

The Way through the Desert

Be alert, be present! I'm about to do something brand-new. It's bursting out! Don't you see it? There it is! I'm making a road through the desert, rivers in the badlands.

Isaiah 43:19 MSG

"You should not see the desert simply as some faraway place of little rain," said journalist William Langewiesche. "There are many forms of thirst."

The Tibetan Plateau, the Antarctic, the Sahara, the North Slope of Alaska's Brooks Range, Death Valley—all deserts. All lands with incredibly rough terrain, eroded by wind and water, difficult to navigate, too harsh and potentially deadly for life to thrive.

Grounds for divorce, hospital surroundings after a grim diagnosis, a hostile work environment, family atmosphere strained to the breaking point—all parched, uninhabitable places where our endlessly faithful God promises to make a road. A road where, in His compassion, He can walk with and comfort His people on their way *through.*

He creates the road to show His wondrous love, to demonstrate His power in affliction, to introduce the miracle of the gospel. And then He adds a river…to refresh, to revive. He bursts through with fresh mercies like the coldest, clearest water in the thirstiest of times.

So watch for Him. Count on Him. Be ready. And then praise His glorious name.

Lord God, Your faithfulness is unshakable. Remind me to look for Your road when I'm stuck in the desert.

Everyday Gifts

If you, then, though you are evil, know how to give good gifts to your children, how much more will your Father in heaven give good gifts to those who ask him!

MATTHEW 7:11 NIV

Everyone loves a good birthday party. Some say the birthday party finds its origins among European royalty long ago. According to legend, during this time some people believed that evil spirits would seek out members of royalty and haunt them on their birthday. In response, friends and family would gather together with their royal loved one in hopes of preventing the evil spirit from coming near. In time, these superstitious beliefs diminished, the gatherings morphed into times of celebration, and the custom was adopted by commoners as well. Birthday parties eventually included things such as cakes and gift giving.

To have friends and family celebrate your life by giving you gifts is a special thing. This demonstrates that they love you and are mindful of you. The Bible says that God is a gift-giving God. In addition to the ultimate gift of His Son, God blesses us with everyday kinds of gifts: food, shelter, friends. But more than that, He gives us joy, peace, and grace. He knows the perfect gifts for us—and He gives them. Every gift we have is a tangible reminder that we have a marvelous God who is ever mindful of us.

Lord, as I consider all the wonderful gifts You have given me, it reminds me of how remarkably loving You are.

Precious in His Sight

Whoever welcomes one of these little children in my name welcomes me; and whoever welcomes me does not welcome me but the one who sent me.

Mark 9:37 NIV

During the American Civil War, composer George F. Root wrote a tune for the war song "Tramp, Tramp, Tramp." Later, one of Root's favorite lyricists, C. Herbert Woolston, would provide these lyrics for the wartime melody:

Jesus calls the children dear,
"Come to me and never fear,
For I love the little children of the world."

The refrain to Woolston's song has become a song unto itself, often sung by children. We know it simply as "Jesus Loves the Little Children."

Woolston was right; Jesus does indeed love all the children of the world. On more than one occasion, Jesus would bring children to His side to illustrate what He was teaching at the time. If someone tried to turn those little ones away, that person would be greeted with a firm rebuke. Why? Because Jesus loves the little children.

Here is a wonderful thought to consider: God refers to those who believe in Him as His children. With eyes of affection and tender hands of mercy, God welcomes us as His very own. What a wonderful Father!

To be called Your child is overwhelming! Your lovingkindness compels me to honor You.

Heavenly Shepherd

Do not be afraid, little flock, for your Father has been pleased to give you the kingdom.

LUKE 12:32 NIV

Early on in human history, sheep became valued for their ability to provide milk, meat, and wool. However, maintaining large flocks of these prized animals required moving them from pasture to pasture. The average farmer did not possess this skill, so shepherding developed as a separate occupation. As shepherding skills advanced in certain parts of the world, milk, wool, and meat became more accessible and affordable. Were it not for shepherds, the flocks of sheep would never survive their many predators. And if the sheep did not survive, the people in need of the sheep's resources would suffer loss.

Our heavenly Father speaks of Himself as a shepherd to His people. He is, in fact, the Good Shepherd. Because we have the ultimate shepherd watching over us, we do not have to fear. Our enemy will never devour us. And because we have the Good Shepherd guiding us, we know that our existence will not be in vain. God makes us useful to the world and for His kingdom. What a wonderful God who would lovingly tend to us as His very own sheep!

God, You watch over me like a shepherd over his sheep. The God of the universe is my Good Shepherd!

The Knowable God

I have made your very being known to them—who you are and what you do—and continue to make it known, so that your love for me might be in them exactly as I am in them.

John 17:26 msg

The early Romans believed that everything in nature was inhabited by *numina*; that is, spiritual forces. In other words, they believed that gods and spirits inhabit places, objects, and living things too. This probably explains why there were so many Roman gods: there was a different one inhabiting every separate thing in their world.

Into this cacophony of unknowable gods came the revolutionary, world-changing message of Jesus: there is one God, and He can be known.

Jesus came to show us God. The love between Father and Son has been transferred to us through the miraculous power of God. It is *in* us—in our souls and spirits. Somehow God has made it possible. May His name be praised.

Jesus, we know that Your life demonstrated who God is and what He can do. Praise You for showing us the Father.

An Invited Friend

And I will ask the Father, and he will give you another advocate to help you and be with you forever—the Spirit of truth. The world cannot accept him, because it neither sees him nor knows him. But you know him, for he lives with you and will be in you.

John 14:16–17 NIV

In elementary school we learn about these things called "compound words." A compound word is two words put together to create a single word with a new and specific meaning, such as *doghouse*, *warlord*, and *bagpipes*.

The Greek word that we translate "advocate" is a compound word (*parakletos*). Made up of the Greek words *para* ("beside") and *cletos* ("called" or "invited"), it is used to describe the work of the One sent to be with us and help us, the Holy Spirit. He is invited to stay beside us. He is there to prompt us to action and lead us to right decisions. And best of all, we know His voice for He lives in us.

Just for God's children, there is a Friend to help. What an amazing gift from the Father!

Dearest God, You are wonderful to me. You have provided an Advocate to dwell in me. I cannot help but worship You.

Follow the Leader

Every person is to be in subjection to the governing authorities.
For there is no authority except from God, and those which exist are established by God.

Romans 13:1 NASB

From Augustus (the first emperor) to the division of the empire into eastern and western empires in AD 395, there were 147 Roman emperors. In England there have been sixty-nine monarchs, if you count the three who were disputed and the Cromwells and Henry the Young King. Americans have elected forty-four presidents. Each leader has had his or her own plans and ideas about what to do and when to do it. Some of those agendas have been fulfilled, but many others have not.

Behind every leader in every nation and in all the world since the beginning of time stands the One True God. It is only by His authority that they were ever permitted to lead in the first place. Kings and rulers come and go like the seasons, but God's Word stands forever. His designs about what to do and when to do it will be fulfilled according to His perfect plan. He reigns over the affairs of men as the Lord of lords, our Judge, and our King.

You are the righteous authority above all earthly leaders, and Your plans will be fulfilled.

God's Classified Ad

Isn't it obvious that God deliberately chose men and women that the culture overlooks and exploits and abuses, chose these "nobodies" to expose the hollow pretensions of the "somebodies"?

1 Corinthians 1:27 MSG

Imagine God's classified ad: "Seeking uneducated, reckless, addicted, broken, downcast applicants to promote a worthy cause. Those with prison and bankruptcy records preferred. Education, wealth, and social connections not helpful."

You know who could apply? Samson. Jeremiah. D. L. Moody. Chuck Colson. These men had no reason to brag when they were called to God's purpose. And since the eternal, all-powerful, sovereign Lord will not, *should not* share His glory with anyone, He seeks those who will humbly deliver His message of grace and peace.

God knows that simple faith becomes harder to embrace when coupled with privilege, sophistication, power, and academic knowledge. For His work to be accomplished in His people's lives, they must first acknowledge their need. Then their chains will be broken.

God called Noah, a quiet, diligent farmer, to build an ark on dry land. He called Rahab, a fearful prostitute living along the city wall, to save Joshua's spies. Jesus called Peter, a brash, impulsive fisherman, to follow Him. Each of them met God's qualifications: ordinary people who did extraordinary things for their faithful God…all to His glory.

I will follow Your call, gracious God. You are the Deliverer of the oppressed and the Redeemer of the lost.

New Creature in Christ

Therefore if any man be in Christ, he is a new creature:
old things are passed away; behold, all things are become new.
2 Corinthians 5:17 KJV

Forrest Gump said many wonderful things, but "My Mama always said you've got to put the past behind you before you can move on" has particular resonance regarding new beginnings.

We've all seen those before-and-after pictures: the "before" picture of the forlorn, ninety-pound weakling; the "after" picture of a smiling Mr. Universe. It looks so easy in all those advertisements for millions of products and procedures. We somehow think a nip here and a tuck there is going to make us all new creatures. At best, it's a temporary fix on a used model.

"New creature" does not mean putting on a fresh coat of paint or putting a used part in a broken appliance. It means *a completely new creation*. The beauty of our "after" picture is glorious and eternal. Think of God creating order from chaos. And what was His opinion of His work? It was good. Through the redemptive work of Jesus Christ, God has done the same with us. Perhaps this is the most wondrous part of the Father's nature: He can make all things new!

We praise You, O God, for making us new creations through the atoning sacrifice of Your Son.

Heaven's Artwork

And God raised us up with Christ and seated us with him in the heavenly realms in Christ Jesus, in order that in the coming ages he might show the incomparable riches of his grace, expressed in his kindness to us in Christ Jesus.

Ephesians 2:6–7 niv

When a woman ponders Degas' ballerinas in oil, when a man circles Rodin's *Thinker* in marble and bronze, when schoolchildren gawk at Ebbet's photo of construction workers in *Lunch atop a Skyscraper*, the question is rarely "Who are they? Who is that thinker? Who are those ballerinas, those workers?" It is usually, "Who created that?" The craftsmanship of these famous works of art is so skillful, so perfect, that the focus is on the artist rather than the subject.

Such is the work your wonderfully creative God has done in you.

We see the craftsmanship of his work *now* in His unspeakable mercy, His extraordinary kindness in redemption, painted in His likeness, framed in Jesus. He will reveal more splendor *then,* when He seats you within His heavenly realm, carved into perfection through His matchless grace.

It will be magnificent. Breathtaking. Immense glory we can only imagine.

How beautiful are the riches of His grace!

Heavenly Father, Your promise of Heaven is irresistible. I wouldn't miss it for the world.

In the Name of the Lord

Whatever you do in word or deed, do all in the name of the Lord Jesus, giving thanks through Him to God the Father.

COLOSSIANS 3:17 NASB

"I come in the name of..." is a phrase used throughout history by those who officially represent someone else. They speak on the authority of the one who sent them, careful to never bring dishonor upon the name of the one they represent.

We have the joy and privilege of representing Jesus Christ in all that we say and do as well. When we speak or act in the name of the Lord Jesus, we are speaking and acting on behalf of the most powerful name in the universe. His is the name to which every creature will eternally give honor and lift up in praise. Make sure you are representing Him well. Then be bold in your words and deeds, knowing you have His authority backing you.

In everything thing that I do and say, Lord, may You be glorified today.

The Worst of Sinners

But for that very reason I was shown mercy so that in me, the worst of sinners, Christ Jesus might display his immense patience as an example for those who would believe in him and receive eternal life.

I Timothy 1:16 NIV

Archibald Alexander, an American clergyman in the 1800s, wrote: "God is not glorified in any transaction upon earth so much as in the conversion of a sinner." And it matters not how far a person has fallen, for God's mercy is equal to it. No one should ever despair of mercy. No one should think that they are so great a sinner that God's forgiveness is unavailable to them.

Paul's title, "worst of sinners," was not a badge of honor. Jesus Christ was the focus of his declaration of mercy—Jesus Christ and His immense patience. God never tires. He never grows weary of extending mercy. He has the highest degree of compassion for our weakness.

Every person ever rescued by His grace stands as a display of His powerful ability to extend His mighty mercy to the lost of the world.

Dear God, have mercy on me, a sinner. You are able to save me.

The Death of Death

This grace was given us in Christ Jesus before the beginning of time, but it has now been revealed through the appearing of our Savior, Christ Jesus, who has destroyed death and has brought life and immortality to light through the gospel.

2 TIMOTHY 1:9–10 NIV

In the novel *The Picture of Dorian Gray,* the protagonist bargains away his soul in order to live a life of perpetual youth. It's a familiar theme in literature: to discover the fountain of youth, the magic potions of immortality. We mortals are not very comfortable with our mortality. We wrestle with the notion that physical life will end, our bodies won't last, and we will one day die.

Why do we seem surprised by the unavoidable fact of death? Simple. We weren't created for it. We were made to live and commune with our Creator forever. Working its evil in one man, sin brought death to the scene, but we are eternal beings. Just as an eagle is happiest soaring on high or a cactus is healthiest in the desert, men and women were made to thrive as co-inhabitants of a perfect world.

With Jesus's great sacrifice, death was destroyed. Right now, that wondrous reality must be embraced by faith, but deep in our beings, the truth resonates. Our heavenly Father has restored what was stolen—life everlasting. And it will be ours one day.

Lord, I stand amazed at Your great plan to conquer the grave.

The Kindred Spirit

For this reason he had to be made like them, fully human in every way, in order that he might become a merciful and faithful high priest in service to God, and that he might make atonement for the sins of the people.

Hebrews 2:17 NIV

Humans are on a lifelong quest to find kindred spirits—people who "get" them. The Rogers to their Astaire, the Laurel to their Hardy, the Gayle to their Oprah. Put two Americans in a bustling European city, two Midwestern kids in an Ivy League college class, two surfers at an electronics convention—and they'll somehow find each other. And if something goes wrong, there's an understanding that those kindred spirits will have each other's backs.

But people—even Christians—have situations in their lives where they feel God doesn't "get" them. How could He? He's sitting on His throne in heaven, surrounded by His creation, creating galaxies. All-powerful, all-knowing, untouchable.

But we must remember: Jesus left that throne to become human...with all the frailties and pain and trials that man can suffer. He was mocked, sold out, unfairly punished, questioned, abused, weary...He wept over a friend who died too young.

He gets you. And that's important, because He stands before God as your high priest, atoning for your sins with all the mercy and compassion only a kindred spirit could express.

Jesus, You understand the road I walk. You are my sovereign Savior in whom I trust.

January 26

Sure Sign of Life

But Christ has indeed been raised from the dead, the firstfruits of those who have fallen asleep. For since death came through a man, the resurrection of the dead comes also through a man.

1 Corinthians 15:20–21 NIV

Firstfruits were the gifts offered to God at the beginning of harvest—the traditional offering of the first produce gathered each season.

As firstfruits were a sure sign that the harvest had begun in the biblical era, so Jesus's resurrection was proof of bodily life after death. More than that, His resurrection was the dedication to God of all who would follow Him into eternal life.

Jesus made it clear to His followers that He was going to be resurrected, and that by the same miraculous power of God, all people could have the same experience. All through the New Testament there is repeated affirmation of this promise: through Christ's resurrection, all humanity can experience resurrection as well.

Death came into the world in the Garden of Eden. Death was defeated on the cross. We are all subject to death, but through Christ, we have life eternal.

I praise You, Lord and Savior, for rising from the dead and destroying the power of death.

Not Guilty

That is why he is the one who mediates a new covenant between God and people, so that all who are called can receive the eternal inheritance God has promised them. For Christ died to set them free from the penalty of the sins they had committed under that first covenant.

Hebrews 9:15 NLT

When two parties have a dispute and wish to avoid the legal intricacies of litigation, they may call in a mediator to facilitate an equitable solution. While many people are suspicious of lawyers and attorneys, mediators are more likely to be considered neutral and trustworthy. Jesus Christ, the one Mediator between God and humanity, was wise and trustworthy.

He was not neutral…He was on our side, desiring that we receive the promised inheritance of God. That is far more generous than some "equitable" solution. That is grace—a gift we did nothing to deserve, the bestowing of innocence on our guilty lives. This was more than the act of a disinterested, impartial mediator; this was the doing of a Savior who loved us. We are now free to worship the living God because of His Son, the divine Mediator.

Your perfect sacrifice, O Lord, has made me free. Thank You for being on my side.

The Righteous Judge of the Heart

Since you call on a Father who judges each person's work impartially, live out your time as foreigners here in reverent fear.

1 Peter 1:17 NIV

In his book *Poetics,* Aristotle wrote that "action is character." While his point to clarify story structure and character development in Greek tragedy, it is true that what a person does repeatedly reveals his or her character. Faith in God *looks* like something. Pious words are easy and often cheap, but the inward grace we receive from God will certainly be manifested outwardly.

Because God has nothing to fear from anyone, He can be impartial. He is answerable to no one. The prince and the pauper have no advantage or disadvantage. God looks upon the heart and judges its condition, not the wealth or external beauty of a person.

The offer of salvation is for everyone, but those who have experienced the miraculous, life-changing power of God live with a certain understanding of their place in the world, and they speak and act in accordance with their faith in Him. How well are you putting your character into action right now? Let God help you.

Dear God, Help me to live out my faith to Your honor and glory.

All for His Glory

Do you have the gift of speaking? Then speak as though God himself were speaking through you. Do you have the gift of helping others?Do it with all the strength and energy that God supplies. Then everything you do will bring glory to God through Jesus Christ.

1 Peter 4:11 NLT

An actor prepares to take the stage by knowing not just the arc of the story, but the habits, thoughts, and gestures of his or her character. Just think of the way Meryl Streep "inhabits" the people she plays—like "Iron Lady" Margaret Thatcher. She knows how to be a "servant of the dramatist," as Sir Cedric Hardwicke, the noted English actor, once described it.

Hardwicke was saying that all good actors understand their responsibility is to stay true to the script. Even when they receive acclaim for their performance, the true professionals in the acting world give credit to the playwright or scriptwriter, for it is that person's message, that person's words, which set the course for the entire film or play.

As our dramatist—our Author and Playwright—God supplies the words we need, when we need them, as we present His message to the world. Yet God goes beyond providing the lines; He also provides the gifts we need to carry out His acts of service and the power to perform the ministry to which He has called us. When we remember this, our words, our works—our very lives—will bring glory to His name.

Dear God, You are the Author and Finisher of our faith. Let my words and actions bring You praise now and forever.

Revealed from Heaven

For at the right time Christ will be revealed from heaven by the blessed and only almighty God, the King of kings and Lord of all lords.

1 Timothy 6:15 NLT

The *Sh'ma Yisrael* is the centerpiece of Jewish morning and evening "Hear, O Israel: the Lord is our God, the Lord is one." It is the central statement of Jewish belief, and a foundational belief of Christianity. An ancient recitation, but revolutionary still. Many, many rulers and kings throughout the ages have sought to take God's place, but He stands alone. In the end, it will be made clear that there is but one God, the King of all kings and the Lord of all lords.

His magnificent power and awesome hand of strength will one day make the ultimate statement of sovereignty, when He reveals Christ from heaven and receives the praise of every being that ever existed. Glory and honor to His name forever!

Heavenly Father, You are the one and only God. You are the Lord of all lords, and I give You all of my worship.

Word of Life

That which was from the beginning, which we have heard, which we have seen with our eyes, which we have looked at and our hands have touched—this we proclaim concerning the Word of life. The life appeared; we have seen it and testify to it, and we proclaim to you the eternal life, which was with the Father and has appeared to us.

1 John 1:1–2 NIV

Eyewitness accounts are the backbone of the American justice system. Systematic proofs are the backbone of science. These systems don't operate on the basis of faith. Yet faith is important, especially in our life with God. Thomas Aquinas, a thirteenth-century Dominican priest, wrote: "To one who has faith, no explanation is necessary. To one without faith, no explanation is possible."

It was of vital importance for Jesus, the Word, to become flesh so that when the reports of Him were passed along by credible witnesses, future generations could be assured that their faith was not misplaced. And yet Jesus Himself said, "Blessed are those who have not seen and yet have believed."

Faith is an essential partner to testimony. God revealed Himself in a touchable, tangible Man in the flesh. He calls us to respond with the heart—in faithful words and decisions, evidence and trust working in tandem.

Dear Jesus, I am ever indebted to You for coming into the world and giving me eternal life.

Rejoice

They triumphed over him by the blood of the Lamb and by the word of their testimony; they did not love their lives so much as to shrink from death. Therefore rejoice you heavens and you who dwell in them! But woe to the earth and the sea, because the devil has gone down to you! He is filled with fury, because he knows that his time is short.

Revelation 12:11–12 niv

We will suffer troubles in this life. We may be persecuted. We may even be martyred for our faith. But that is not the final word. We play a role in that story, but God gets to write The End. Not any human being. Not death. Not our adversary, the devil, or his henchmen. God alone, the Alpha and the Omega, will write the ending.

When and how God decides to conclude His story on this earth is His call. But regardless of our circumstances at any point in our life's journey, we are encouraged to rejoice. The word "rejoice" in the Greek means "to put in a good frame of mind." Are you feeling weak? Rejoice, for there is no power greater than God's. Are you discouraged? Rejoice, because Jesus Christ is the Author and Finisher of your faith. Are you weary? Then rejoice, because your soul can rest in the completeness of God's grace and mercy, now and for eternity. Whatever difficulty you're experiencing, rejoice—because this too shall pass, and your enemy knows it.

I find joy in Your life-changing power, Your abundant mercy, and Your overwhelming love.

As Sure as the Sun

The LORD said in his heart, "I will never again curse the ground because of man....
While the earth remains, seedtime and harvest, cold and heat,
summer and winter, day and night, shall not cease."

GENESIS 8:21–22 RSV

Every day of your life, the sun has risen. Every year of your life, there has been a change of seasons. That means that by the time you are fifty years old, you will have experienced almost twenty thousand sunrises. These things are sure. This is why you don't lay your head on your pillow at night and wonder if the sun will come up in the morning. Or ask in February, "Do you suppose the weather will be warmer in August than it is now?" The sun always rises, and the seasons always change.

The wonderful reality is that these are tangible demonstrations of the compassion of God. In the days of Noah, rebellion against God reached an all-time high. God could have pulled the plug on humanity—and would have been justified in doing so. But instead, He made a promise—a promise that His love would endure for all time, *despite* mankind's sin and rebellion.

Take a look outside right now. Step beyond your front door for a moment and feel the air. What you feel is the promise of God that though you turn your back on Him, He will never turn His back on you. Nothing can change His commitment toward you. It's as sure as the sun's rising, on display for us every day and in every season.

God, thank You for standing by my side through my most rebellious days.

February 3

God's Purpose

But I have raised you up for this very purpose, that I might show you my power and that my name might be proclaimed in all the earth.

Exodus 9:16 NIV

History points to Pharaoh in Moses's time as being either Amenhotep II or his father, Thutmose III. Regardless of which of the two was the ruler who haggled with Moses over the fate of the Israelites, one thing was certain: Pharaoh was proud and attributed his greatness to no one but himself.

God told Moses to let Pharaoh know that his position of power had been granted to him by God Himself and that it was not for Pharaoh's purposes but for God's. Pharaoh might have disputed the point, but it's interesting to see how the story played out. Paul even referred back to this episode in Romans 9:17.

Paul's point in Romans—and perhaps even God's point in Exodus—was not that God is concerned with planting despots and tyrants in positions of authority. No, the more true and lasting emphasis is this: God is the *ultimate* authority. His word overrules all others. In the final analysis, His wondrous name will be proclaimed throughout the earth.

O God, all authority is Yours in heaven and on earth. I proclaim Your almighty name!

Everything Is God's

Yours, Lord is the greatness and the power and the glory and the majesty and the splendor,
for everything in heaven and earth is yours.
Yours, Lord, is the kingdom; you are exalted as head over all.

1 Chronicles 29:11 niv

Question: How much does the earth weigh? Answer: six and a half sextillion tons.

That's just the earth. If you added the heavens, well, that figure lies somewhere beyond our ability to measure. Probably the best way to respond to how much the heavens and the earth weigh is to say "everything." It is a single word that sums it all up. And that is exactly the word used to describe God's kingdom.

Everything in heaven and earth is the Lord's. As the old folk song used to say, "He's got the whole world in His hands." This includes galaxies and planets, as well as "the little bitty babies" and "you and me, brother." Everything belongs to Him. He is the head over it all and He rules over it all. He can only be described by words like *glory* and *majesty* and *splendor*—words that fall short but remind us of just exactly who He is. He is the God of everything.

Yours, O Lord, is the glory. I thank and praise Your name.

February 5

Do Not Be Afraid

"Do not be afraid," Samuel replied. "You have done all this evil; yet do not turn away from the LORD, but serve the LORD with all your heart.... For the sake of his great name the LORD will not reject his people, because the LORD was pleased to make you his own."

1 SAMUEL 12:21–22 NIV

The most frequently spoken words in the Bible are "Do not be afraid." The statement appears about seventy times—used by prophets, angels, Jesus, and God, and spoken to calm the natural tendency of the human heart to be fearful. There is certainly a place for reverence and fear in the comprehensive relationship we have with God. He is our Creator after all. Yet it is God's desire to draw us into His love and keep us there.

This is not a halfhearted invitation. This is not a halfhearted commitment. God is "all in," and He asks the same of us. No matter the spiritual condition of our souls, for the sake of His great name, God's invitation is always available. This is a glimpse into the wonder of God's sovereignty. Through the redemptive work of Jesus, we are all offered this divine option to accept the enfolding love of God's embrace.

Throughout Scripture, God was constantly making His presence known to those who had open and eager hearts. It is no different now. "Do not fear" is an invitation to accept His wonderful love. It is an offer to let go of those things that hinder us from finding refuge in God's loving arms.

Thank You, God, for loving me far beyond what I deserve or could ever imagine.

February 6

The Vastness of an Infinite God

You alone are the Lord. You made the skies and the heavens and all the stars.
You made the earth and the seas and everything in them.
You preserve them all, and the angels of heaven worship you.

Nehemiah 9:6 NLT

Imagine spending an entire year in a car. You get in, buckle up, and drive seventy-five miles per hour without stopping for an entire year. If you did this, you would travel over 650,000 miles. Now here's a staggering thought: if you drove at this speed and distance every day for seventy consecutive years, you would have traveled not even half the distance to the nearest star in our solar system! The sun sits 93 million miles from where you are right now. It would take over 140 years driving in your car just to span that distance. Arriving at the next closest star would take nearly 37 *million* years of car travel!

The size of our universe is impossible to fathom. The immense space between planets and stars reaches lengths that our minds do not comprehend. Yet this massive amount of created space that comprises our universe is exactly that—created space. Above it all stands the Creator. With a simple spoken word, God made vast spaces—planets, stars, and galaxies—all finding their origins in the infinite mind of God.

If created space is unfathomable, how much more so our Creator! Stand amazed. He is an awesome God.

Lord, my mind is filled with wonder as I consider the work of Your hands.

Going Deep with God

Then the LORD answered Job out of the whirlwind and said:
"Have you entered into the springs of the sea, or walked in the recesses of the deep?"
JOB 38:1, 16 ESV

In March 2012, filmmaker James Cameron eased into his tiny submersible vessel and dove almost seven miles down into the deepest point of Earth's ocean: the Mariana Trench.

It was a record dive into a valley 120 times larger than the Grand Canyon and deeper than Mt. Everest is tall. A mile deeper. It was a dangerous, thrilling dive, and Cameron filmed it all for the National Geographic Society. He made history.

But he didn't *walk* there...only God has. No man could walk the Trench—not Job, not Cameron, not the Navy's most sophisticated diver. The water pressure is extreme—like three trucks sitting on you.

And that was the point of God's reply. He wasn't avoiding an answer to Job's searching questions. He was saying, "You cannot fathom the depths of My counsel. I made the mysterious, deepest, darkest parts of the ocean—parts not yet discovered and perhaps undiscoverable. I walk there. I start at the beach and stride through the ocean, running My fingers along the tropical forests, the tectonic plates, the rugged mountains. I can do this because I am God. And you, Job, are man."

He is the great and mighty One. His counsel is perfect, and His answers are always true.

Holy God, Your wisdom is indeed unfathomable. Speak to me in life's storms and remind me of Your unlimited power.

February 8

Marvelous Things

Blessed be the L*ORD* *God, the God of Israel, who alone works wonders.*
And blessed be His glorious name forever;
and may the whole earth be filled with His glory. Amen and Amen.

Psalm 72:18–19 NASB

In the Bible, when you see the name "LORD" in capital letters, it's more than just a generic title for God. It's a translation of the name God gave Moses when he asked God who He was. God answered Moses's question with the word "YHWH," which means "I will be." God told Moses, "Whether past, present, or future, I AM."

Israel was always plagued with the temptation to worship the gods of their neighbors. Many different gods with many different names were presented before them as they occupied the land God had promised them. But time and time again it was proven that only the LORD, the God of Israel, could work wonders.

God's very name—I AM—reminds us that His marvelous nature is not relegated to the past. Many things in life lead us to think they can give us hope and make us complete. But these counterfeit gods can't deliver. In the end, we will discover that these lesser gods are both ordinary and temporary. But Yahweh is more. He is the self-existent One. His works are marvelous. And they always will be.

Marvel today at the great I AM. There is none like Him.

Lord, there is none like You. Lesser gods might offer ordinary and temporary pleasures, but Your works are both wonderful and everlasting.

God's Unfathomable Love

For as the heaven is high above the earth, so great is his mercy toward them that fear him. As the east is from the west, so far hath he removed our transgressions from us.

Psalm 103:11–12 KJV

The Neil Armstrong quote, "One small step for man, one giant leap for mankind," gave the world a sense of pride when man landed on the surface of the moon. Still, the moon seems puny in comparison to the vast expanse of space yet to be seen or explored. Like the Energizer Bunny, there are spacecraft traveling through deep space today that keep going and going with no known end point.

We measure distance in space by lightyears. One lightyear is estimated at 6 trillion miles, and the farthest galaxy the Hubble space telescope has seen so far is 13 billion lightyears away. Incredible.

Unfathomable.

But not as immense as God's great mercy toward us.

His miraculous love sweeps away the weight of our sin through the redemption of Jesus Christ, removing it so far from us that no trace of it is left. There are no corners in heaven where our sins are stockpiled. God alone accomplishes this wonderful feat. Hallelujah!

O Lord, the height and depth of Your love is too wonderful to grasp. May I always be grateful for Your great mercy toward me.

Rock of Refuge

Those who fear the Lord are secure; he will be a refuge for their children.

Proverbs 14:26 NLT

Their slogan is "Your Safety Is Our Priority." They are known by an abbreviation—three letters that can evoke a number of emotions: TSA, the Transportation Security Administration. The goal of this government agency is to remove fear from the mind of the general public by ensuring secure travel. Security = the absence of fear.

God's slogan, however, could well be stated: "Your Salvation Is My Priority." His nature is to be there for us regardless of what life presents. He is a refuge for us and for our children, always present, a safe place for those who fear Him. So for us, security = the presence of the Lord.

There is security in revering Him too. It is no coincidence that He is known by a name that evokes emotion, a word that some among the faithful refuse to pronounce: Yahweh—the God of Abraham, Isaac, and Jacob. Call Him the Creator of all that is, the Redeemer of our hearts, our Strong Tower, our Rock, our Refuge—they all spell S-A-F-E.

Your abiding presence with us is safety and refuge and salvation.

The Source of All

The beasts of the field will glorify Me, the jackals and the ostriches, because I have given waters in the wilderness and rivers in the desert, to give drink to My chosen people.

Isaiah 43:20 NASB

The human body can only survive three to five days without water, and to be without it for even one day produces a desperate situation. The blood thickens and the heart labors. Circulation shuts down and the organs begin to malfunction. Water is an essential element for our survival; we dare not stray very far from a source.

In a combination of His miraculous power and His excellent goodness, God supplied water in the wilderness, so intent was He to answer the needs of His people. Even the wild animals noticed and honored Him!

When Jesus told the woman at the well in Samaria that He could provide her with "water" that would quench her thirst forever, she was at first confused but came to understand that such an offer was divine and could only come from God. The extent of God's grace to us is abundant. Our response should be nothing less than gratitude and praise.

Dear Lord, thank You for Your abundant love and mercy. You are the source of all I need.

The Rainbow Connection

Like the appearance of a rainbow in the clouds on a rainy day, so was the radiance around him.
This was the appearance of the likeness of the glory of the Lord.
When I saw it, I fell facedown, and I heard the voice of one speaking.

Ezekiel 1:28 NIV

The way I see it," said Dolly Parton, "if you want the rainbow, you gotta put up with the rain."

Ezekiel was a street preacher, and he brought a lot of rain—twenty-two years worth of it—reminding upper-class Babylonians of their sin and of God's judgment and salvation. He begged exiles to repent and obey. He used gripping object lessons, saw sensational visions, and suffered incredible sadness. High drama.

Sometimes it takes a lot of drama to make a point. In this case, it was a vision of glory, complete with a rainbow. It was impossibly perfect and completely untouchable...a vivid reflection of an unbearably hot and bright sun burning through the last drops of rain. It was an optical and meteorological phenomenon, as well as Ezekiel's picture of the unchangeable holiness of God.

Life is going to have a lot of rain—it's just part of the human experience. But your wonderfully compassionate God will look through those storm clouds, see the rainbow, and remember His covenant of forgiveness and mercy. He shines in radiance and glows with glory. He is our loving and merciful God.

Merciful God, help me to remember Your glory in the midst of my failures. Remind me to cling to Your covenant.

February 13

All Roar, No Bite

He delivers and rescues; he works signs and wonders in heaven and on earth,
he who has saved Daniel from the power of the lions.

DANIEL 6:27 ESV

William Wilberforce was working hard to make a name for himself as an up-and-coming politician in Britain. But following his conversion in 1785, Wilberforce's lifestyle underwent a radical transformation. No longer able to turn a blind eye to the horrific realities surrounding slave trade in the Middle Passage, Wilberforce decided to make abolition of slavery in England his lasting legacy. With the help of others and a relentless determination, Wilberforce was able to see Britain's Slave Trade Act received by Royal Assent on March 25, 1807, which paved the way for the emancipation of slaves in Britain and the United States. Though most slaves never knew Wilberforce, he worked to set them free.

This is what God does today: He frees the hearts of those held captive by sin in ways we don't even see. The Bible says in 1 Peter 5:8 that the devil prowls the earth like a roaring lion, looking for people to devour. But we have an Advocate who has the power to close the mouth of the lion. God literally saved Daniel from the power of the lion. And He saves you from your enemy's jaws, even when you don't realize it.

God, I praise You for all the unseen ways You have saved and rescued me.

No Holds Barred

Their Redeemer is strong, the LORD of hosts is His name;
He will vigorously plead their case so that He may bring rest to the earth,
but turmoil to the inhabitants of Babylon.

JEREMIAH 50:34 NASB

The earliest written use of the term "No holds barred" was found in a Manitoba newspaper in 1892 describing a Greco-Roman-style wrestling match. Any wrestling move or hold was legal. If there was a rule book, it got tossed out the window.

Our enemy has a "take no prisoners" attitude. No holds barred. So when our Redeemer declares He "will vigorously plead" on our behalf, we can be secure in the knowledge of how our divine Protector will approach the enemy to defeat him. He will "grapple," as it says in the original language.

Make no mistake: this is a cosmic struggle for our souls. We need a strong God. Our souls suffer under the weight of sin, and the enemy dangles a death sentence over our heads. Only the miraculous power of God could defeat such an enemy, and only by the death and resurrection of Jesus Christ could such a thing be accomplished. It is to God's glory that He loved us so much that He would go to any lengths to save us from the dominion of sin and death.

O Lord my Redeemer, may I always be grateful for the power of Your redeeming love for me.

Right Side Up

You have heard the law that says the punishment must match the injury: "An eye for an eye, and a tooth for a tooth." But I say, do not resist an evil person! If someone slaps you on the right cheek, offer the other cheek also. If you are sued in court and your shirt is taken from you, give your coat, too. If a soldier demands that you carry his gear for a mile, carry it two miles.

MATTHEW 5:38–41 NLT

In his book *The Different Drum*, M. Scott Peck described Jesus's total upheaval of the entire social order that occurred the Thursday before the crucifixion. Jesus was already on top, so to speak, but He lowered Himself and washed His disciples' feet. It was a revolutionary moment where everything was turned upside down. But as far as the kingdom of heaven was concerned, everything about that moment was right side up.

It's the same in Matthew 5. Jesus overturns everything that seems natural to us and says, "Listen to what I say—here's how to really march to a different drummer." Jesus contends that by abiding in Him and His power, we can outlove any revenge, outlast any court case, and outwalk any of this world's expectations. His way is constantly turning perceptions upside down, while setting reality right side up.

That's our God: His solutions are surprising but powerfully perfect.

Lord, You are the truth and the life, and You're also the way to make everything right.

Something New

For I was hungry and you gave me something to eat, I was thirsty and you gave me something to drink, I was a stranger and you invited me in, I needed clothes and you clothed me, I was sick and you looked after me, I was in prison and you came to visit me.

MATTHEW 25:35–36 NIV

The life-changing power of King Jesus always creates the possibility of something new. In Matthew 25, the "something new" is a kingdom where hunger and thirst are not an issue. It is a living, breathing reality that makes sure strangers are welcome, the naked are clothed, the sick are tended to, and the incarcerated are not forgotten.

The Bible contains over three hundred verses that refer to the poor—God's heart for them, His commandments regarding them, our responsibility toward them. The modern church sometimes overlooks this, focusing instead on other cultural issues like politics and international problems. But the Word of God is not trendy. It is everlasting and true, like its Author. His deep, transforming mercy toward the least of His children is miraculously replicated in the heart of every believer. He is supernaturally able to provide for the desperate out of the riches of His hand.

Many have tried, Lord, but only You have the power to make the world new.

Powerful Peace

Then He arose and rebuked the wind, and said to the sea, "Peace, be still!" And the wind ceased and there was a great calm. But He said to them, "Why are you so fearful? How is it that you have no faith?" And they feared exceedingly, and said to one another, "Who can this be, that even the wind and the sea obey Him!"

Mark 4:39–41 NKJV

Max Planck was one of the founders of quantum theory back in 1900. This "big-brain" stuff studies the interaction of frequencies, energy, speed of light, atoms, and so forth, but Planck had to concede that it was impossible to comprehensively explain the action and interaction of all these invisible energies. In other words…how do you explain the miraculous?

With a single word, "Peace," which literally translates "Hush," Jesus had command over these forces as well as the elements of nature. When you think about it, this display of His miraculous power was pretty easy for the One who actually created the forces of nature. But it goes deeper than that. Here is a vivid display of Jesus's personalized deliverance.

Certainly we can marvel at the wonder of His sovereign power over creation, the world He spoke into being. But in Mark 4 is a perfect example of Jesus—fully divine God yet fully human flesh and blood like us—attending to human fears and distress, calming the stormy sea with a simple word to soothe a group of frightened men in a small boat.

Just imagine what He can do in our world today.

O God, You alone are our Deliverer and Savior.

February 18

The Greatest Mentor

Jesus answered, "My teaching is not my own. It comes from the one who sent me."

John 7:16 niv

Harvard University sponsors a web page with an interesting purpose. It is called "Who Mentored You?" and on the site, well-known personalities recount the stories of adults who greatly influenced them.

A mentor can make an astounding difference in an individual's life. A great teacher pulls from his or her own experience and informs the decisions of others in a real and personal way.

Informed by the Father, Jesus possessed words that had eternal implications. He made it clear that His knowledge was not merely human speculation or hypothesis when He stated, "My words are not My own." His message was divine in origin. His own teacher was God the Father, whose "understanding is infinite," according to the psalmist.

As great as the best teachers and mentors are, they cannot compare to our God. He alone "reveals deep and hidden things; he knows what lies in darkness, and light dwells with him" (Daniel 2:22 niv). May the name of God, the only wise One, be praised forever and ever!

God, You sent Your own Son to make sure I would have the very words of life. I worship You for the gift of Your good news.

First Love

Father, I want everyone you have given me to be with me, wherever I am.
Then they will see the glory that you have given me,
because you loved me before the world was created.

JOHN 17:24 CEV

Parents love a child before it ever arrives. Announcements are mailed, rooms are redesigned with vibrant colors and cribs, siblings are prepared for the arrival, and the family begins the Herculean task of name selection. All of this takes place before the baby is delivered. The parents' love comes first; the child doesn't earn the love of its parents. The love is present before that baby boy or girl even enters the world.

The Father loved the Son before there was anything. Before the creation of light and dark and fish and birds and creeping things and trees and fruit and man and woman. God loved His Son before the world was breathed into being. And that same wondrous love is what the Son showers on us by His life, death, burial, and resurrection.

God's love is always first, before anything else. He is the initiator of love, of our communion with Him. We don't earn His love; it is unconditional and a gift of His grace. Before the world was created, the Father loved the Son. Before we knew Him, God loved us.

Your love, Lord, is always first. Hallelujah!

A Heart to Help

In everything I did, I showed you that by this kind of hard work we must help the weak, remembering the words the Lord Jesus himself said: "It is more blessed to give than to receive."

Acts 20:35 NIV

A young boy read an ad in the paper that said "Puppies for Sale." Having saved his money all summer, he went to the man selling the dogs. After showing the owner his pocket full of dollars, he was escorted to the backyard where he saw the litter of puppies. "Pick any one you want, son," the man said to him. Within a few minutes, the little boy had made his choice: the runt of the litter. The man tried to convince him to pick another, explaining that this one might not grow up to be as playful as the others. But the boy insisted, "This is exactly the one I want." And as the young boy walked joyfully out the door carrying his new puppy, the man couldn't help but notice a slight limp and the imprint of leg braces pressing against the boy's pants.

It is a beautiful thing to see the effect of a tender heart. Often this is how God works: we identify with others because we have felt similar pain, hunger, heartache, or despair, and we reach out to help. Empathy goes deeper than that, though. The beauty of our God is that even when we are separated from others who are hurting—perhaps by distance or circumstances—He supplies us with the ability to feel compassion and then to work hard to help meet the need. Only His gracious love can accomplish such work in our lives.

God, it is wonderful that You can make my heart tender toward the needs that exist all around me. Show me how to respond.

Ultimate Love

But God demonstrates his own love for us in this:
While we were still sinners, Christ died for us.
Romans 5:8 niv

Oscar Wilde once said, "Every saint has a past, and every sinner has a future." Pretty simple, really. We were lost, and yet while we were wandering hopelessly, God sent His Son to atone for our sin though we did not deserve or earn His mercy. God's love was demonstrated in tandem with His unsurpassed grace, so that now we with our sinful pasts have a future.

It's a powerful show of love. We mortals can try to understand it, and offer gifts to the Father in return, but eventually we come to the truth: He loves us. He wants to share life with His created ones. He chose to demonstrate His love in an excruciatingly costly gift—His Son.

To Him be the glory for this unmatchable, indescribable act of love.

Dear God, You sent Jesus to die for us while we were yet sinners. I thank You and praise You forever for Your gift of love.

Trading Places

God made him who had no sin to be sin for us,
so that in him we might become the righteousness of God.
2 Corinthians 5:21 niv

Dr. Evan O'Neill Kane was sure that anesthesia could successfully be applied locally during surgery. While it made sense in theory, people were not volunteering to prove it. But on February 15, 1921, Dr. Kane did finally use a local anesthetic for the first time while performing an appendectomy. Having performed over four thousand appendectomies, you would think Kane would have been at ease. But he wasn't. To prove that a local anesthetic would be effective during an appendectomy, Dr. Kane performed the surgery on himself! The doctor became a patient so that future patients would not suffer.

Jesus, the Great Physician, brought us healing by putting Himself in our place. He surrendered Himself to a sinner's cross, and in exchange draped us with a sinless position before God. But He did more than trade places with us, for our deaths would not have delivered us from the power of sin or its curse. Only the sacrifice of the Holy Lamb of God could pay the price and conquer the grave.

How incredible that Jesus would demonstrate His love by placing Himself on the operating table of sin's judgment. Praise God for His radical gesture of love on our behalf!

Lord, today I stand righteous before You—not because of my own righteousness, but because of Your love!

Give Peace a Chance

Dear brothers and sisters, I close my letter with these last words:
Be joyful. Grow to maturity. Encourage each other. Live in harmony and peace.
Then the God of love and peace will be with you.

2 Corinthians 13:11 NLT

"It isn't enough to talk about peace," said Eleanor Roosevelt. "One must believe in it. And it isn't enough to believe in it. One must work at it."

Peace does not come easily for nations at war, families in conflict, or companies in distress. But it is worth the effort.

The kind of devoted, everlasting harmony that eludes many people came at great cost to God, the Author of peace. Through the sacrificial grace of Jesus and the fellowship of the Holy Spirit, there is great freedom from strife. But one must cultivate that freedom… one must *pursue* peace, nurturing it, living in it. So, where there is sorrow, the apostle Paul urged joy. Where there is conflict, Paul recommended building a bridge to restoration. Where someone needs encouragement, true words from the heart can be offered.

It is a worthy goal to find a reason to agree with the disagreeable. To *believe* in peace… then make peace. Though it takes *hard* work to love others, the infinite, benevolent God—the Author of all love, of lasting joy—abides within when the call to peace is answered. He is the way to true peace.

God of love, Your sacrifice is reason alone to pursue peace. May Your spirit of benevolence wash over me.

February 24

Christ, Redeemer

Christ hath redeemed us from the curse of the law, being made a curse for us: for it is written, Cursed is every one that hangeth on a tree.

GALATIANS 3:13 KJV

In Paul's day, the practice of buying and selling slaves was common- place. Slave auctions were public spectacles where the cruelty of humanity was on display, and where families were torn apart. Occasionally, however, a slave was redeemed. *Redeemed* is a powerful word. In the Greek it means "to buy up." To redeem a slave was to "rescue" them, to "buy them out" of slavery forever. It cost the purchaser something to pay for this buyout.

Christ became *our* Purchaser, and He assumed a penalty that was not His—becoming a "curse" for us. Most of us will never know what it is like to be the slave of an earthly master, but the apostle Paul makes clear that we are "slaves to sin," and therefore under a curse. Only a pure sacrifice could satisfy sin's price.

The Son of God bought our freedom from the slave auction block, paying the cost for our sin on a public cross. There Jesus took upon Himself the curse of the law, willingly choosing to be the atonement for our sin and redeem us from the enemy.

Praise You, Jesus, my Redeemer and Savior.

The Whole Thing

Praise be to the God and Father of our Lord Jesus Christ,
who has blessed us in the heavenly realms with every spiritual blessing in Christ.

Ephesians 1:3 NIV

James 1:19 says, "Every good and perfect gift is from above, coming down from the Father of heavenly lights." As we consider everything in our lives that we would classify as a blessing, there should be no doubt: God is the giver of all these things.

Paul says in Ephesians 1 that God has blessed us with "every spiritual blessing." In the Greek language in which Paul wrote, he used the word *pas*, which is translated "every." This Greek word carries with it the idea of a sum total. In other words, God has given us the *whole* blessing. And His name is Jesus.

When God gave us Jesus, He gave us everything. For without the salvation Jesus provides, all other "blessings" would be nothing but temporary niceties that ultimately mean nothing. But God has blessed us with all of His blessing. The whole lot. His name is Jesus, and He sits on the throne of heaven.

Lord, I am beyond grateful that You have lavished me with all You have to give. I'm astounded at the extent of Your gracious nature.

Enough

This Christian life is a great mystery, far exceeding our understanding, but some things are clear enough: He appeared in a human body, was proved right by the invisible Spirit, was seen by angels. He was proclaimed among all kinds of peoples, believed in all over the world, taken up into heavenly glory.

1 Timothy 3:16 MSG

"Fuel is running low. Been unable to reach you by radio. We are flying at 1,000 feet." These are the last words the radio operator on the Coast Guard vessel heard from the *Electra*, Amelia Earhart's airplane. She was attempting an around-the-world flight that would have been the longest to date by an equatorial route and the first such feat by a woman. She and her navigator, Fred Noonan, left with 1,100 gallons of fuel in the tank, with an intended destination of Howland Island. But they never made it, and the details of what happened are a mystery to this day. We'd like to understand the whole story, but we don't.

Likewise, some of the details of the Christian life are full of mystery. Yet certain facts are clear: like the amazing truth that Jesus Christ walked this earth as a man, and raised the dead and gave sight to the blind and offered forgiveness to those in the grip of great darkness until His work was done. Then He was welcomed Home by the Father. There is much about His daily life that we do not know, but all that we do know—of His influence, His compassion, His miraculous work and saving grace—is enough to warrant our worship and praise.

I give glory and honor to Your name, O Lord.

Worth the Wait

While we wait for the blessed hope—the appearing of the glory of our great God and Savior, Jesus Christ, who gave himself for us to redeem us from all wickedness and to purify for himself a people that are his very own, eager to do what is good.

Titus 2:13–14 NIV

"What are you waiting for?" It's one of those questions that often gets an immediate answer: "The bus." "A phone call." Or, upon reflection, it can hold great insight into our lives: "Once the weather gets better, I'm going to start taking more walks." "We're hoping to have a baby after we pay off our bills."

We're all waiting for something almost all the time. There's nothing wrong with that—it's how our lives are lived. Yet there is a waiting that's beyond our usual answers, and it's not for a *what* but a *who*.

The "blessed hope" of which Titus 2 speaks is our great God and Savior Jesus Christ. He is the one we're waiting for. So while we await many other things, above all else our Hope is readying a place for us in heaven. Come, Lord Jesus, come.

My hope is built on nothing less than You, Lord. Come quickly.

Head of the House

Finally, all of you should be of one mind. Sympathize with each other. Love each other as brothers and sisters. Be tenderhearted, and keep a humble attitude.

1 Peter 3:8 NLT

At its simplest and most understandable level, the community of faith is a family. Yes, believers are fellow workers too, and a team, and soldiers in God's army, but we operate best when we recognize that spiritually, we are related for life. God is our Father and we are His children.

Pope John Paul II said, "To maintain a joyful family requires much from both the parents and the children. Each member of the family has to become, in a special way, the servant of the others." He was talking about flesh-and-blood relatives, but how much more true that is when we are brothers and sisters in Christ!

Striving to be in agreement, being tender and kind, showing humility—these are not always easy accomplishments in a family. Yet the Head of our spiritual household, Father God, is always near to His children, and He longs to give us the peace that calms discord and softens hard hearts. His mercy and goodness are poured into our family every day, forever.

You, O God, are the good Father. Your mercy toward Your children is such a comfort.

Celebrate!

All the angels were standing around the throne.... They fell down on their faces before the throne and worshiped God, saying: "Amen! Praise and glory and wisdom and thanks and honor and power and strength be to our God for ever and ever. Amen!"

REVELATION 7:11–12 NIV

Envision Times Square on New Year's Eve—a million revelers crammed into the most famous commercial intersection in the world, singing and dancing and celebrating. Now picture the Macy's Day Parade on Thanksgiving—four million parade-goers lining the route, craning their necks to see the marching bands and floats, cheering as iconic balloons like Snoopy and Kermit the Frog float by.

Those crowds...the spectacle...that wall of noise is just a *fraction* of what the apostle John saw in his vision of heaven. Angels—ten thousand times ten thousand, thousands of thousands, a crowd no one can count—standing around the great throne of God, then falling down on their faces, shouting, "Praise and glory! And wisdom and thanks! And honor and power and strength to our God, forever and ever!"

It is the song of triumph to the conquering King who reigns over the enemy, the great and glorious Lord who is the Lamb of God. He has the power! He is victorious! Amen!

Victorious God, I fall on my face and give You praise and glory, honor and thanks. Amen and amen.

The Great Protector

Jacob said to him, "My lord knows that the children are tender and that I must care for the ewes and cows that are nursing their young. If they are driven hard just one day, all the animals will die.

Genesis 33:13 niv

Who of us has not felt the frantic pace that life seems to force on us? Circumstances can sneak up and kick us into overdrive before we know it, threatening our physical and spiritual health.

As Jacob's words in Genesis 33 reflect, we are not so different from sheep. Lambs are especially fragile before they are weaned. They must be watched and coddled by their mothers and by their human guardians. Jacob knew this and was an attentive caretaker of his flock, wise enough to understand the importance of pacing. To be driven too hard and too long would be sure catastrophe for those in his charge.

Is not our good Shepherd even more gentle and caring? Does He not tenderly call us from our busy lives and give us rest? When we look to God as our shepherd, He will guide us—at exactly the right pace—each day of our lives.

Dear God, thank You for Your all-seeing care and powerful protection through the pace of each day.

Showers of Life

Let my teaching fall like rain and my words descend like dew, like showers on new grass, like abundant rain on tender plants. I will proclaim the name of the Lord. Oh, praise the greatness of our God!

Deuteronomy 32:2–3 niv

We tend to take rain for granted, but it is really a miracle. It doesn't just water the earth, but nourishes it, collecting sulfur and nitrogen—both of which are essential to the formation of amino acids and chlorophyll in plants. On its way down, each drop captures mineral-rich dust and delivers it to the soil. Rain is, in reality, food. Rain brings life.

In his final act as leader of Israel, Moses stood before the whole assembly and spoke God's truth to the people. Moses began his oration by telling the heavens and the earth to pay attention. He then poetically describes God's word as "showers" and "abundant rain"—a wonderful expression of the mystery of God's presence in all of creation. God cares so much for each of us that He showers us with the nourishing abundance of His love. How else can we respond except with heartfelt praise?

O Lord, pour out Your abundant Spirit upon me and let me sing of Your greatness.

A Helper from Heaven

I was ashamed to ask the king for soldiers and horsemen to protect us from enemies on the road, because we had told the king, "The gracious hand of our God is on everyone who looks to him, but his great anger is against all who forsake him."

Ezra 8:22 NIV

The nation of Israel had come to a point of excitement and anxiety. It had been eighty years since the first of their kinsmen had gone back to Jerusalem, and the temple had been completed for twenty years. God's people were excited about returning home, but anxious about the potential dangers that awaited them on the trip. Ezra, their priest, considered asking King Artaxerxes—Queen Esther's stepson—for protection. But Ezra remembered that he had once boasted: "Our God is mighty and strong. Our God will keep His people safe."

So Ezra made a critical decision. Instead of turning to Artaxerxes for help, he would turn to the King of heaven. Ezra and the people prayed and fasted, and the Lord heard their prayer.

There are plenty of powerful people in this world who can provide us help, but God is the ultimate Helper. And, wonder of wonders not only does God have the power to protect us, but He is also willing. He welcomes us into His throne room, where He actually gives us His ear. What a wonderful God who hears our prayers for protection and answers them!

God, in You I place my complete trust.

God's Friends

God said to Satan, "Have you noticed my friend Job? There's no one quite like him—honest and true to his word, totally devoted to God and hating evil."

Job 1:8 MSG

It's suddenly so easy! With just a click of your mouse or a touch on your trackpad, you can "friend" someone! No investing time, no getting acquainted, no earning trust. Simply add yet another friend to your cyberspace collection! In this day and age, friend can mean almost anything—or nearly nothing at all: it can mean confidant and soul mate, or it can refer to an Internet acquaintance of a cousin's best friend's veterinarian. Thankfully, God's Word redeems the word friend for us.

Notice, for instance, that God called Job "my friend." Life was about to get difficult for Job, yet God's enduring presence with His faithful friend made it possible for Job to live honestly, true to his faith, hating evil, and choosing to trust in circumstances that raised questions about the Lord's goodness. When we live out our devotion to God as Job did—especially in the dark times—God can draw others to His life-changing mercy, increasing not just the number of His friends but the number of His children. This is our wondrous God: acting on His infinite power and love, creating each of us, and then choosing to call us "friend."

Thank You, God, that You call us friends.

Make Some Noise!

Sing to God, sing in praise of his name, extol him who rides on the clouds; rejoice before him—his name is the LORD. A father to the fatherless, a defender of widows, is God in his holy dwelling.

PSALM 68:4–5 NIV

We don't often hear the word *extol* used today. In fact, it is used sparingly in the Bible, but very specifically. It is a robust word meaning "to heave up", "to be loud" in a vigorous way. At athletic events, we hear the cheerleaders imploring the crowd to "make some noise," and the psalmist in Psalm 68 is doing the same thing.

But in order to extol God—to make noise that pleases Him—we must first know Him and His character. We are able to praise God and rejoice before Him with loud voices when we have experienced the miraculous wonder of His goodness and love. He "who rides upon the clouds," is the Lord, and He never takes His eyes off His children, even when we find ourselves in lonely places and in need of His tender mercies.

In lifting Him up to His rightful place in our lives, we find that everything else finds its place too. Oh, what a Savior!

I shout Your name to the heavens, O Lord. You alone deserve my praise!

March 6

God of the Sea

You gave them charge of everything you made...the birds in the sky, the fish in the sea, and everything that swims the ocean currents.

Psalm 8:6, 8 nlt

In Richmond, Virginia, stands a monument of the "Pathfinder of the Seas"—Matthew Fontaine Maury, who spent much of his nineteenth-century naval career charting winds, currents, and whale migration, publishing an oceanography book still used today.

Before Maury, globetrotter Benjamin Franklin commissioned and published a 1768 chart of the Gulf Stream. But years before Franklin, explorer Ponce de Leon discovered the powerful ocean current that made his fleet traverse the Atlantic faster.

But long before any of these well-traveled, seafaring men—and a thousand years before Christ—David, the poet-musician, wrote about the paths of the seas and the fish and whales that swim there. Mighty King David was a land warrior, ruling from Jerusalem, which was surrounded by valleys. He didn't sail the Mediterranean Sea, let alone feel the pull of the current or hear whales sing. And yet, he was compelled to include these mysteries in a psalm about the grandeur of God and His creation.

God designed many things that we humans have yet to discover, much less explain. It's another aspect of His sovereign splendor. The wonder is that He is everywhere–from the far reaches of the solar system to the deep paths of the sea.

God of wonder, how majestic is Your name in all the earth!

Lord in the Silence

What I do, God, is wait for you, wait for my Lord, my God—you will answer!
I wait and pray so they won't laugh me off, won't smugly strut off when I stumble.

Psalm 38:15–16 MSG

One winter in the fourth century AD, forty members of an elite Armenian bodyguard were forced to stand through the night in a freezing lake, warm baths taunting them on shore. All their commander required of them was to renounce their faith, and bow down to pagan gods. They chose to remain silent.

In 1947, Holocaust survivor Corrie ten Boom had the chance to lash out at a former Ravensbruck concentration camp guard whose cruelty was legendary. But she didn't. Recalling the scene, she wrote, "For a long moment we grasped each other's hands, the former guard and the former prisoner. I had never known God's love so intensely as I did then."

It's a bittersweet kind of suffering to hold back when someone takes a verbal shot at your faith, your reputation, your motives—the very essence of who you are. But in those moments your ever-faithful God stands with you, ready to see you through the valleys of suffering. Come to Him. Rest in Him. Let Him hold you in His powerful arms of love.

Help me to be patient and calm in the face of adversity, knowing that You, Lord, are my strength and salvation.

March 8

Just a Few

He made heaven and earth, the sea, and everything in them.
He is the one who keeps every promise forever. He gives justice to the oppressed and food to the hungry. The LORD frees the prisoners.

PSALM 146:6–7 NLT

The attributes of God are infinite. There are not enough computers on earth, not enough poets and musicians and artists in all of history, to detail the riches of His character. And yet the wonders of His goodness, His kindness, His patience and grace are so great that all of heaven and earth—right down to the smallest molecules in our bodies—displays the truth of who He is.

As a soul-reviving exercise, think for a few moments about the fact that our Creator is all-powerful, all-wise, and all-loving—all at the same time. Our all-powerful God can do anything He pleases. Our all-wise God is pleased to do whatever is best for His kingdom and His people. And because He is all-loving, whatever pleases Him is always good for His creation.

Now think about those traits as they relate to you: God has the best of desires for you. He knows what it takes to turn those desires into a reality. And He is fully capable of making His purposes stand. He is a promise-keeping God, ever faithful and true. There is none like Him.

Lord, I have complete confidence that You will make all things right.

Infinite Wisdom

The fear of the Lord is the beginning of knowledge,
but fools despise wisdom and instruction.
Proverbs 1:7 niv

In 2004 Ken Jennings prepared to appear on a June episode of the television game show *Jeopardy!* But Ken would not appear on just a single episode that summer. He would be victorious in every episode for the next six months, astounding people with his seemingly endless supply of knowledge. Ken's unprecedented run finally came to an end on November 30 of that year.

Knowledge is a good thing—and can sometimes pay off with a big jackpot! But wisdom is even better. The book of Proverbs tells us that true wisdom begins when we fear the Lord. The Hebrew word for "fear" carries with it much more than the idea of being filled with fright. It embodies reverence and awe, the kind that leaves us virtually speechless. If God were to showcase His wisdom, we would stagger backward in astonishment. We would shake our heads in amazement. We would fall down in holy fear. And we would listen.

Stop and consider the reality that God is infinitely wise and that there is no limit to His knowledge. Sit at His feet in awe.

Lord, help me to listen, learn, and live in Your wisdom.

Constant Creator

The Lord will make the tongue of the Egyptian sea completely dry;
and with his burning wind his hand will be stretched out over the River,
and it will be parted into seven streams, so that men may go over it with dry feet.

Isaiah 11:15 BBE

The idea that God created the universe, wound it up like a toy and set it on its course, and then retreated to a position of casual observer is not a new one. Deism takes this view, as does the "clockwork universe theory." The Bible, however, takes a completely opposite view. God is far more than a disinterested bystander. He is actively engaged in His creation—sustaining it, writing its history, redeeming its losses, bringing beauty out of its ashes.

We read the words: "In the beginning God created the heavens and the earth." If we can accept this first wonder of His miraculous power, then anything and everything else God has done or will do—from flooding the earth to drying up seas to creating a new heaven and new earth—is a cakewalk.

The Lord's power is inexhaustible, and His involvement in creation is constant. How magnificent is our God!

Help me to be mindful of Your involvement and care as I go about this day.

Forever

"The God who made you is like your husband. His name is the LORD All-Powerful.
The Holy One of Israel is the one who saves you. He is called the God of all the earth.
You were like a woman whose husband left her, and you were very sad.
You were like a wife who married young and then her husband left her.
But the LORD called you to be his," says your God.

ISAIAH 54:5–6 NCV

The poet David Whyte has written a piercing line, the kind that stops you in your tracks: "I want to know if you belong or feel abandoned."

Our lives seem to tip in one of those two directions: we either have a sense of belonging and worth in this world, or we feel alone, adrift, abandoned. The "who" or "why" behind that hollow feeling is explained by the specifics in our stories, but the feeling is universal.

Yet so is the presence of our God. The prophet Isaiah described the Holy One of Israel as He who will never abandon us. God is the One who saves, but He doesn't just save and then forget. No, He is the One who saves and then remains faithful to His own, faithful now and forevermore. God has called us to be His, and His we will remain. Amen.

While others may forget and abandon me, Your faithfulness endures, O God.

The Finder and the Keeper

We all, like sheep, have gone astray, each of us has turned to our own way; and the LORD has laid on him the iniquity of us all.

ISAIAH 53:6 NIV

We've all seen the signs posted around our neighborhoods: "Lost dog! If found, please call…" Below the plea is the photo of a sweet, furry face looking at its beloved master.

Pet owners know all too well that a dog or cat can go astray no matter how long they have been in the family or how much they are loved. When a pet does disappear, it causes panic. No effort or expense is spared to retrieve that lost family member.

Like the straying pet are the wayward sheep in a Hebrew shep-herd's flock. Even more to the point, we humans are like that wandering pet or sheep. The word "all" in the Hebrew and Greek means…ALL. We *all* are like the animal that too easily wanders away. The apostle Peter himself fled the scene when Jesus was arrested and then denied knowing His Savior three times. But the One who forgave Peter is the same One who bore Peter's sin—and ours. And Jesus, the Good Shepherd is eager to forgive every sorry sheep that longs to return to the fold.

What a wonder it is that God spared no expense to make a way for *all* of us to be found when we go astray. This love is truly beyond our comprehension; this mercy reaches to the heart of our sin.

God, You gave Your only Son as atonement for our iniquities. Thank You for sparing no expense for me.

March 13

No Limits

Ah, Lord God! Behold, You have made the heavens and the earth by Your great power and outstretched arm. There is nothing too hard for You.

Jeremiah 32:17 NKJV

Theories exist, but no one knows exactly why the Great Pyramid of Giza was built. Even more perplexing is *how* this ancient wonder was built. At nearly five hundred feet tall, this pyramid stood as the largest man-made structure nearly four thousand years! Assembling such a structure at that point in history should have been impossible, but the mastermind behind its blueprint didn't let that deter him.

Consider now the impressive nature of all that God has created. God's creation dwarfs the greatest of manmade structures. Stars, planets, galaxies, all are the work of our Creator, along with animals, cells, DNA—life itself. Nothing is beyond the power of Almighty God. He truly is a God with no limits!

God, nothing is too hard for You. You are my all in all.

Acts of God

For he makes his sun rise on the evil and on the good,
and sends rain on the just and on the unjust.
MATTHEW 5:45 ESV

"Act of God": a sudden and violent act of nature completely outside human control. An environmental rampage. A catastrophe that guarantees, according to humorist Alan Coren, "that you cannot be insured for the accidents that are most likely to happen to you."

The thing about these unpredictable events of nature is that they're totally impartial. You can get hit with a deluge of rain, buckets of hail, or a tornado, earthquake, or volcano regardless of your income, social standing, genealogy, or religion.

But that's also the beauty of God's "acts of grace." They too are impartial. Because God is good and perfect and compassionate beyond comprehension, He blesses people—believer or not, righteous or unrighteous, whether they *deserve* it or not—with sudden love, impulsive kindness, unexpected decency. No discrimination. No prejudice.

Can you imagine a world modeled after God's immutable character, God's pattern of goodness? Sudden and violent grace. A calamity of forgiveness. A rampage of love.

He is the only One to emulate. Praise His wonderful name.

Holy God, help me emulate Your acts of grace.

God's Good Pleasure

At that time Jesus came from Nazareth in Galilee and was baptized by John in the Jordan. Just as Jesus was coming up out of the water, he saw heaven being torn open and the Spirit descending on him like a dove. And a voice came from heaven: "You are my Son, whom I love; with you I am well pleased."

Mark 1:9–11 NIV

John Charles Ryle was the first Anglican bishop of Liverpool. In the latter half of the nineteenth century he wrote these words: "It was the whole Trinity, which at the beginning of creation said, 'Let us make man.' It was the whole Trinity again, which at the beginning of the Gospel seemed to say, 'Let us save man.'"

That plan of salvation meant Jesus, the Son of God, would walk this dusty planet for three decades, preaching, teaching, healing, and then dying on the cross as the sinless Lamb. Jesus's baptism was an initial step toward the cross. By being baptized, Jesus publicly honored His Father, and God the Father responded in kind by sending the third member of the Trinity—the Holy Spirit—in the form of a dove. As if that wasn't gift enough, God then spoke aloud, affirming His great pleasure in Jesus.

Through the atonement of Jesus's sacrificial death, we are welcomed into God's family as His children. And through the Spirit, we know the Lord's approval.

The plan of salvation is a plan of pleasure—of God's pleasure in His Son, of God's pleasure in you.

Heavenly Father, what a privilege and blessing to be called Your child.

Serendipitous Benefits

I confer on you a kingdom, just as my Father conferred one on me.

Luke 22:29 niv

Portuguese aristocrat Luis Carlos de Noronha Cabral da Camara arranged for an unusual distribution of his wealth after his death. In 1988, thirteen years before he died, Luis and two-witnesses went to a Lisbon registry office where they randomly selected seventy names from a local phone directory. Unbeknownst to those individuals, they were chosen to be beneficiaries of this wealthy man's estate. It was not until after his death that these seventy learned of their inheritance.

This seemingly outlandish choice of beneficiaries is not that different from something that happened two thousand years ago. As the Son of God, Jesus ministered with all authority, ushering in a heavenly kingdom where the Father's reign was both revealed and experienced by those who believed in Him. Amazingly, Jesus has conferred this kingdom on us: He has made you and me His beneficiaries. Not only does the peace of the Father now reside in the hearts of those who have named His Son their Lord and Savior, but we also have the ability to make His kingdom known to others in such a way that they too can understand, embrace, and receive.

Being the beneficiary of a heavenly kingdom is not only a huge responsibility, but it is an unexpected delight. Celebrate and rejoice that God chose you to be His child! The blessings of His choice will last—literally—forever!

You have chosen me to be among the recipients of Your heavenly kingdom. That's yet another reason why I stand in awe of You.

What Love Looks Like

This is how everyone will recognize that you are my disciples—
when they see the love you have for each other.

John 13:35 MSG

In a December 2008 auction, environmentalist Tim DeChristopher raised a bidding paddle in an attempt to outbid oil and gas companies wanting to lease Utah's public lands. That raised paddle started a chain of events that eventually resulted in a 2011 courtroom scene where DeChristopher was sentenced to two years in a federal prison. Minutes before receiving his sentence, the young man turned to the presiding judge and said, "This is what love looks like." He was quickly taken away, but his love for the land was unmistakable.

Jesus's love wasn't for the land but for the people; it was, in fact, for the whole world. And His love was unmistakable. Jesus walked among the least and the lowest, showing them immeasurable love. He healed the sick and raised the dead, all the while ignoring the status quo. Then He laid down His life, the God-designed means to conquer death once and for all for His children—a love far greater than one man's love for the land.

Living out that kind of sacrificial love for one another is the most powerful witness we can give for our Christian faith. When others see love in action—love that costs—they see Jesus. In our mercy, kindness, sacrifice, and charity, they see the love of a wonderful Redeemer.

Jesus, may Your love be the unmistakable sign of Your wonderful grace in our lives.

Ready and Deployed

As You sent Me into the world, I also have sent them into the world.

John 17:18 nasb

During World War II, a group of African-American pilots were ready to serve their country. However, no African-American had ever served as a United States military pilot. The Jim Crow laws and the segregated military of the day made the combat assignments that these pilots so deeply desired seem like nothing more than wishful thinking. Despite the discrimination of the day, however, their skills and readiness for service captured the attention of their superiors. In time, these pilots received the assignment for which they had worked so hard and waited so patiently. Now known as the Tuskegee Airmen, these trailblazing servicemen were deployed as bomber escorts in Europe, where they were highly successful in virtually all of their missions.

Will the same be said of Jesus's followers and their mission? When the Son of God walked the earth, He used the language of mission to explain that the Father sent Him to this world for a specific purpose. And Jesus not only invites but actually commands His followers to work with Him in this divine mission.

God does not send us without help, however. His Spirit empowers and accompanies us, readying us for our assignment. To Him be the glory!

You have not only commanded me to join You in Your kingdom work, but You have also prepared me and—by Your Spirit—You go with me.

The Ambassador

All that belongs to the Father is mine; this is why I said,
"The Spirit will tell you whatever he receives from me."
John 16:15 NLT

Every world power needs a great ambassador, and God sent two of them straight from the throne room of heaven.

As part of His perfect plan, the Lord dispatched two diplomatic envoys of the highest rank to Planet Earth. He charged them to protect His interests by negotiating peace and understanding between sinful humanity and Himself. Jesus was the first of the Father's ambassadors, and after He returned to heaven, the Holy Spirit came, vested with Christ's authority and charged with interpreting and executing His will.

With their Savior and Lord no longer present physically with them, the disciples desperately needed a Guide in this dark world—and so do we. The disciples needed reliable information and instruction if they were to stay strong in their faith—and so do we. The disciples needed help conveying, in the most persuasive way possible, the truth about the Sovereign God, the risen Jesus, and every human's need of a Savior—and so do we.

By God's gracious provision, we have all this and more in His Holy Spirit. Sent from God Himself, the Spirit is here as our supernatural Guide and Helper, Teacher and Comforter. Worship and glorify Him.

Holy Spirit, You are a God-given source of hope and strength. Point me to Jesus, that I may prove faithful in all things.

Eternal Blessing

God raised Jesus from the dead, and he will never go back to the grave and become dust. So God said: "I will give you the holy and sure blessings that I promised to David."

Acts 13:34 NCV

Many times in Scripture, God repeated the promise He made to King David, Israel's great ruler. One place it appears is Psalm 132:11-12: "One of your own descendants I will place on your throne. If your sons keep my covenant and the statutes I teach them, then their sons will sit on your throne for ever and ever" (NIV).

This promise of a Messiah was what Paul referred to—and what his audience understood—when the apostle mentioned the "sure blessings that I promised to David." Jesus had come to earth, teaching and healing, appearing to be the hope of their salvation.

When Jesus was crucified on the cross, some of His followers were shocked and disillusioned, but Jesus rose from the grave, fulfilling in His life, death, and resurrection every single Old Testament promise about the Messiah's first coming. Consider the wonder of our promise-making and promise-keeping God! For hundreds of years, while hope languished and His people despaired of deliverance, God remembered.

David's Successor does indeed sit enthroned. The promises of our mighty, everlasting God are sure, and His mercies continue from generation to generation.

Almighty God, Your blessings to King David extend even to me. How can I ever express my gratitude for Your willingness to make promises and keep them?

God Loves Nobodies

Get along with each other; don't be stuck-up.
Make friends with nobodies; don't be the great somebody.
Romans 12:16 msg

"One of the greatest diseases," said Mother Teresa, "is to be nobody to anybody." Recognizing this truth, Mother Teresa chose to be a special friend to the world's nobodies—to the homeless, the hungry, the diseased, the disenfranchised, the unloved. This amazing woman was definitely a powerful "somebody," but she was also a reluctant one. She won the Nobel Peace Prize, dined with celebrities and world leaders, and, to help rescue trapped children, brokered a temporary ceasefire at the height of the 1982 siege of Beirut.

And yet Mother Teresa considered herself, first and foremost, a representative of a compassionate God who is wildly generous in His protective care and provision. She emulated Jesus, who was a Friend to children and Companion of common fishermen and tax collectors. She lived out the apostle Paul's 1 Corinthians 13 guidelines for sincere, committed love. And her life illustrated the wisdom she spoke: "Intense love does not measure. It just gives."

Mother Teresa was known for her love for the poorest of the poor in Calcutta just as Jesus was known—and widely criticized—for associating with tax collectors, prostitutes, rule-breakers, and other "nobodies." Yet neither was deterred. Jesus loved people and continues to love them indiscriminately. All because of who *He* is rather than who we are.

Teach me to love with the kind of love You extend to me, that others may come to know You too.

Lord of the Living and the Dead

For to this end Christ died and lived again,
that He might be Lord both of the dead and of the living.
Romans 14:9 NASB

Every day we see right in front of us some part of the birth-to-death cycle. We see trees burst with buds in the spring, and we marvel at a newborn baby. We say our farewells at a funeral, and we gaze at the bare branches of winter.

Jesus Himself lived through this same cycle: He was born of a virgin, and He died on a cross, but then He added a spectacular twist to the life cycle when He emerged—alive!—from the tomb. Jesus's resurrection from the dead stands at the heart of all that Christians believe. Without the Resurrection, the apostle Paul said, "Our preaching is in vain." Jesus performed miracles, preached great sermons, and gave us a moral code to live by, but without His resurrection, Christ would be just another great person written about by admiring biographers.

By God's miraculous power, the stone was moved away from the tomb, and Jesus was very much alive, fully qualified to be "Lord both of the dead and of the living"—of those who have died and gone before, those presently alive, and those yet to be born. While death claims the body, it cannot claim the soul. And for those of us who believe in and celebrate the Resurrection, we will joyfully proclaim for eternity the lordship of Christ and the great wonder of God's life-giving—and eternal-life-giving—power!

Because You are the Victor over sin and death, I can spend eternity celebrating Your resurrection power and love.

March 23

Face to Face

For now we see in a mirror dimly, but then face to face.
Now I know in part; then I shall know fully, even as I have been fully known.

2 Corinthians 13:12 ESV

When you stop to think about it, the human imagination is truly amazing. We can imagine being someone other than who we are, we can imagine being somewhere other than where we are, and we can imagine realities other than any we've ever known.

As remarkable as our ability to imagine is, this faculty is nevertheless limited. We can imagine eternity. We can try to picture what Jesus is like. We can daydream about the next phase of life after this earthbound phase is complete and wonder what it will be like to experience that new reality. We can imagine, but we can't know. At least not yet.

But the time is coming when we will see and understand God with absolute clarity. God has revealed Himself generally through nature and more specifically through Scripture and His Son, but there will come a time when we actually see Him and know Him in all His glory. At that point, He will miraculously increase—even perfect—our understanding so that it is no longer imagination that fills our minds but reality that fills our eyes. In that moment, the wonder of who He is will become the source of our joy forever.

My heart races as I think about standing face to face with You, Lord. I am filled with humble anticipation at the thought of that wondrous day in Your presence!

Blessing to Be a Blessing

Now he who supplies seed to the sower and bread for food will also supply and increase your store of seed and will enlarge the harvest of your righteousness. You will be enriched in every way so that you can be generous on every occasion, and through us your generosity will result in thanksgiving to God.

2 Corinthians 9:10–11 niv

Generosity begins with God. The Almighty bountifully supplies all that His beloved children need, and often He supplies much more. The agricultural imagery of 2 Corinthians reflects not only the beautiful cycle of God's provision but also something about His purpose. The Lord does indeed meet our physical needs, and one reason He does is so that we, in turn, can be generous to others.

Consider for a moment the phrase "he who supplies." We human beings like to think of ourselves as independent and self-made, but this term speaks not of a one-time supply but of someone furnishing one thing after another. It is an apt phrase for our faithful and generous God who blesses us not just once but continually.

When we choose to be generous with what God has so freely given us, those people with whom we share are blessed—but so are we. When we share our God-given blessings, we are blessed with the heartfelt joy that comes with giving, and God is glorified. We are blessed by God…to be a blessing to others.

Heavenly Father, give me a cheerful and generous heart so that as I receive Your blessings, I will joyfully share them with others.

The Burden-Bearer

Carry each other's burdens, and in this way you will fulfill the law of Christ.

GALATIANS 6:2 NIV

"Preach the gospel at all times, and when necessary, use words." This famous quote, attributed to St. Francis of Assisi, builds on the adage that our actions speak louder than our words.

Action is essential because the burdens of those we love do, in fact, have weight. To come alongside someone who is struggling under the weight of difficult circumstances can be a great blessing to that person. To be present with a heart of compassion—a heart ready to serve however and whenever needed—is to be present with the heart of Jesus.

But there's more. This bearing of one another's burdens entails a mystery you may have already been blessed to experience. You see, miraculous and life-changing power is released when one human being shares another's pain.

The greatest Burden-Bearer ever, Jesus Christ, healed the diseased, fed the hungry, washed feet, and died on a cross for our sins. When He walked this earth, He reached out to the hurting and the outcast, to the rejected and the dejected, and He literally took on the weight of their burdens. Even today, Jesus continues to share His power with us, enabling us to discern the place He has for us to serve, the person He has for us to love, and the avenue to walk as we take His heart into our world. Amazing! What a beautiful privilege from our wonderful Lord.

God of mercy, enable us to bear each other's burdens with a compassion and love that reflects Your compassion and love.

The Lord of Life

All honor and glory to God forever and ever! He is the eternal King, the unseen one who never dies; he alone is God. Amen.

1 Timothy 1:17 NLT

He was the sixteenth president of the United States and led our nation through its greatest internal struggle, the Civil War. If not for Abraham Lincoln, the United States might be two countries today, hardly "united." Lincoln also signed the Emancipation Proclamation, abolishing slavery in America. No wonder he is widely considered to be one of the great leaders in US history!

Great as he was, though, Mr. Lincoln was not eternal. He is buried at Oak Ridge Cemetery in Springfield, Illinois.

In sharp contrast with even the best of human leaders is our holy and wise, great and eternal God. Our King of kings who will never cease to exist.

He alone is God. If not for God's sovereign and sacrificial plan for our salvation, every man, woman, and child through all history would be lost in sin and destined for everlasting death. Easter morning marked the greatest emancipation proclamation ever, for when Jesus arose from the tomb in Jerusalem, He broke the chains of sin and death.

I can be awed by excellent leadership, stunned by brilliant strategies, stirred by unexpected victories. Yet nothing on the human scale compares, Lord God, with You!

The Price of Grace

We do see Jesus, who was made lower than the angels for a little while, now crowned with glory and honor because he suffered death, so that by the grace of God he might taste death for everyone. In bringing many sons and daughters to glory, it was fitting that God, for whom and through whom everything exists, should make the pioneer of their salvation perfect through what he suffered.

Hebrews 2:9–10 NIV

Eugene O'Neill, the American playwright who won a Nobel Prize for literature, once wrote, "Man is born broken. He lives by mending. The grace of God is the glue."

We are indeed a broken people, and we do need "mending." Only by God's grace does that mending—that healing—come.

God's grace was extremely costly. Not only did the only begotten Son leave heaven, but when He did so, He took on the nature of a human being. That choice to become flesh and blood made Jesus vulnerable to suffering and death. Yet His suffering and death were the means by which God's plan of salvation would be carried out. Jesus's sacrifice opened the door to our reconciliation with the Father.

We humans can do absolutely nothing to reconcile with God. That reconciliation required a sacrifice. The perfect sacrifice. The shed blood of a spotless Lamb. No angel met these standards. No human being could do this. Only the Son of God was qualified. And Jesus willingly embraced that role.

Dear Jesus, You left heaven for the confines of a human body. What wondrous love is this!

Participation in the Divine

His divine power has given us everything we need for a godly life through our knowledge of him who called us by his own glory and goodness. Through these he has given us his very great and precious promises, so that through them you may participate in the divine nature, having escaped the corruption in the world caused by evil desires.

2 Peter 1:3–4 NIV

Once C. S. Lewis once compared the gap between holy God and sinful humans to the gap between human beings and the lowly ant. Despite this vast gulf between us, God passionately desires to be connected—to be in relationship—with us. At the same time, God has made a way for us to lead a godly life.

God wants us to know life in every sense of the word. In fact, He calls us to enter into His glory and goodness, and this call is not only for a special few. It is for all who accept the gift of His grace through Jesus Christ.

The Lord Almighty invites everyone to enter into relationship with Him. He longs for us to know His goodness as evidenced in Jesus and to then receive, by the power of His Spirit, all that we need to live a God-glorifying life.

God offers us this wonderful invitation to be transformed by His divine and marvelous nature. And it's an invitation we accept not only at the moment of conversion but again and again as we walk through life with Him.

It is a miracle that You desire to be in relationship with me. Forgive me for neglecting our relationship. Turn my heart back to You.

Holy Energy

And the earth was without form, and void; and darkness was upon the face of the deep. And the Spirit of God moved upon the face of the waters.

Genesis 1:2 KJV

Any artist will tell you that before they dive into a creative work, there is a time of contemplating, pondering, meditating. Before action is taken, time is spent focusing the imagination. God's creative process remains a wonderful mystery, but Scripture does tell us that just before God made His first creative choice by speaking light into existence—kicking off six days of amazing originality—the Spirit of God "moved" over the surface of the waters.

"The waters" of Genesis 1 were a liquid mass suspended in dark space, according to Bible scholars. (Imagine a lava lamp with its boiling bubbles.) The prime root meaning in the Hebrew of the word "moved" is "to brood," yet this brooding is not a passive action; inherently it means a sense of movement, a holy energy building until it is released when God speaks, "Let there be light."

It is true that no one can know the mind of God, but surely the results of "brooding" before creative action could only be called good. From chaos and disorder came this astounding creation. We stand in awe of such a magnificent God!

Creator God, how awesome is Your power; how wonderful are Your marvelous works!

Fame

There is no other nation on earth like Israel, whom you rescued from slavery to make them your own people. The great and wonderful things you did for them have spread your fame throughout the world. You drove out other nations and their gods as your people advanced, the people whom you set free from Egypt to be your own.

2 Samuel 7:23 GNT

Every year *TIME* magazine offers their "100" issue, a list of the one hundred most important people in our world. From leaders to thinkers to artists and champions, it's an annual compilation of the planet's best and brightest.

In recent years names like Kathryn Bigelow, Sachin Tendulkar, and Elizabeth Warren have graced the list. What? You don't remember those names or why they made the list? You're not alone. The world's fame changes annually, if not daily, and names come and go in the public consciousness. But there is One whose fame has spread throughout the world, and His fame does not depend on seasons of taste or whims of popular opinion.

The Lord's fame is everlasting because of His great and wonderful works toward the ones He has called His very own. He is the Lord, the Famous One.

Lord, You and You alone are the Famous One, and You alone deserve my praise and admiration.

Melody Maker

Accompanied by trumpets, cymbals and other instruments, the singers raised their voices in praise to the LORD and sang: "He is good; his love endures forever." Then the temple of the LORD was filled with the cloud, and the priests could not perform their service because of the cloud, for the glory of the LORD filled the temple of God.

2 CHRONICLES 5:13–14 NIV

In 2009 the National Science Foundation funded a documentary, *The Music Instinct: Science and Song*, to explore the mysteries of music. Musicians were interviewed to explain how melody and harmony are created, and neuroscientists explored how the brains of musicians interact when they play together. It was a valiant attempt to understand, through science, the beautiful power of the medium.

How did music come to be? Why does music evoke such an emotional response? These and other questions about the universal language can't fully be answered by scientific exploration. God, the original Composer, created music. Angels sing around His throne. All creation is commanded to sing His praise. And when the Ark was brought to the temple, He responded to the sound of the singers and the instruments by filling the place with the cloud of His glory.

Perhaps nothing more gloriously shows the wonder of our God than the miracle of music. He is the magnificent Maker of all the harmony of our world.

Father God, I am amazed by You. Your creation is altogether inspiring.

Fearfully and Wonderfully Made

For thou hast possessed my reins: thou hast covered me in my mother's womb.
I will praise thee; for I am fearfully and wonderfully made:
marvelous are thy works; and that my soul knoweth right well.

Psalm 139:13–14 KJV

When poet Emily Dickinson wrote that "the brain is wider than the sky," it's doubtful she knew the science behind her imagery. Brain, spinal cord, and peripheral nerves make up the central nervous system in the human body. This trio regulates all the facets of a person's life, both conscious and unconscious. The brain is made of 100 billion nerve cells that are busy gathering and transmitting electrochemical signals 24/7. And somehow this complex process of cells and signals produces all that a person thinks and imagines: a grocery list, a Broadway play, a violin concerto, or a dream in the night. Such wonder and mystery can only be summed up in poetry.

And the wonder goes beyond the physical. The Hebrew word for "possessed" does not mean "to own" but "to found" or "to create." And the word for "reins" in the Hebrew, surprisingly, means "kidneys," which in this setting means the soul, the place of deepest passions and desires. God created the profound, hidden parts of every person and has woven each part together like threads in a delicate cloth.

He is all-knowing, even to the deepest yearnings of the human heart. How marvelous He is!

Dear God, You made my body and my soul. With all my being, I worship You.

The Immovable Anchor

The seas have lifted up, Lord, the seas have lifted up their voice;
the seas have lifted up their pounding waves.

Psalm 93:3 NIV

Ahhh...the soothing sound of crashing waves. Unless you're in the thick of it. Standing at the edge of the water, the sound will hit you at 80 decibels—too noisy for normal conversation. A train whistle is louder, as is a power saw, a trombone, and a nearby thunderclap. Physical pain leading to permanent hearing loss begins at 125 decibels. Raging waters smashing against a rocky shore produce a sound somewhere between a jet engine and a shotgun blast.

So when the psalmist describes seas lifting up their voice, he's not being poetic or even romantic. He's speaking of raw power—furious monsters of churning water and clouds of foam; walls of seawater that sink ships and flood towns, renewing their attack again and again.

But this is nothing compared to God's power. He is greater than a roaring sea. His voice is mightier than a jet engine, a sonic boom, a volcanic blast. Massive rogue waves can never reach His throne, disturb His rest, defeat His purpose.

He is an immovable anchor in the storm. So when the next crushing wave sends turmoil your way, remember God's irresistible power. Unlimited. Unshaken. Triumphant.

All-powerful God, be my immovable anchor when my spirit is terrified.

Faithful

Not to us, Lord, not to us but to your name be the glory,
because of your love and faithfulness.

Psalm 115:1 NIV

On September 18, 1870, Nathaniel Langford and other members of an exploration team were making their way through a remote part of the United States. What they saw that day blew their minds. Bursting out of the ground came a tight shaft of boiling water stretching over one hundred feet into the air.

Langford and his team raced toward the scene, realizing they had just stumbled upon a geyser. Amplifying their delight was the realization that the geyser would erupt again. And again. And again. This geyser put on a show for them all day long at remarkably predictable intervals of time. Langford recorded in his journal that his team began to refer to the geyser simply as "Old Faithful." Today, thousands of people from all over the world journey to take in the glory of Old Faithful, not because it is the biggest geyser, but because it never fails to deliver.

God's faithfulness is worthy of our wonder. From eternity past to eternity future, His faithfulness has never failed. His commitment to us is astounding. It is marvelous. And when you really stop and take it in, it will blow your mind.

I am amazed at how Your faithfulness toward me has never wavered, and I know it never will.

April 4

God's Timeless Word

Your word, LORD, is eternal; it stands firm in the heavens.

PSALM 119:89 NIV

Psalm 119 is one of several acrostic or alphabetic psalms in the Bible. It uses the order of the Hebrew alphabet, with eight lines per stanza—twenty-two stanzas total—each line beginning with the next letter. Most likely this clever format was used to make the psalms easier to memorize and sing, and it was a perfect device for planting the most important precepts of Yahweh in the hearts of the Israelites. One of these treasured precepts is "the word of the Lord."

By God's Word the heavens were made, and their very existence confirms His Word. Our God spoke the heavens into glorious existence, and by this same power the heavens are held together in perfect order and splendor. His Word maintains order in the cosmos and in our lives as well.

Though the earth revolves on its axis, the Word of the Lord stands firm. Of this we can be sure. As Paul states in his letter to the Romans, "Who is like our God? For from Him and through Him and to Him are all things."

Lord, the power of Your word is boundless. Today I will hold it and cherish it in my heart.

Bright Lights, Big God

He counts the stars and assigns each a name.
Our Lord is great, with limitless strength;
we'll never comprehend what he knows and does.

Psalm 147:4–5 MSG

Twinkle, twinkle, little star/How I wonder what you are?

That lyrical question is one we can actually answer. Stars are flaming balls of luminous plasma. And while most stars are not visible to the naked eye, some can be clearly seen in the night sky. We've given these bright lights names like Sirius, Canopus, Arcturus, and Vega. But beyond a few very distinct stars, we lose count. Scientists tell us the number of stars is infinite, meaning, beyond our limited comprehension. In other words, there are just too many.

But the Lord is the truly infinite One, and He not only knows how many stars there are, but He knows each and every star by name. Not the names we've given them, many of which are derived from Greek mythology. No, these are God's appointed names, uniquely bestowed on each and every star by its Maker.

If our magnificently all-knowing Creator cares so much to name stars that scientists will never lay eyes on, we can trust that He is intimately concerned with each of our lives.

Limitless God, I am humbled that You care so much about me.

Worth Celebrating

LORD, you are my God; I will exalt you and praise your name,
for in perfect faithfulness you have done marvelous things, things planned long ago.
ISAIAH 25:1 NIV

Do you remember this iconic ad campaign from the 1980s? A dinner party is in full swing when a young professional casually remarks to another that his broker is E. F. Hutton. All conversation peters out, silverware clatters on plates, guests lean toward the young man, and the announcer says, "When E. F. Hutton talks, people listen."

Isaiah was the E. F. Hutton of 700 BC. As a prophet, he was used to large crowds leaning in to hear what he had to say...and it usually wasn't good news. But in Isaiah 25, God's spokesperson changes it up and foreshadows a time at the end of time—a glimpse of life where there is no death, no tears...just a celebration of God's perfection, His victory over evil, His faithfulness to His purpose, His testimony of loving concern.

What a day to anticipate! What a dinner party! What a crowd! And what a comfort to know that when God speaks, you can take Him at His Word. He has done fantastic things, and all the world praises Him!

Lord God, thank You for Your untiring faithfulness when mine wavers. You are my Rock, my Refuge, my Strength.

Beneath the Surface

I the Lord search the heart and examine the mind, to reward each person according to their conduct, according to what their deeds deserve.

Jeremiah 17:10 NIV

Years ago, law enforcement started training dogs, hoping they could locate illegal drugs that eluded police detection. This experiment proved to be a huge success. Thanks to "sniffer dogs," countless illegal drugs have been confiscated, removing those drugs from the streets. Not only that, our canine friends are now being used to unearth underground explosives, detect illegal cellphones in prisons, and even locate endangered bumblebee nests to prevent them from extinction! God has equipped these animals with remarkable abilities, but His power to search our hearts and minds is beyond imagination.

God sees what no one else can. When harmful things are lurking nearby, He is able to expose and uproot them. And when God sees what is right in us, He is able to reward and preserve it. The penetrating eyes of God always work for our good and His glory.

Thank God today for His awesome ability to see what needs to be seen.

You rightly correct and encourage my heart, Lord. You see clearly and act according to Your divine wisdom.

The Lord's Great Love

The steadfast love of the LORD never ceases; his mercies never come to an end; they are new every morning; great is your faithfulness.

LAMENTATIONS 3:22–23 ESV

I am a most noteworthy sinner, but I have cried out to the Lord for grace and mercy, and they have covered me completely. I have found the sweetest consolation since I made it my whole purpose to enjoy His marvelous Presence." These words were written by the man who set out to find a New World—and succeeded. Christopher Columbus could have basked in his accomplishments, but he chose instead to remember his place before God and the function of God's mercy on his behalf.

Mercy comes from God's steadfast love for us. In the Hebrew, "mercy" means "kindness, an act of favor, a good deed." When this term is rendered "mercies," think of mercy coming forth in multiples.

We are all in need of multiple mercies. God's mercies are not a one-time offer. God's mercies are never exhausted. God's mercies are in perpetual flow—a free and sovereign choice He makes on behalf of His children every day.

It is easy to be consumed and overwhelmed by the worries of this life or our own sinful nature. Aren't you glad that in the wonder of God's eternal faithfulness, He pours out His mercies upon us with each new day?

Dear God, may I always remember my place before You and be forever grateful for Your tender mercies toward me.

Burning with Glory

Suddenly, the glory of the God of Israel appeared from the east. The sound of his coming was like the roar of rushing waters, and the whole landscape shone with his glory.

EZEKIEL 43:2 NLT

When Jesus ascended to heaven from the Mount of Olives just outside the eastern walls of Jerusalem, an angel appeared to His followers and told them that Jesus would return in the same manner He left. But Jerusalem looks much different now than it did when Jesus ascended from that place. The city has been destroyed and rebuilt several times. The eastern gate of Jerusalem has been sealed shut, and a graveyard runs along the area where people used to enter. Some have even speculated that since Jewish tradition forbids one to walk over dead bodies, the Messiah will not be able to enter through Jerusalem's eastern gate, even if it were not sealed shut. But the prophecies in Scripture say otherwise!

Ezekiel looked ahead to a far distant day and saw the whole earth shining with the brightness of the Lord. The eastern sky burned with light, and he heard the deafening roar of a mighty body of rushing water. This is the Messiah, come to set up His kingdom forever and ever. This is our God, who at last in glory will rule over all the earth!

Lord, I know You have promised eternal life for those of us who believe. I praise You and long to see Your glory.

Awesome and Opposite

The burden that I ask you to accept is easy; the load I give you to carry is light.

MATTHEW 11:30 NCV

Jesus was rather fond of oxymorons—verbal opposites. He was constantly taking contradictory figures of speech and weaving them together. Take Matthew 11:30, for example. Jesus presents us with "easy burdens." Really? Have you ever heard of such a thing? Isn't a burden, by definition, *hard*? Then He continues, speaking of "light loads." He's got to be kidding, right?

Jesus was also fond of redemption. He was constantly taking people's preconceived notions and turning them inside out. He loved taking the ironclad theories of His day and inviting His listeners into something fluid and unexpected and life-giving—like saying that those who are last shall be first, and whoever wants to become great must serve.

Yes, Jesus loved reordering perceptions. In Him, burdens are no longer burdensome and loads end up light as feathers. Others have promised such things, but only Jesus delivers the goods. He is awesome and able.

You, O Lord, are the only One who can redeem the contradictions of this world and weave them into something beautiful.

Undercover God

But among you it will be different. Those who are the greatest among you should take the lowest rank, and the leader should be like a servant.

Luke 22:26 NLT

On February 7, 2010, a major network aired a reality-style pilot television episode that featured the CEO of a major corporation going undercover in his own business, hoping to get a true sense of what works and what doesn't work inside his organization. The pilot was met with rave reviews, and the network ordered up several more episodes featuring more CEOs and their companies.

While watching these corporate bigwigs perform humiliating tasks provides some comedic appeal, the show's primary reason for success seems to come from the feel-good outcomes that result from the employers' discoveries. There are always tears of joy in the end.

Jesus was the ultimate example of an important person lowering Himself for the good of others. Think about it: God clothed Himself in human likeness, was born to common parents who He obeyed as a child, washed the feet of His followers, and touched members of society who had been shunned by everyone else. He laid aside His royalty and became the servant of all, not as part of a reality show or a publicity stunt, but because of the great love He had for us. What an amazing God, that He would humble Himself for us!

Dear Lord, as I consider the way You humbled Yourself out of Your love for us, I am filled with awe.

To God Be the Glory

And whatsoever ye shall ask in my name, that will I do,
that the Father may be glorified in the Son.

John 14:13 KJV

It's all about who you know.

In the world today, using someone's name can open doors and create opportunities. But the truth is that the power and influence of any human name has limits.

Jesus, however, stated emphatically that *whatever* we ask in His name, He will do. Who would have the audacity to claim affinity with God and then back it up with an equally audacious promise of action? Only the Son of God. Jesus could offer the power of heaven itself, for He had been with God from the beginning; He had come into the world to bring life to mankind and reveal the glory of the One who sent Him. Even in the final hours before His death, Jesus was thinking of what future glory He could bring to God the Father.

Jesus gives one condition for the petitioner: the glory must go to God alone. Jesus sacrificed Himself on our behalf for one reason: to glorify the Father in accord with His eternal promise of redemption.

Dearest Jesus, Your name is my shelter. I am astounded that You would back Your promises with the power of heaven, just for me.

Who's behind Who We Are

And he gives us the power to live, to move, and to be who we are.
"We are his children," just as some of your poets have said.
ACTS 17:28 CEV

Picture yourself standing in the wings, just about to step out into the spotlight and stand before the watching eyes of a massive audience. You're nervous, but you've practiced the required hours and beyond. Then, only moments before you step onto the stage, a fellow performer whispers in your ear: "Just be yourself."

Of all the things people say to us, that phrase—"Just be yourself"—may be the most profound and the most challenging. In our own power that's almost impossible, even when we have been gifted with extreme talents. But we are children of the Most High God who empowers for many things, including the ability to be who we are.

God created all that is. He crafted and designed all of nature, along with the scientific and mathematical properties that bind it together. From the beginning of time—which He set in motion—He has monitored the progress of life itself. And then He formed you in your mother's womb.

The next time someone whispers, "Just be yourself," remember that you *can* because you are a child of our most awesome Creator and heavenly Father.

I'm so grateful that I can be who You meant me to be because of Your incredible power.

Full of Wonder

Therefore, since we have been made right in God's sight by faith, we have peace with God because of what Jesus Christ our Lord has done for us.

Romans 5:1 NLT

Chapter 5 of Romans begins on the heels of something the apostle Paul called "this wonderful truth"—that Jesus died and was raised to make us right with God.

The writer David James Duncan says wonder is his second favorite condition to be in, second only to love, and that "maybe love is just wonder aimed at a beloved." While we were still the enemies of God, Christ died for us. It was the love of Jesus Christ our Lord that took our wrong and made us right before God so that now He sees us through the lens of peace. No one else could have done that. No one else would have done that. Only Jesus, God's Son, was sufficient and willing for such a task.

That is a truth that is wonderful—*full of wonder*. He is a Savior who is full of love.

Your love for us, O Lord, is a wonder that brings peace and rights every wrong.

Patient Power

May our dependably steady and warmly personal God develop maturity in you so that you get along with each other as well as Jesus gets along with us all.

ROMANS 15:5 MSG

It was a battle of epic proportions: two maidens in mortal combat, each defending her intrinsic worth, cheered on by a thousand martyrs. One waited staunchly as the other attacked, flung insults, and struck with a sword that eventually shattered.

Is this a scene from a super hero movie? No. It's two characters in the epic Latin poem "Psychomachia" from fifth-century Rome. The Late Antique poet Prudentius wrote the popular allegory as a conflict between seven pairs of virtues and vices. Ira—Anger—is the aggressor. Patientia—Patience—is the defender.

Isn't that the way of anger: to insult and attack and injure? But we are encouraged in Scripture to strive after patience, just as Jesus is patient with our offenses. It's a process, to be sure. A process through which our dependable God enables us to become mature believers who are slow to anger and quick to forgive.

Only an Almighty Father can work that kind of transformation and grant us victory over anger. His power to mold and patiently train us is truly awe-inspiring.

Ever-patient God, You are virtuous beyond compare. Help me to emulate Your extraordinary endurance.

Divine Direction

There are different kinds of spiritual gifts, but the same Spirit who is the source of them all.

1 Corinthians 12:4 NLT

Behind every brilliant movie is a brilliant director. A great film will draw in viewers and almost cause them to forget that it's just a movie. Creating such a cinematic experience is no easy task. It requires a masterful mind who can direct the actors and film crew, not just controlling the film's artistic and dramatic aspects but also guiding the technical elements.

In a similar way, the Holy Spirit is directing God's global church, known as the body of Christ. Within the body there are members who minister, who teach, who encourage; others evangelize or lead; some oversee; and others exercise other gifts. The church is a living organism with various parts working in remarkable synchronization. And behind all of this work is the Spirit of God. The Spirit determines which gifts are necessary, infuses individual believers accordingly, and then guides the body into action.

It is a complex work, expertly directed by One who knows exactly how to make a beautiful and dynamic masterpiece.

Lord, as I consider everything being accomplished through Your church, I'm amazed at how You are orchestrating such a complex work.

Mirror, Mirror

Nothing between us and God, our faces shining with the brightness of his face. And so we are transfigured much like the Messiah, our lives gradually becoming brighter and more beautiful as God enters our lives and we become like him.

2 Corinthians 3:18 msg

Look into a mirror. What do you see? If you have high-end lighting, you might get a charitable reflection—your features shadowed and smoothed in all the right places, your eyes brighter, your hair softer. Enchanting. If you were a first-century Corinthian, you looked into polished metal. If strong light—streaming sunrays, a bank of candles—filled the room, your reflection was brilliant, glowing. Exquisite.

Now imagine God's glory—dazzling, so much splendor, so extraordinarily magnificent that Moses had to veil his radiant face after seeing it. Life-changing.

How can you reflect that?

God, in His infinite wisdom, sent His Son, Jesus—the gospel, the Word—so that you could meet His eye in the mirror. No veil, no obscurity, no soft lighting. Just full-on glory that you could behold, absorb, and reflect out to the world, inspiring others to be transformed into Christ's image.

Lift your face, catch the light, and bask in the fullness of God's glory.

God, Your justice, mercy, and goodness are so marvelous. Help me to reflect Your glory today.

Lavish Love

In him we have redemption through his blood, the forgiveness of sins, in accordance to the riches of God's grace that he lavished on us with all wisdom and understanding.

Ephesians 1:7–8 NIV84

Have you ever "paid it forward"? Has someone ever shown you a kindness that you didn't ask for and didn't expect, and you were so warmed by it that you went right out and showed an equal kindness to another?

The pay-it-forward mind-set is trendy now. You might have seen the movie back in 2000 or noticed the recent commercials promoting random acts of kindness. There's even a Pay It Forward Day worldwide. But this is not a new concept.

It started with the Godhead—Father, Son, Holy Spirit—putting together a plan in eternity past. A *lavish* plan comprising wisdom and understanding, sacrifice and grace. A plan for people who had not yet been created on a planet that had not even been formed. A plan only an all-powerful, all-seeing, infinite God could devise.

Redemption is a powerful thing. You can't earn it. You can't buy it. You can't demand it. But you can receive it. It's already been paid for—and paid forward—by a God who has lavished His unfathomable grace on you.

Loving God, Your grace is a rich and wonderful gift to me. Thank You.

Citizenship

But our citizenship is in heaven.
And we eagerly await a Savior from there, the Lord Jesus Christ.

PHILIPPIANS 3:20 NIV

Each year across the United States, you can observe something wonderfully beautiful: a group of people being sworn in as US citizens. There are some things you are sure to find at each ceremony: American flags, special guests, new citizen packets…and lots of tears as they celebrate the hope that there are better opportunities now in store in their new homeland. Though the participants may look and sound different from one another, their longing is exactly the same: to be blessed with all the rights and privileges promised by their splendid new country.

The very moment you began to hope in Jesus, you became a citizen of heaven! You gained a new home—a new country—and a bright future. Jesus Himself has prepared this perfect place for His redeemed. His deep love and care for us extends even to eternity.

Lord, You have secured a place for me in heaven. I praise You for receiving me into Your divine kingdom.

The Best Is Yet to Come

He will take our weak mortal bodies and change them into glorious bodies like his own, using the same power with which he will bring everything under his control.

PHILIPPIANS 3:21 NLT

It's little wonder that so much time, energy, and money is spent on trying to stay young. The process of aging can be humiliating. Eyes grow weak over time and need bifocals. Knees wear out after many years and need to be replaced. Even our minds can begin to fade and lose touch with the present as time takes its toll.

Such a reality can be incredibly depressing …*or* it can be a constant reminder that there is One who will someday use His cataclysmic power to bring everything under control. In one powerful sweep of His hand, God will take our weary and broken bodies and make them glorious. Far greater than being or looking or feeling young, this will be the experience of becoming *like Him* and seeing Him as He is.

Praise the One who transcends time and mortality. He will make all things new!

We are humbled by Your wondrous power that can re-create all things.

The Truth Revealed

The mystery in a nutshell is this: Christ is in you, therefore you can look forward to sharing in God's glory. It's that simple.

Colossians 1:27 msg

Remember the telephone game? Kids sat in a circle and one player gave a phrase to the next player, who then whispered it as quietly as possible to the next person, and so on, until the message was passed along to the last kid, who shouted it out. And it was usually completely, hilariously wrong.

The religious leaders in biblical times played that game for centuries—passing along secret rules for spiritual perfection within a very limited, exclusive circle, maintaining power by constant correction. And it worked beautifully…until Christ came along and delivered the true message to His followers, and Paul brought "telephone" to a screeching halt by shouting out the secret: Christ dwells within our hearts and is the *only* hope for experiencing God's salvation.

This was a huge revelation—so huge that Paul was stoned, dragged, beaten, chased out of town, thrown into prison, and eventually martyred. The secret was out! The exclusivity gig was up! No more mystery, no more manipulation. Jesus opened the door of heaven for all. Incredibly, wonderfully.

It was a glorious secret, held at the heart of God's throne until it pleased Him to release it to the world. Game over.

Glorious God, Your revelations are extraordinary and freeing. Christ now dwells in me!

April 22

A Faithful Conclusion

Here is a true message: "If we died with Christ, we will live with him. If we don't give up, we will rule with him. If we deny that we know him, he will deny that he knows us. If we are not faithful, he will still be faithful. Christ cannot deny who he is."

2 Timothy 2:11–13 CEV

Grammar is that subject in school that is full of difficulties for most kids: when to use a comma, what constitutes an incomplete sentence, should it be *who* or *whom*…and the list goes on. One rule of grammar that's fairly easy to recognize, though, is the conditional phrase, which usually begins with the word *if*: if *A* (the premise), then *B* (the conclusion). That's exactly the equation the apostle Paul used in 2 Timothy 2, and the conclusions are amazing.

To the premise "If we died with Christ," Paul concludes, "we will live with him." And to the premise "If we don't give up," Paul concludes, "we will rule with him." Wrapped up in both statements is the gift of eternal life and a glimpse into our eternal roles as children of the King. But it is probably that last premise—"If we are not faithful"—that has the most humbling conclusion: "he will still be faithful."

Our true and perfect God will never forsake us. It's a conclusion that calls for nothing less than overflowing praise.

Even if I stumble and fall, still You are faithful. Thanks be to Your name, O Lord.

God's Double-Edged Sword

For the word of God is alive and active. Sharper than any double-edged sword, it penetrates even to dividing soul and spirit, joints and marrow; it judges the thoughts and attitudes of the heart.

Hebrews 4:12 NIV

We've all seen what happens with a kid's science fair project when you mix soda, vinegar, and soap flakes. The chemical reaction of the ingredients sends the mixture spewing over the rim of the papier-mâché volcano—and potentially all over the room!

There is a similar type of reaction when you combine the Word of God and the heart of the believer. God's Word—the *Logos* that is Jesus and the written word of Scripture—is not a vague concept or a dead law. It is "alive and active," which means powerful and present.

The term "double-edged" appears only twice in the New Testament. In both cases, it literally means "double-mouthed." John's description of Jesus in his vision while on the isle of Patmos was "out of his mouth came a sharp double-edged sword."

This sword is invasive—and able to perform spiritual surgery. Painful as that may be sometimes, it is always beneficial to our souls.

If we allow Him into our hearts, God gives life-changing power. All-gracious, all-merciful, He is faithful to keep His promises.

Lord, make my heart a pure and holy dwelling place for Your Spirit.

April 24

The Mercy Seat

We don't have a high priest who is out of touch with our reality.
He's been through weakness and testing, experienced it all—all but the sin.
So let's walk right up to him and get what he is so ready to give.
Take the mercy, accept the help.

Hebrews 4:15 MSG

Johnny Cash, in a song he recorded called "The Mercy Seat," sang that he was both "yearning to be done with all this weighing of the truth," and that his head was burning at the thought that the mercy seat was waiting.

What is mercy? And why does the thought of accepting it cause such conflicting emotions? The human characterization of mercy usually involves a judge and guilt and fair payment. But *divine* justice radiates grace that only Jesus the High Priest could offer.

Why Jesus? Before He came, God spoke through prophets and priests, appearing rarely, usually in judgment. There was no rush to the mercy seat, no urge for enlightenment. Then, in His infinite wisdom and perfect timing, God sent Jesus—divine Man tasting human nature, tempted, taunted, weary, disappointed. A Man of Sorrows but not regrets. A Man who became sympathetic to the trials of being human—*your* trials, *your* pain, *your* temptations.

Now He holds out His holy hand, beckoning—*Come to Me...come boldly to the throne of grace.* Take the mercy, dear one. Accept the help being offered by our perfect and loving God.

Holy God, grant me Your mercy as I go through this day.

Beautiful Butterflies

Consider it a sheer gift, friends, when tests and challenges come at you from all sides. You know that under pressure, your faith-life is forced into the open and shows its true colors. So don't try to get out of anything prematurely. Let it do its work so you become mature and well-developed, not deficient in any way.

James 1:2–4 MSG

Caterpillars aren't typically lauded for their beauty. Conspicuous-looking things, caterpillars are voracious feeders and are considered by farmers to be pests.

The appearance of a caterpillar usually mimics its habitat: some caterpillars look like weeds, thorny brush, or even bird droppings! But in time, something happens to these ugly little critters. After a caterpillar has eaten all it can, it finds a safe place to settle and be still, and begins to spin its cocoon, encasing itself inside a "shell" of its own making. During the caterpillar's time inside this safe little home, it undergoes a metamorphosis and eventually exits as a new being. The ugly creepy crawler has become a beautiful winged butterfly.

As fascinating as this change is, the metamorphosis of the human heart is greater still. Science can explain the process of change for the caterpillar, but the only explanation for what happens to a transformed heart is that God has done something supernatural.

When you consider the metamorphosis that God has performed in your heart, don't just feel a sense of gratitude. Feel the wonder!

Lord, You are able to transform the heart and create a completely new nature. You are marvelous!

April 26

Leap of Faith

Though you have not seen him, you love him; and even though you do not see him now, you believe in him and are filled with an inexpressible and glorious joy.

1 Peter 1:8 NIV

Leading nineteenth-century clergyman and abolitionist Henry Ward Beecher wrote, "Faith is spiritualized imagination." In this day and age, so much is done for us that the gift of our imagination does not get the exercise it needs. We appreciate it and know it's available; we just don't tap in to it often enough.

Loving someone you have not seen or do not know personally is a challenge. It requires the proverbial "leap of faith." By faith in Christ, we have a direct connection with those who saw Jesus in the flesh. By faith Jesus dwells in our hearts. By faith His qualities are manifested in our lives. By faith His mysteries are revealed in our imagination.

Here is the beauty of faith: it is the great equalizer among believers, from the first century to the present day. We all needed a Savior, and God has responded in full with the redemptive work completed in Jesus, a work that is the same yesterday, today, and forever.

Who but God would ever have imagined such a solution?

O God, I am amazed by who You are. Thank You that You are ever the same.

Light of Fellowship

But if we walk in the light, as he is in the light, we have fellowship with one another, and the blood of Jesus his Son cleanses us from all sin.

1 John 1:7 ESV

The Greek word for "fellowship" is *koinonia.* It is used nineteen times in the New Testament and is also translated as "contribution, sharing, or participation."

A close study of the usage of this word shows that action is always included in its meaning. So fellowship is not just being together; it is doing together or walking together. And it's a specific kind of walking.

In order for fellowship to be a reality and not just a word, it is imperative that we walk in the light as Christ walked in the light. There can be other aspects to fellowship, but there must at least be the glow of the light of Christ's love and forgiveness of sins. There is no other bond as strong. We are to be joined together in *koinonia*—the true, honest connection that can only be sealed by the miraculous love of God.

Your light and love, Lord, create the only path to true fellowship. Help me to walk in it today.

Royalty One Day

He lets us rule as kings and serve God his Father as priests.
To him be glory and power forever and ever! Amen.
REVELATION 1:6 CEV

Under British common law, the crown is currently passed on by "male-preference primogeniture." In other words, succession passes first to royal sons, in order of birth, and subsequently to daughters, again in order of birth. One can ascend to the throne only because of the blood found in their veins. The eldest son of Queen Elizabeth II is Charles, the Prince of Wales. He is the heir-apparent to the throne. He will one day be king.

Because of our new birth as children of the King, we now have royal blood in our veins. The implications of this reality are staggering: we will rule as kings and queens. Our position is not due to anything we have done or any gifts or talents we have. We didn't earn the title or have to go to war for it. The fact that our Father is King confers this privilege on us.

Our God reigns! His is the kingdom, and the power and the glory will be His forever.

That we will one day rule as kings is only because of Your great mercy, Sovereign God.

All the Way Home

We know that we have passed out of death into life, because we love the brothers. Whoever does not love abides in death.

1 John 3:14 esv

When Sara Tucholsky of Western Oregon University stepped up to the plate and swung the bat, she did something she had never done in high school or college: she smashed the softball over the centerfield fence, hitting her first-ever home run. But the thrill of victory quickly turned into the agony of defeat when she unexpectedly collapsed with a knee injury on her way to first base.

Not knowing what else to do, Sara crawled to the base and just sat on it. If her teammates helped her, she would be called out. What could she do? Well, something happened that no one expected. Two members of the opposing team—one of whom was the conference's career home run leader—picked up Tucholsky and carried her around the bases so that her three-run homer would count…even though the three runs meant a playoff-eliminating defeat for Western Oregon's opponent.

When God placed His people within the body of Christ, He did an even more wonderful thing: He joined us together with other believers in whom His Spirit also dwells. Being connected to these people, we find ourselves unexpectedly carried along through life's weakest moments. How wonderful that the God who is love filled His people with that love! And how marvelous it is that we are part of that body!

Thank You for the body of Christ. What a wonderful thing You have done by making me part of Your family.

Caring Love in Correction

As many as I love, I reprove and chasten: be zealous therefore, and repent.

Revelation 3:19 ASV

Scottish minister Oswald Chambers wrote this in his seminal book *My Utmost for His Highest*: "Get alone with Jesus and either tell Him that you do not want sin to die out in you—or else tell Him that at all costs you want to be identified with His death."

The love of Christ is remarkable. Motivated by pure love, Jesus came down to earth and died. That was His action, and as Sir Isaac Newton set forth in his third law of physics: "For every action there is a reaction." Accepting Jesus's love as demonstrated on the cross prompts in us a reaction of zealousness and repentance. In the Greek, "zealous" means "to move with heat," and "repent" means "to exercise the mind; to observe and comprehend; to think differently."

Jesus implored us to move with passion into His embrace, to identify with His death by acknowledging that it is our sin that nailed Him to the cross, and to experience the life-changing power of His forgiveness and grace. In every moment He disciplines and corrects us, may we come to know more deeply the wonder of His ever-watchful love.

Lord, I thank You that You continue to have mercy on me, a sinner. May I respond with a life that honors You.

Maker of Heaven and Earth

By the word of the LORD were the heavens made and all the host of them by the breath of His mouth.

PSALM 33:6 KJV

The first line of the Apostle's Creed reads: "I believe in God, the Father almighty, Creator of heaven and earth." This belief is basic to our understanding of the great God we worship. The God of the Bible is the Creator of all: He made the universe out of nothing. By His word He spoke the heavens into existence, and by His breath He created the starry canopy of the sparkling night sky.

Word and *breath*. In the original Hebrew the word for "breath" is the same as the word for "spirit." At the beginning of John's Gospel, we read that "in the beginning was the Word, the Word was with God, and the Word was God.... All things were made by Him" (1:1, 3). Jesus the Word was present at creation, the Word of God laid out the heavens, and the Spirit of God sustains all of creation.

What a glorious occasion: the Trinity working in concert to speak and breathe the heavens and the earth into existence. It is impossible not to marvel at the wonder of this awesome display of divine creativity and power.

Lord, each time I look into the heavens, may I rejoice at the evidence of Your creative power.

Thunder

The LORD also thundered in the heavens, and the Most High uttered His voice, hailstones and coals of fire. He sent out His arrows, and scattered them, and lightning flashes in abundance, and routed them.

PSALM 18:13–14 NASB

Thunder is a mysterious thing. Simply stated, it is the sound made by lightning, but the actual cause of this sound has puzzled scientists for centuries. Ancients thought that we hear thunder when clouds collide. Later on, scientists proposed more complex theories about this mysterious sound. Some hypothesized that lightning creates a vacuum, which then produces a thunderous noise. Others suggested that the higher temperature caused by a lightning strike creates a shockwave of sorts that results in a rumble. Though much about thunder is not understood, one thing is certain: thunder signals power in the skies that is beyond our control.

The psalmist David spoke of God Almighty having a voice of thunder, and that metaphor was undoubtedly a source of comfort. Being pursued by men wanting to kill him, David could think about himself as protected and defended by the thundering One of heaven, the God who is not controlled by mankind.

Mysteries about thunder and lightning remain, but both are the handiwork of God, pointing to Him who is even more powerful than the forces of nature.

When I turn to You, I find refuge and shelter in Your vastness and strength—and I thank You, Almighty God.

Humble Praise

Lord, let all the kings of the earth praise you when they hear the words you speak.
They will sing about what the LORD has done, because the LORD's glory is great.
Though the Lord is supreme, he takes care of those who are humble,
but he stays away from the proud.

PSALM 138: 4–6 NCV

The word "humble" comes from the Latin root word *humus*, meaning "of the earth or the ground." It's the same root that is the basis for our English words *exhume* and, of course, *human*. So while *humble* can mean many things to many people, at its essence the word at least means something along the lines of "one who remembers where he or she came from." The word refers to origins, and that doesn't just mean your parents. It primarily means…the dust.

Remember that from dust you were created and to dust you will return. It's a familiar phrase that can be either depressing or encouraging. Why encouraging? Because the words remind us of the One who promises to take care of us, the One *not* made from dust but the One who existed before the dust even came to be; the One who reigns over all, the One whose glory is great, the One who is supreme, the Lord.

No other gods are like You, O Lord. You are supreme, and Your glory is great.

Tradition!

Give praise to the LORD, proclaim his name; make known among the nations what he has done. Sing to him, sing praise to him; tell of all his wonderful acts.

PSALM 105:1–2 NIV

"Tradition!" Tevye sings as the classic musical *Fiddler on the Roof* opens. In this rousing song, the family patriarch refers to Hebrew customs and responsibilities, practices that exist even today.

Moses laid out certain traditions and instructions in Deuteronomy, but his admonition in chapter 6— "Impress them on your children ...talk about them when you sit at home and when you walk along the road" (vv. 6-9)—gave parents an idea for making God's truth relevant.

Now consider what would happen if you became Hebrew for a day. Imagine fervently calling out to God. You tell everyone about His unparalleled wisdom, miraculous abilities, unsurpassed goodness. And you sing about His creation and divine sovereignty, about His grace and salvation. You do all of this for just one day.

What do you think would happen the next day if you invited others—if you invited your spouse and your children—to join you? What if you started the daily practice of praise, thanksgiving, and song in your family? Would you soon have a...tradition?

Probably. So what's stopping you?

Holy Lord, help me establish the right kinds of traditions within my household.

The Greatest Teacher

I will instruct you and teach you in the way which you should go;
I will counsel you with my eye upon you.

Psalm 32:8 NASB

Alexander Pope wrote "An Essay on Criticism" in 1709. In it he proclaimed that "A little learning is a dangerous thing." And that's true. People with a small amount of knowledge often think they have more expertise than they actually do. Their limited knowledge, however, goes hand in hand with their limited understanding, and the results can be disastrous.

Thankfully, according to His Word, we find in God a willing teacher whose wisdom is perfect and divine. Yet God takes His role as teacher one step further. He not only instructs you, but He will "watch over you" and provide counsel and guidance for each step of your way.

Don't misinterpret this phrase to mean that God is like some troll under a bridge, ready to bash you when you slip up. Exactly the opposite is true! God loves you, His child, so much that He made the commitment to care for you in every way necessary. We might remember a favorite teacher in our academic careers, but only God, in His wondrous goodness, cares enough to be always present in our lives to shepherd us along the righteous path.

Teach me Your ways, O perfectly wise Lord, and by Your Spirit and Your truth, keep me on the righteous path.

A Delighted Father

God can't stand pious poses, but he delights in genuine prayers.

Proverbs 15:8 MSG

What does it mean to be pious? Is piety simply devotion to the God of the Bible? Is it showing loyalty and reverence for the Almighty? Or is piety too often a "holier than thou" stance of self-righteously looking down on the regular-Joe sinner? Yes, yes, and yes.

Piety itself—heartfelt devotion, humble godliness—is not what God despises. A pious *pose* is what the Lord cannot tolerate.

Far too easily our sincere prayers can degenerate into empty words repeated in hopes of buying off God, avoiding the consequences of sin, or attempting to elevate ourselves. We too often assume the pious pose in front of fellow sinners in the desire to be considered "religious." What God prefers to all of this, however—what He absolutely *delights* in—is the simple prayer spoken genuinely from the heart.

Imperfect grammar is fine; religious rhetoric is not. Rather than having His children approach Him with polished speeches, God prefers our honest stammerings, humble cries, fervent pleadings, earnest confessions of sin, and childlike gratitude for His grace.

Of course, the God who longs for a relationship with us doesn't want pretense or posing. He desires for us to approach Him openly, hiding nothing, so He can bestow on His children the blessings of His affection for them.

Help me to approach You in all honesty and genuineness so that You may delight in me and I may delight in You.

May 7

Around the World

The wind blows to the south and turns to the north;
round and round it goes, ever returning on its course.
Ecclesiastes 1:6 niv

In the science of meteorology, the term *cyclone* doesn't refer to a tornado-like system of weather. Instead, *cyclone* describes a normal, always-occurring movement of air. A cyclone is a large system of air that circulates between the equator and either of the poles. The air circulates clockwise in the southern hemisphere and counterclockwise in the north. So, round and round the air circulates…

This is just one of the myriad plans devised by our Creator God. This constant movement of wind creates air currents that carry rain, fresh air, seed spores, and more to the far reaches of the globe, helping to maintain the life God put in place.

He is a God of wonder, always surprising us when we learn something new about His intricate, precise, perfectly planned ways.

When I pause to closely examine even a single aspect of Your amazing world, O God, I can only praise You.

The Ultimate Living Room

God's Message: "Heaven's my throne, earth is my footstool.
What sort of house could you build for me?
What holiday spot reserve for me? I made all this! I own all this!"

Isaiah 66:1 MSG

Followers of Hinduism believe that the gods live in several places: Shiva is said to live on Mt. Kailasa in the Himalayas and Vishnu on an ocean of milk. Practitioners of voodoo believe that one of its powerful beings lives under bridges and assumes the form of a policeman. The Assyrians of Isaiah's time worshiped idols fashioned by human hands, idols that were inhabited by every kind of god. Logically, manmade gods can live wherever their maker desires. After all, these lowercase-*g* gods are only as big as the limits of human imagination.

In the splendor of heaven, however, our Jehovah God of Scripture sits on a magnificent throne, commands the universe with kingly authority, holds court with angels and winged creatures, and oversees His vast creation. God's mere *presence* fills both heaven and earth. It isn't possible to create walls around Him, for He is the creator of all that is. And He reigns with heaven as His throne room and the earth beneath His feet.

As the one true and eternal King, His majesty extends to every star and sun, from the deepest sea to beyond the highest heaven.

God in heaven, how I long for the day when I can behold You—in all Your glory—high and lifted up, on Your everlasting throne.

The Watchful One

Like flying birds so the Lord of hosts will protect Jerusalem.
He will protect and deliver it; He will pass over and rescue it.

Isaiah 31:5 NASB

The red-tailed hawk is unique. This bird seldom flaps its wings, so its flight is slow and deliberate, punctuated by deep wingbeats. It has the ability to hover and remain stationary as it watches over its young or searches for prey. Even when it soars, the red-tailed hawk's speed is typically slow, but when it dives, it can reach up to 120 mph. Blessed with vision that allows it to see great distances, the red-tailed hawk keeps its eye on its young and flies to their assistance whenever there is danger.

The instincts of this grand bird are a marvel, and they reflect the guardian relationship that God has with His people. Our heavenly Father has a tenderness and affection for those in His care, and He will act with deliberate speed and swiftness to deliver His people whenever there is danger.

God watches over His people to protect and defend us. What a comfort to know that you are never out of God's sight! Nothing can separate you from His loving care.

As my Protector and Provider, thank You for allowing absolutely nothing to separate me from Your care.

Everlasting Compassion

When he saw the crowds, he had compassion on them, because they were harassed and helpless, like sheep without a shepherd.

Matthew 9:36 NIV

Some people are born compassionate—you may have looked into a child's eyes and seen an old soul full of tenderness and humility. But most compassionate people have earned it the hard way.

C. S. Lewis discovered a depth of tenderness he had never known when he met, loved, then lost his wife, Joy. Chuck Colson took a long, hard fall from a prestigious White House position to a prison cell—where he heard the Lord's call to a different line of work and service. Walk down the halls of any cancer ward for children, and you'll see hard-won compassion there as well.

But God did not earn or learn compassion the hard way, nor did He uncover it when He first experienced great pain. Compassion is part of His very nature, existing in Him eternally even as He has existed eternally. And that compassion undoubtedly brings Him heartache. Not a day has gone by without Him being ridiculed, blasphemed, cursed, denied, or ignored. He also witnesses the harsh persecution of His people. And yet...God graciously continues to extend His boundless compassion.

The Almighty's kindness is real. He will never stop reaching out to the hurting, the hopeless, and the helpless.

Lord, even if I have to learn the hard way, help me be more compassionate so I may point the lost and hurting to You.

The God Who Can Be Found

You will seek me and find me when you seek me with all your heart.

Jeremiah 29:13 niv

We all like to be appreciated and, from time to time, even praised for who we are and what we have accomplished. But none of us likes it when someone pours on the flattery for the sole purpose of getting something from us. Virginia tobacco growers in the 1600s recognized this "blowing smoke" tactic when a buyer used empty flattery to try to get a cheaper price from the farmers.

The same vast difference exists between flattery and appreciation when it comes to approaching God. The difference between flattering God and praising God is enormous. Flattering God arises out of a self-serving agenda, and the resulting prayers sound more like bargaining with God than acknowledging His greatness. In sharp contrast, praise comes from the soul of someone sincerely and wholeheartedly seeking—even striving after—our awesome God.

How God blesses us when we put aside our personal agenda and silence a flattering tongue! God delights in us when we seek after Him with our whole heart and enjoy simply being in His presence. Graciously, our infinite and holy God, Ruler of all history and Lord of our lives, lets us find Him. All praise to Him both now and forever!

Lord of my life, thank You for letting Yourself be found by me and known by me, for in You I have purpose and hope, direction and peace.

A Father's Devotion

And even the very hairs of your head are all numbered.

Matthew 10:30 NIV

Have you ever seen a daddy who is absolutely lovestruck with his newborn infant? His adoring gaze at the new little person who has captured his heart is sweet to behold. A first-time father will sit in a hospital chair for hours and just stare at this child he only just met but who he now loves beyond comprehension. He will examine little fingers and toes, look carefully at the shape of the lips and nose, and offer prayers of thanksgiving and pleas for blessings and protection. This is *his* child, and he is smitten.

If you have ever wondered about the extent of God's love for you, consider this: God knows the exact number of hairs on your head. He has gazed upon you and counted them. Furthermore, it is estimated that 7 billion people live on the earth right now, yet our Creator knows every single detail about every single one of us.

God's love is like no other. His awareness of our innermost thoughts is simply the outworking of His tremendous affection toward us. It's remarkable that the God who created the universe and holds it all together nevertheless sits quietly, at right this moment, captivated by us. How long has it been since you've delighted in the reality that God the Father utterly delights in you?

Your love truly exceeds anything I have ever known. That's amazing.

Salty

Salt is a very good thing; but if it should lose its saltiness, what can you do to restore its flavour? You must have salt in yourselves, and live at peace with each other.

Mark 9:50 Phillips

Many sermons have been delivered about the Bible's talk of salt, most of them reminders of salt's basic properties: it is both a seasoning and a preservative—essential properties in our sinsick world. But have you ever noticed how Jesus turned our usual definition of peace on its head?

Peace is the absence of struggle and the absence of grit. Yet Jesus encouraged us to "have salt" in ourselves. Salt is, by nature, gritty and rough. Interestingly, *gritty* and *rough* could be used to describe Jesus's own nature: He never hesitated, for instance, to boldly speak confrontational truth and words of disarming honesty with anyone and everyone.

Jesus went on to say that we can have salt in ourselves yet still be at peace with one another. Many spiritual communities would wince at that thought. How can gritty words result in smooth relationships? Only by the transforming power of Jesus. With His blessing, the world can taste and even welcome our peaceful-salty witness. It really can happen; it really does happen.

Jesus makes the peaceful-salty paradox possible. He brings kingdom growth out of apparent contradictions. How mighty are His ways!

Fill my life with Your peace that it may overflow into the lives of those around me who so need it.

Out of a Good Heart

A good man produces good things from the good stored up in his heart,
and a bad man produce evil things from his own stores of evil.
For a man's words will always express what has been treasured in his heart.

Luke 6:45 Phillips

Cellular memory—at this point it is only a theory, but the stories around it are intriguing. Basically, *cellular memory* refers to the supposed phenomenon that occurs when an organ is donated to another human being and the recipient takes on some of the donor's characteristics. For example, a heart transplant recipient suddenly finds herself craving pastries and later discovers that the donor was a pastry chef who couldn't get enough of the sweets.

Luke 6 implies that our hearts have a memory of sorts—a storehouse of either good or bad. In fact, that storehouse is the source of our words. Thankfully, Jesus's promise of a new heart is not a transplant story but rather the re-creation of the old. The Great Physician overcomes and overhauls the sinful desires of our old memories and replaces them with good things—the seed of good words.

Only God Almighty is able to clear away a storehouse of evil and replace it with a treasure trove of things wonderful and fresh, beautiful and new.

Father, You alone possess the ability to make my bad heart good, my hardened heart soft. Keep me in Your loving care.

The Voice

I assure you that the time is coming—and is here!—when the dead will hear the voice of God's Son, and those who hear it will live!

John 5:25 CEB

We know some people in our lives so well that they don't have to identify themselves when they call us on the phone. Usually the first few words from a spouse, a mother, a sister, or a best friend are all that is needed for us to know who's calling.

Isn't it amazing how the ear picks up frequencies that are meaningful to us?

Similarly, Jesus promised that those who name Him Savior and Lord will recognize His voice when He calls out. He didn't tell us what or when He would call. But we can be sure that when Jesus does beckon, no introductions will be necessary. The dead will know whose voice it is. The faithful will recognize the eternal voice of Jesus, the Son of the living God.

For those who listen and respond, life everlasting is promised. Hallelujah! What a Savior!

Your voice, Jesus, is the lifeline to everlasting joy and peace. May I never miss You when You call.

Our Great Bridge

Jesus spoke these things; and lifting up His eyes to heaven,
He said, "Father, the hour has come; glorify Your Son, that the Son may glorify You,
even as You gave Him authority over all flesh,
that to all whom You have given Him, He may give eternal life.

JOHN 17:1–2 NASB

Construction of the Golden Gate Bridge began on January 5, 1933, in an effort to span the Pacific Ocean's entrance into San Francisco Bay. Then, several years later, on the so-called Pedestrian Day of May 27, 1937, an estimated eighteen thousand people lined up at six a.m. to cross the bridge. They were thrilled to see the fulfillment of this dream, and they wanted to experience for themselves the opportunity to walk between the two shores.

A more remarkable bridging occurred two thousand years ago when Jesus came to span the infinite distance between holy God and sinful humanity. Serving as our great High Priest, Jesus prayed to God on behalf of the entire human race just before the countdown to the cross began. Sinless Jesus had authority over all humankind, so He could be the perfect sacrifice that would reconcile us to God.

And what are two divine results of Jesus's crucifixion and resurrection? *Glory* for the Father and the Son, and *eternal life* for humankind. It was God's original design that we should have eternal life, and by the atoning sacrifice of Jesus, it is accomplished.

O Jesus, You are the great bridge to the Father. To You be the glory and honor forever.

Trustworthy

Now my soul is troubled, and what shall I say Father, save me from this hour? No, it was for this very reason I came to this hour. Father, glorify your name! Then a voice came from heaven, "I have glorified it, and will glorify it again."

John 12:27–28 niv

Author Anne Lamott has said the two best prayers she knows are *Help me! Help me! and Thank you! Thank you!* And she's right. In fact, most of our prayers can be distilled into one or the other of these options.

But consider the possibility of another "best" prayer, one that we can pray only after we've lived a little and witnessed the surprising tender mercies of God. It's a prayer of spiritual maturity. It's the prayer Jesus prayed before He went to the cross: *Father, glorify your name*. Or, in other words, *I trust You.*

It's impossible to pray that prayer half-heartedly. Those simple words are an all-in prayer—a verbal declaration to anyone who's listening that, whatever the circumstances, distress, or grief, the desired outcome is always glory to God. A prayer like that in no way diminishes the genuine need that prompts our cries for help or our sincere gratitude for safe passage. Rather, *Father, glorify your name* is a plea that we will be able to hold tightly to something beyond ourselves. It is a very best prayer by which we cling to the enduring faithfulness of our almighty God.

I trust You, Father. I really do. Yet I want to trust You more. May Your holy and perfect name be glorified!

They Are One

Stephen, full of the Holy Spirit, looked up to heaven and saw the glory of God, and Jesus standing at the right hand of God.

Acts 7:55 NIV

A number of verses in the Bible report that Jesus is at "the right hand of God." This position indicates the Father's approval of the Son, but more importantly, it places Jesus as God's equal in power and authority. That's the vision the apostle Stephen saw, which explains the message He was conveying to his accusers that day. This truth, however, was more than they could handle, and Stephen became the first Christian martyr.

Whether or not the onlookers—whether or not you and I—could handle the truth that Jesus is co-equal with God is really beside the point. Again and again Scripture presents evidence in support of the truth Jesus spoke earlier in John's Gospel: "I and the Father are one." The authority and power Jesus holds is the same power and authority God the Father possesses. God the Father and God the Son are one.

Not surprisingly, the glory of Stephen's vision dropped him to his knees. At that point, the angry mob threw its lethal stones. Yet from Stephen came a cry of praise and forgiveness as he entered the eternal presence of the Lord. At that moment, in a very tangible way, Stephen stepped from mortality to eternity. All glory goes to our awesome God, who pulls aside the veil and shows Himself to those He graciously grants eyes of faith.

Worthy are You to be praised, Lord. May I do so every day I live and—like Stephen—even when I die.

Steadfast Faith

Without weakening in his faith, he faced the fact that his body was as good as dead—since he was about a hundred years old—and that Sarah's womb was also dead. Yet he did not waver through unbelief regarding the promise of God, but was strengthened in his faith and gave glory to God, being fully persuaded that God had power to do what he had promised.

Romans 4:19–21 NIV

Before God gave us His laws and commandments, He gave us His promises.

When God spoke to the fallen Adam and Eve after the serpent had tempted them, He spoke of her offspring that would crush the deceiver's head. He promised the ultimate defeat of the enemy.

When God instructed Noah to build an ark the length of a football field in anticipation of never-before-seen rain, Noah obeyed. Noah trusted God's promise that He would preserve him as well as his family.

When God told Abraham that he would be the "father of many nations," Abraham didn't ask for it in writing or call a notary as a witness. He accepted the truth of the promise based on the One who made the promise.

Choosing to believe in the face of contrary circumstances—deciding to feed faith instead of counting doubts—builds one's spiritual strength. All glory goes to the Lord, who is able to accomplish all that He promises to do. His Word is sure, and He will not fail His people. He will not fail you.

My prayer is simple: help me keep trusting You, even when I struggle to.

Conquering Love

No, in all these things we are more than conquerors through him who loved us. For I am convinced that neither death nor life, neither angels nor demons, neither the present nor the future, nor any powers, neither height nor depth, nor anything else in all creation, will be able to separate us from the love of God that is in Christ Jesus our Lord.

Romans 8:37–39 NIV

Oswald Chambers said, "It is a shameful thing for a Christian to talk about getting the victory. The Victor ought to have got us so completely that it is His victory all the time, and we are more than conquerors through Him." Yet it is sometimes hard to feel like a conqueror. Life can be brutal, and we may not live with any sense of victory at all. That's when we must choose to believe what we know but don't necessarily feel. We must choose to focus on the truth expressed in God's Word: that by the redemptive power of Jesus Christ, we are *more* than conquerors.

Our resurrected Savior's victory over sin and death was complete and total. It was not a mere gesture, hint, or tease. Jesus won victory on the cross once and for all. Nothing from the lowest depths to the greatest heights, nothing from the darkest past to the bleakest future, can weaken the victory or threaten to take it away. So Chambers was absolutely right: for Christians to talk about someday *getting* the victory is absurd. Jesus has already won it.

May I daily testify of Your victory over sin and death and bear witness to Your sacrificial love.

What You Need

God can bless you with everything you need, and you will always have more than enough to do all kinds of good things for others.

2 Corinthians 9:8 CEV

Mick Jagger and Keith Richards of the Rolling Stones would hardly be considered theologians, but one of their most famous songs has a few lines the faithful would do well to ponder:

No, you can't always get what you want.

But if you try sometimes, you just might find you get what you need.

That said, the apostle Paul would hardly be considered a rock star, but in a single verse, he focused in on the truth that Mick and Keith only hinted at. And Paul kept going where the Rolling Stones stopped.

The apostle Paul wrote that God pours out His riches on His people. God's grace, mercy, love, forgiveness, and kindness overflow in our lives—He blesses us abundantly—when we come to Him by naming His Son as our Savior and Lord. God gives us all that we need and much more. And He gives abundantly, not only so we will have what *we* need, but so we can bless and serve others.

You never know when doing good things for someone else in God's name might lead them to recognize Jesus as their Savior and Lord. We should expect it. After all, our God is the the One whose infinite supply meets and surpasses all demand.

Your provision is astounding, Lord. I pray I never take Your generosity for granted or fail to thank You for the abundance of gifts that come from Your hand.

May 22

Nudge

The love of Christ compels us, because we judge thus: that if One died for all, then all died.

2 Corinthians 5:14 NKJV

Different Bible translations offer different descriptions of what the love of Christ does to us. Examples include *compel, rule, constrain*, and *control*. All of these words hint at force or obligation, but there is another way to understand how Jesus moves us to act. Specifically, Max Lucado has written that the Christ-possessed heart is *nudged* by Christ. And that is a good thing to remember.

If we forget that *the love of Christ nudges us*—if we're always listening or looking for something big and bold from the Almighty—we may miss His gentle voice or the tender, guiding movement of His hand. God does speak boldly, but He also nudges us in smaller, subtler ways. Maybe in your own life it was a friend's kind and timely word, the generous offering of financial assistance, or a warm welcome when you first visited the church you now call home. The love of Christ is in the nudging as much as it is in the bold proclamations. In the nudging, Jesus's love is a quieter compelling, a softer controlling, a gentler rule. His is the soft voice in our hearts, moving and urging us to reach out in His name. May we never miss His promptings.

Compel, control, rule, constrain, and nudge me for Your glory, Lord, I pray.

May 23

Forever Sealed

Do not grieve the Holy Spirit of God, with whom you were sealed for the day of redemption.

Ephesians 4:30 niv

There is a beauty in the scrolls and seals—in the parchment, the clay or the wax, the intricate imprints—of ancient times. We look at them in museums and marvel at the painstaking work, the craftsmanship, the attention to detail.

Any document that required a seal was, by implication, quite valuable. Typically carved into a ring, each seal was unique, like a signature. The ring-bearer would stamp his "signet" into a spot of clay or wax that had been melted onto the rolled parchment. Once it dried and hardened, the signet impression could not be changed. When a scroll sealed by royalty or a governing authority was presented, people may well have come running in anticipation of the message, but they looked on solemnly as the intended recipient broke it open.

Today, this process of sealing a scroll offers a picture of what the Holy Spirit has done for you. He has gently rolled you up like an invaluable scroll, validated your faith, and then stamped you with His unique seal, which *cannot be changed.* When He placed you—a precious scroll of great value—into God's mighty hands, it was a solemn and stirring moment. Sealed by God's Spirit and placed in the Lord's hands, you are secure in His kingdom for all eternity.

Lord, I am forever safe in Your kingdom and love because of Your choice to bind me to Yourself.

Choosing Good

That you will see the difference between good and bad and will choose the good; that you will be pure and without wrong for the coming of Christ; that you will be filled with the good things produced in your life by Christ to bring glory and praise to God.

PHILIPPIANS 1:10–11 NCV

Does one bad apple really spoil the bunch? Yes, it can definitely happen. Given time, a moldy apple can contaminate the fruit around it, which in turn will contaminate the other apples, until the whole barrel is spoiled. So it is vitally important to remove any blemished apples from the bunch.

The apostle Paul probably knew that one tiny cut in a piece of fruit can start the process of rot. Perhaps this is why he prayed for the Philippians as he did. Paul warned about the presence of a bad apple and the potentially far-reaching consequences of its mold and rot. He prayed with total faith that God would bless believers—then and now—with discernment, with the wisdom and insight necessary to identify the bad, the wrong, the sinful and to only keep the pure and good.

God's Word teaches that we can—with the Spirit's guidance—choose good. Such wise choices point to God, the Giver of all good things.

I ask You, by the power of Your Holy Spirit, to grant me the discernment I need in order to know when the enemy is at work.

I Love My Boss

Do your work willingly, as though you were serving the Lord himself, and not just your earthly master. In fact, the Lord Christ is the one you are really serving, and you know that he will reward you.

Colossians 3:23–24 CEV

If you're dissatisfied at work, you're not alone. In fact, a Google search of the phrase "I hate my job!" will yield more than 40 million results. That's right—40 million! But you don't have to stay in the hate. In fact, one of the best ways to improve your job situation is not to change jobs, but to stay right where you are and adjust your attitude.

For those of us who follow Christ, this attitude adjustment comes by way of knowing and remembering who our Boss *really* is. As Paul stated, whatever our line of work and whoever signs our paycheck, the One we are actually serving is the Lord. When we work as unto Him—when we are mindful of our witness and we want to glorify God in all we do—He promises to reward our efforts…and God always keeps His promises.

With the eyes of our heart focused on the Lord, we can find satisfaction and meaning in the most mundane of tasks. We can discover joy in the simplest of duties. And here's one more perk to this plan. With this simple adjustment of our attitude, we may find that our "I hate my job!" mantra has been replaced with a new one: "I love my Boss!"

Remind me today that it is You I serve, O Lord. My labor is not in vain.

Never Unfaithful

The one who calls you is faithful and he will do it.

1 Thessalonians 5:24 niv

In the early 1980s, no one would have imagined that the leader of the Soviet Union would eventually have such fond feelings toward America's commander-in-chief. But he did.

When Ronald Reagan died in 2004, former Soviet leader Mikhail Gorbachev boarded a plane headed for Washington, DC—to pay his last respects. In recounting his relationship with the former president, Gorbachev shared that his feelings toward Reagan had changed over the years. What eventually won the Russian leader over? Reagan was "a man of his word."

If it is possible for leaders of entire nations to be won over simply because someone was true to their word, how much more should we trust our promise-making, promise-keeping God? Having existed for all eternity, God has made promise upon promise, and He has yet to fail on a single one. Great is His faithfulness!

Lord, enable me to be a person of integrity, a person of my word.

The Place of Highest Honor

After he finished the sacrifice for sins, the Son took his honored place high in the heavens right alongside God, far higher than any angel in rank or rule.

Hebrews 1:3 MSG

Seating arrangements do matter! Often a given culture or a certain setting will require specific guidelines, and those established rules are carefully adhered to. A wedding reception, a state dinner, the Supreme Court, the United Nations Security Council—much thought goes into planning who will sit with whom. The higher the office or the more important the occasion, the more significant the decisions.

At the beginning of time, the Almighty—the God of order—brought the universe into being, and He too determined the seating arrangement. And the plan He established gave Him great pleasure.

But first some of the backstory. There was a birth, a family, a thirty-three-year visit to Planet Earth. A sacrificial death and a purging, three days of other-worldly battle, a forty-day return to earth, a Great Commission, and a glorious ascension into heaven. At that point, Jesus had done all He had been called to do. Having perfectly fulfilled God's plan for the salvation of humanity, Jesus took His place next to God, His sacrificial work finished.

There, at the right hand of God, in the traditional place of highest honor, Jesus sits today—patient, calm, anticipating the day that you will be with Him, seeing Him in all His glory, as He really is.

Help me to always keep my eyes on You, and please grant me glimpses of Your glory to sustain me.

The Good and Perfect Gift-Giver

Every good and perfect gift is from above, coming down from the Father of the heavenly lights, who does not change like shifting shadows.

James 1:17 niv

What comes to mind when you think about the worst gift you ever received? We've all gotten that…uh…indescribable Christmas gift we can't return, exchange, or regift quickly enough! And who hasn't purchased something, only to get it home and find that a vital piece is missing?

In sharp contrast to our human efforts, God is the perfect Giver of perfect gifts. His giving is merely an extension of His generous and compassionate nature. The gifts—of forgiveness, righteousness, grace, mercy, and love—come at great cost, yet they flow from Him in abundance, always ideal for the recipient, with no missing parts, no confusing instructions, no catches, no hidden fees.

The origin of these life-changing gifts is "the Father of heavenly lights," and our heavenly Father has absolutely no intention of turning away His children or being tightfisted. This generous Giver has offered us the ultimate gift of eternal life through Jesus Christ. Clearly, as poet Elizabeth Barrett Browning wrote, "God's gifts put man's best dreams to shame."

You have provided so much for me, dear Father. Show me how to pay it forward.

Our Suffering, His Strength

If you suffer as a Christian, do not be ashamed, but praise God that you bear that name.

1 Peter 4:16 niv

"We must learn to regard people less in the light of what they do or omit to do," said Dietrich Bonhoeffer, "and more in the light of what they suffer."

Bonhoeffer himself knew about suffering. A pastor during Hitler's reign of terror, Bonhoeffer was part of the German resistance movement. He ended up being arrested and imprisoned in concentration camps. But far from being bitter about this course of events, he was described by even German authorities as "lovable."

Ever since the people of Antioch slapped Jesus's followers with the nickname, Christians have suffered for their faith. Just as Jesus's peers insulted Him because of His holiness, subsequent generations have been just as willing to abuse His followers.

Against this backdrop, one wondrous aspect of God's nature comes into sharp relief. When those who bear the name of His Son suffer—when they are insulted, rejected, or even imprisoned for His sake—God reveals His presence with them. His power, His goodness, and His strength are evident in His suffering children. His supernatural grace in our lives gives us the ability to persevere—and makes the world sit up and take notice.

Lord Jesus, what a privilege to be known as a Christian. May I, by the power of Your Spirit, wear Your name well.

Remarkable Resemblance

Dear friends, we are already God's children,
but he has not yet shown us what we will be like when Christ appears.
But we do know that we will be like him, for we will see him as he really is.

1 John 3:2 NLT

After the birth of a child, comments like "Oh, she has her mother's nose" or "He definitely has his father's eyes" are common. In reality, it's truly hard to tell when a child is so young. We see what we want to see when we look at a newborn. What parents do know for certain in those moments is "This baby is my child." Who that child will end up looking like remains to be seen.

Similarly, who knows how much God's children will end up looking like Jesus on this side of heaven? We are God's children if we have recognized our sin and accepted the grace and forgiveness that are available through Jesus. As our lives here on earth unfold, we will grow up to be…to one degree or another…like Jesus.

What will we ultimately look like when Christ appears? Scripture says only that "we will be like Him." We will resemble our heavenly Father; we will unmistakably be the sons and daughters of God. In the meantime, the longing of our heart should be to grow in purity and wisdom, in grace and kindness. How marvelous to resemble our beautiful Savior now and forever!

Father, keep up Your ongoing, persistent, patient effort to transform me into the likeness of Your glorious Son. Forgive me when I fail.

A Reverential Fear

The fear of the LORD is the beginning of wisdom;
all who follow his precepts have good understanding. To him belongs eternal praise.

PSALM 111:10 NIV

What do you think of when you hear the word *fear*? Maybe you thought first of phobias—those persistent anxieties associated with a place or an object, like spiders or heights or darkness or flying. Sometimes even simple worry is characterized as fear. In 1915, Professor Walter Cannon, chairman of the Department of Physiology at Harvard Medical School, coined the term "fight or flight response" to describe the physiological responses in animals (later in humans) in threatening situations. All these kinds of fear are temporary reactions to passing circumstances, and they are a very normal part of being human.

The fear that the psalmist refers to in Psalm 111—the fear that births wisdom—begins when we come before God in reverence. Certainly the Lord is powerful enough to warrant heart-pumping terror, for He can raise His righteous hand in fearsome ways. But as God's children, we need no longer be afraid of His eternal judgment. Our reverence fuels our worship; our awe and wonder lead to praise. Our reverence also motivates us to follow the teachings of God's Word, and as we obey, we grow to know and love the Lord in a deeper way.

Reverence for the Holy One who is all-loving, all-powerful, all-wise, all-knowing is fear that prompts worship, devotion, and a closer relationship with Him. We are, understandably, to be humbled in His presence. Yet He also enfolds us in His love.

Teach me not only to worship You with all my life, but to fear You in a life-giving, wisdom-bearing way.

It's in Our DNA

God spoke: "Let us make human beings in our image, make them reflecting our nature so they can be responsible for the fish in the sea, the birds in the air, the cattle, and, yes, Earth itself, and every animal that moves on the face of Earth." God created human beings; he created them godlike, reflecting God's nature.

Genesis 1:26–27 msg

About 3.5 billion females and just over 3.5 billion males—that's a ballpark number for how many human beings are on the planet right now. Now consider this: every one of those 7 billion people—and that obviously includes you—is created in the image of God. Sure, you may sound like your father or have your grandmother's temper, but the primary image we all carry around inside us, down deep in our DNA, is God's. Have you ever wondered what that looks like?

The early chapters in Genesis indicate our created nature is to be responsible, to take care of people, places, and things. Consider the implications of 7 billion responsible people caring not only for themselves and their families but for friends and neighbors and widows and orphans and steelhead trout and magpies and magnolia trees and Ponderosa pines.

Doesn't this reveal what our Father is like? He is a wonderfully caring, beautifully generous, perfectly responsive God.

Your generosity is overwhelming, O God. May my life reflect Your image.

The Battle Cry

The Lord will fight for you; you need only to be still.

Exodus 14:14 niv

Their pre-battle speeches are the stuff of legend. "Will you fight?!" William Wallace roared to the Scottish Army at Stirling atop his war horse, his face painted blue. "Aye, fight and you may die…they may take our lives, but they'll never take our freedom!"

King Aragorn shouted, "Hold your ground!" to his army at the Black Gate in *Lord of the Rings*. "A day may come when the courage of men fails…but it is not this day. This day we fight!"

Of all those speeches in cinema and in history, however, Moses's exhortation to the Israelites to "Be still" as Pharaoh's army charged them may just be the most uninspiring. The Israelites had left Egypt armed for battle. They'd marched out boldly. They'd followed a mysterious pillar of fire. They'd been a bit cocky…right up until they were trapped in a strait between the mountains, the sea, and the Egyptian troops.

Then Moses did the unthinkable: he let the Israelites know they'd have no part in the honor of the upcoming battle. God would bring salvation. God's loving-kindness would rule the day. God would gain the glory through Pharaoh and his army.

God always has a purpose and always to His glory. You need only to trust and be still.

All-powerful God, the heart of the battle is Yours. Help me to be still in faith and hope.

Declare His Glory

Declare his glory among the nations, his marvelous deeds among all peoples.
For great is the LORD and most worthy of praise; he is to be feared above all gods.

1 CHRONICLES 16:24–25 NIV

Oswald Chambers wrote, "If in preaching the gospel you substitute your knowledge of the way of salvation for confidence in the power of the gospel, you hinder people from getting to reality."

The focus of the gospel is the resplendent nature and the magnificent work of God. Methods or doctrines are no substitute for that reality. When Jesus gave His mandate to preach the gospel, it was a simple instruction: if His glory and His deeds are declared, the world will be drawn to Him.

The Hebrew meaning of the word translated "deeds" is literally "action." God takes action in His creation and in the lives of His people. The exuberant response is to talk about it—what He has done, what He is doing, and what He will do.

The salvation of God through Jesus reveals the glory and wonder of God's excellent goodness to us. It is a reality we can always celebrate and a truth that can never be exhausted. He has done wonderful things. Talk about it!

Dear God, You are great and worthy of praise, and I declare Your glory.

June 4

Love Wins

I know that my redeemer lives, and that in the end he will stand on the earth.

Job 19:25 NIV

Poor Job. He didn't know he was starring in an Old Testament "Movie of the Week"—an epic riches-to-rags-to-riches story.

Behind the scenes, Satan the Screenwriter takes a righteous character living a blessed life, hits him with death and destruction—raiding parties that strip him of his livestock, freak acts of nature that strip him of his children—then Satan throws in itching, oozing sores and gleefully lets the action play out with sympathetic but misdirected minor characters and an unlikable wife.

But Job, poor Job…he suffers mightily, unaware of the conversations between God the Author/Director and Satan the Screenwriter. Job didn't know the ending like you do. He never thought he'd advance beyond the "rags" portion of his long, sad story. He said, in fact, "My spirit is broken; my days are cut short; the grave awaits me."

But God is sovereign—He cannot be tested by a fallen angel. The test was for Job. And Satan. And you. For no matter what Job lost on earth, no matter the inconceivable reason for his loss, he had one unshakable belief: an all-powerful, all-knowing Redeemer God directs everything from above. In the end, all else will fade away, and His good purpose will stand.

Almighty God, remind me during times of trial that love is stronger than suffering and that You are Love.

Final Destination

Then they cried out to the LORD in their trouble;
He delivered them from out of their distresses.

PSALM 107:6 NASB

Forty years in a desert. The phrase rolls off of our tongues with ease, but forty years is an awfully long time. For Moses and the Israelites, it must have felt like an entire lifetime. For many of them, it *was* their entire lifetime. In fact, by the time the Lord told Joshua to conquer Canaan, a completely new generation was in charge! How hard it must have been to keep believing that they would end up in a good place, to remember that these first years were just part of the journey. Yet year forty-one would not be like year forty.

Israel would indeed leave that desert. When they cried out for help, the Lord answered them and led them out by a "straight way" to a good place to settle. When God's people trust in Him, He leads them down straight paths. And the destination to which He leads His people is one of promise. It's a good place.

Isn't it amazing to realize that though God is bigger than we can imagine, He hears our cries for help? Be filled with wonder today at the God who sees, knows, and answers. He is preparing a wonderful destination for you.

God, I trust in You completely. I know that You have wonderful plans for me and that my destination will be better than I can even imagine.

God's in His Heaven

But our God is in the heavens; He does whatever He pleases.

Psalm 115:3 nasb

God's in His heaven, all's right with the world" is a line from "Pippa's Song," Robert Browning's poem about a young orphan girl who lived in a town in northern Italy. If you don't know the context of this poetic line, you'd think Pippa is uttering a naïve platitude about her precious faith. But if you read the rest of the poem, you find that she was exploited by unscrupulous people who forced her to work long hours in terrible conditions.

Context is everything, and within it, Browning's readers understand that this statement is one of praise in spite of personal circumstances, a statement of faith grounded in reality. Pippa is claiming that despite the evil and injustice in the world, one can still believe that God is omnipresent. And as long as He is ever with us, all is right with the world.

This God in heaven is our God, sovereign and absolute in power and majesty. The essence of His wonder is incomprehensible. His ways are above our ways, His thoughts above our thoughts. He rules with boundless power and His throne is not shaken by disbelief, by any sinister chaos devised by humanity or the evil one, or by disruptions in nature. In heaven and on earth, His awesome and perfect purposes are ultimately accomplished.

Not to me, O Lord, but to You be glory and praise.

Eternal Light

You, Lord, keep my lamp burning; my God turns my darkness into light.

Psalm 18:28 NIV

When it is night and the power goes out in the house, it can be disorienting. A place that is familiar and comfortable no longer feels safe. We stumble around until a candle is lit or a flashlight is found. The visibility the light provides immediately brings a sense of calm. Though the darkness is still present, the light allows us to find our way.

The God who lit up the universe on the first day of creation is the same God who focuses His radiant goodness on each of His children. Even at the time of creation, God did not completely dispel the darkness. Instead, He made the darkness distinct and gave it boundaries.

It's a given that we will face dark times in life, but just as God was present at creation, so too is He present in our lives in the midst of those frightening periods of darkness. The apostle John tells us in his first letter, "God is light, and in him is no darkness." The light emanates from His goodness. The purity of this light dazzles us with wonder. It is redemptive. It is healing. And it can never be extinguished.

God, let me be ever mindful of Your astounding goodness toward me so that I may always find joy, even in times of darkness.

Spontaneous Tribute

The Lord reigns forever, your God, O Zion, for all generations. Praise the Lord.

Psalm 146:10 NIV

The final moments of the big game. Your team needs to score to win. The seconds *tick, tick, tick* in agony, the ball is in the air, and...TOUCHDOWN! Do you sit passively in your seat, nodding and smiling? Or do you jump up, arms raised in victory?

The parade marches down the street. The color guard appears, shoulder to shoulder, flags and rifles in precise order. Do you stand, hand over heart or in salute?

The orchestra plays the familiar introduction to Handel's magnificent "Hallelujah Chorus." You can hear the words in your head long before they're sung. Do you leap to your feet in noble tribute?

If you do any of these things, you are joining in an act of praise, much like the writer of the "hallelujah psalm" in Psalm 146. You get caught up in the moment, emotions are high, and you *just can't help yourself*...you praise!

This is the kind of activity God delights in—exuberant, demonstrative tribute to His extraordinary loving-kindness and constant provision. He takes pleasure in your shining face when the choir sings, "For the Lord God Omnipotent reigneth." Your joyful adoration brings God joy as well. So go ahead—throw a hand in the air and praise!

King of kings and Lord of lords, Your strength and mercies are everlasting. I rise up and sing "Hallelujah!"

Loving Discipline

But don't, dear friend, resent God's discipline; don't sulk under his loving correction. It's the child he loves that GOD corrects; a father's delight is behind all this.

PROVERBS 3:11–12 MSG

The American satirist P. J. O'Rourke once remarked, "Because of their size, parents may be difficult to discipline properly."

Ah, discipline…that firm-handed instruction necessary for growth, that painful part of good development, that sometimes excruciating blow to adult pride. Yes—*adult* pride.

Adults naturally tend to get defensive when corrected; try shushing grown-ups in a movie theater. And that's why this proverb is so critical.

Your wise and merciful God, understands the adult reaction to discipline. He knows you resent it. But He also knows that every act of rebellion against Him and His holy principles is a wound to your own soul, so He acts in your best interests.

Sometimes He uses guilt. Sometimes He allows a crisis. Sometimes He sends a quiet word through another person. But at *all* times, He enfolds you in His everlasting and unchangeable grace, drawing you back to Him.

Our wonderful Father—even His correction is an expression of His amazing love.

Father God, Your patience and wisdom are beyond compare. Help me submit to Your teaching and correction.

Just Right

The LORD alone is God! He created the heavens and made a world where people can live, instead of creating an empty desert. The LORD alone is God; there are no others.

ISAIAH 45:18 CEV

For well over half a decade now, astronomers have been searching for a "Goldilocks planet"—one not too hot and not too cold that harbors oceans on its surface. In other words, scientists are looking for another habitable planet similar to Earth. Recently a discovery was made of the planet called Kepler 22b, about 2.4 times wider than Earth, circling a star about six hundred light years away. It is truly an amazing discovery that in no way diminishes our planet but actually emphasizes what an incredible creation Earth really is.

Our planet is one where people can live, sustainably. Earth is not like the vast rocks that are our neighbors: extremely hot (Venus) or deathly cold (Mars). The gift of a planet that is "just right" for us is no fairy tale but the result of the divine intentions of the Lord alone, the Creator of the heavens and the earth.

What a magnificent Architect! Everything we humans need for a thriving, fulfilling, healthy life exists here on Earth, provided by His hand. He alone is God!

Father God, Your creation of the Earth is perfect, as are You.

No Comparison

Can you compare me to anyone? No one is equal to me or like me.
Some people are rich with gold and weigh their silver on the scales.
They hire a goldsmith, and he makes it into a god.
Then they bow down and worship it.

ISAIAH 46:5–6 NCV

Of the many types of gods we worship, some are made of gold, some of silver, some of other precious metals or stones. But what those external idols have in common is that they were made by humans. Someone—a goldsmith or jeweler or artisan—took the raw material and fashioned it into an image. None of those items came to be by their own will or desire; they were dependent on another being to cause them to be.

Not so with God. No one created Him, no one fashioned Him from raw materials. He is primary, first, before all others, and above all others. He is the Source of all that is. Lesser gods may have eyes or ears but they cannot see, they cannot hear. God hears our prayers, He sees our needs, He upholds us, He bestows mercies that are new each morning. He has no equal. There is nothing that compares to Him. Nothing.

There is no created thing that is Your equal, Lord. Nothing compares to You.

Commander of the Sea

I am the L*ORD your God, who stirs up the sea so that its waves roar—*
the L*ORD of hosts is his name.*

ISAIAH 51:15 ESV

On the night of July 9, 1958, William Swanson and his wife anchored their houseboat in an Alaskan bay and went to bed. They were soon wakened by the violent shake of an earthquake. Swanson looked outside and saw what he thought was a landmark glacier flying through the air. Suddenly, he lost sight of the glacier and could only see a wave of water. Minutes later, Swanson's boat—still anchored—was lifted up by the wave and carried along like a surfboard. Swanson noticed that they were soaring approximately eighty feet above the trees. Amazingly, the Swansons' boat rode the crest and landed safely, and a fishing boat eventually rescued them. William Swanson and his wife survived the largest tsunami that had ever been recorded, one that had risen 1,720 feet above the shoreline.

The power of a tsunami reminds us it is God's command that can rattle the earth and tell the waters to rise. The mighty waters show us the mighty God to whom they submit. He is the Lord of hosts! Stand in awe of His matchless power today.

Lord, Your power causes me to stand in awe of You. You are the Lord of hosts.

Transforming Words

The word of the Lord came to me, saying, "Before I formed you in the womb I knew you, before you were born I set you apart; I appointed you as a prophet to the nations."

Jeremiah 1:4–5 NIV

By the year 626 BC, Assyria had ruled the world from its capital, Nineveh, for three centuries, but the contest for supremacy was ramping up. Babylon, to the south, was growing more powerful. Egypt, a super-force centuries before, was again getting ambitious. Into this cauldron stepped Jeremiah. His task was overwhelming: to speak truth in dangerous and difficult places, calling his people—the Israelites in Judah—back to their God.

Jeremiah was faithful through terrible, devastating years, yet Judah did not repent. Babylon swept across the land and conquered it. Jerusalem was destroyed and God's people taken into captivity. Through all of this, Jeremiah continued to listen to the voice of God, never giving up on the people. He was known by the Lord, who spoke to him specifically, privately, in his inner being. God strengthened him for the job. He chose him.

Jeremiah personifies obedience to the call, but he knew from the beginning he was not alone. The Lord's words are life and sustenance for all who will heed them. What is the Holy Spirit whispering to you today?

All-Knowing God, You are the Lord of all time and every nation. I praise You for Your words of life.

The Greatness of God

All the peoples of the earth are regarded as nothing.
He does as he pleases with the powers of heaven and the peoples of the earth.
No one can hold back his hand or say to him: "What have you done?"

Daniel 4:35 NIV

The nations of the world send their greatest athletes to compete in the Olympic Games. Millions upon millions of people across the globe tune in to watch as records are set and players excel in a multitude of sports. We thrill to watch their accomplishments because our world craves achievement. We take personal pride in our power; nations proclaim their feats. Still, individuals and entire nations rise and fall. Only God endures forever.

To think that whatever "greatness" we attain as an individual or a country is comparable to the greatness of God is pure folly. There is no comparison between the work of mankind and the excellence of God. If God intends to do something, nothing and no one may oppose His divine purposes.

Who can resist His will? Who can arrest His power? Who can stop His mighty hand? Who can challenge His decisions? Who can prevent Almighty God from completing that work which He has begun in the world or in an individual's life? In the words of King Nebuchadnezzar: no one.

Dear God, may I be ever mindful of Your greatness as You work Your will in the heavens and the earth.

Awesome Authority

And Jesus came and spoke to them, saying,
"All authority has been given to Me in heaven and on earth."
Matthew 28:18 NKJV

In his book, *Mere Christianity*, C. S. Lewis argues that to just consider Jesus as a great human being with a moral message is nonsense. "A man who was merely a man and said the sort of things Jesus said would not be a great moral teacher. Either this was, and is, the Son of God, or else a madman or something worse."

In case anyone thought Jesus was confused as to His identity, His words to His disciples—and by extension to all of us—should clear up that misconception. What's more, Jesus—by right of His death and resurrection—established His authority in all of creation and asserted His identity in His role within the Godhead.

And it all came with a promise: this unified Godhead with its miraculous, life-changing power would be available and present in our lives from the moment we accept Jesus into our hearts until we are ushered into eternity. No moral teacher could ever make such a claim or back it up with such a promise.

The weight of the authority of God in Christ is a reality changer. Fully, forever, He is trustworthy and able.

Dear Lord, You have authority over heaven and earth, and I praise You for Your life-changing power at work in me.

God's Glorious Salvation

For my eyes have seen your salvation, which you have prepared in the sight of all nations: a light for revelation to the Gentiles, and the glory of your people Israel.

Luke 2:30–32 niv

At its essence, Christianity could be called a rescue religion. The word for "salvation" in the Greek means "rescue," and salvation is at the heart of the Christian faith. There's light coming toward us down the dark tunnel. There's air to breathe, and food for the desperately starved soul, and an exciting life waiting ahead.

Through His Son, Jesus Christ, God has prepared a great banquet. He has set the table. He has sent out the invitations. He has expanded the guest list to include all nations—anyone who has "eyes to see."

It is a grand mystery why God chose this method of salvation—taking human form and dying for the sin of humankind. But that is the wonder and prerogative of God. In His loving-kindness, He knew we were in need of rescue, and so He sent us His salvation—a revelation of His redeeming love.

Dear God, in Your wondrous love You sent Jesus Christ, our Rescuer and Redeemer. You are my life and the hope of every nation!

Bright and Beautiful

When Jesus spoke again to the people, he said, "I am the light of the world. Whoever follows me will never walk in darkness, but will have the light of life."

John 8:12 NIV

Light is a wonderful thing. Technically speaking, it is a form of energy that results when electrons change their orbits around nuclei. Practically speaking, therapeutic light is used in lasers, fluorescent lamps, or bright, full-spectrum lights for the treatment of skin disorders, sleep disorders, and even some psychiatric disorders. Lasers emit light through optical amplification and are used in medicine, law enforcement, science, the military, entertainment, and thousands of other fields. So light isn't just about vision. It's about *healing*. It's about *power*. It's about *life*.

Jesus stated that He is the light of the world. Think of His statement in light of what we now know about light. Without the Light of the world, life would be bland and colorless. Jesus brings vibrancy to our existence. He lights our paths and adds beauty along the way.

Look around you right now. The colors you see are an explosion of electromagnetic activity that God has set into motion! See all of that light? It's a reminder of the God who not only made light, but the God who *is* Light.

Lord, the light I see right now reminds me of who You are. I stand amazed.

He Is Life

Before long, the world will not see me anymore, but you will see me. Because I live, you also will live. On that day you will realize that I am in my Father, and you are in me, and I am in you.

John 14:19–20 NIV

It was the film director Billy Wilder who said, "Hindsight is always twenty-twenty." Jesus's disciples would have benefited from that understanding. Imagine the emotions, thoughts, and memories swirling within their souls after a few years with Jesus. They had to be scratching their heads at the mysterious things He told them.

But perhaps they weren't surprised. After all, the Son of God had been making bold and, to their mortal minds, puzzling statements all along. Jesus was trying to help them grasp the concept of death and resurrection—His death and resurrection. Twenty-twenty hindsight would soon prove to be their greatest wonder when they would see their risen Lord and recall all that He had said.

As it was for them, it will also be for us. We will see our glorious risen Savior. We will finally know as we are known. We will worship Him because He died to give us life, and we will live forever because our awesome, wondrous God is faithful to all His promises.

Praise You, Jesus! You've defeated death and given us life forever. I long to see You face-to-face.

His Glory in Our Obedience

"I tell you the truth, when you were young, you were able to do as you liked; you dressed yourself and went wherever you wanted to go. But when you are old, you will stretch out your hands, and others will dress you and take you where you don't want to go." . . . Then Jesus told him, "Follow me."

John 21:18–19 NLT

No can accuse Jesus of varnishing the truth. Yes, it's true that He taught in parables designed to hide things from the wise of this world. But when it came to those closest to Him, like His disciples, Jesus shot straight. And He did that with Peter in John 21. Peter may not have understood every nuance, but He knew Jesus was saying, "Your life is not going to end up like you've thought. But follow Me anyway."

Why would Jesus put that burden on such a dear friend? Four simple words: *Peter would glorify God.* It wasn't about Peter. It was all about God.

Jesus does the same with those of us who are His followers. He tells the truth about our lives, warning that they probably aren't going to turn out like we've planned. But because we are closest to Him—the ones He loves—the same invitation stands: "Follow Me anyway." All the glory will go to Him. He is an all-powerful Savior who can give us the strength to walk whatever path lies ahead.

Thank You, Jesus, for Your challenging, love-filled invitation to follow. May my obedience demonstrate God's glory to the world.

June 20

Can't Get Enough

"Take care that what the prophets have said does not happen to you: 'Look, you scoffers, wonder and perish, for I am going to do something in your days that you would never believe, even if someone told you.'" As Paul and Barnabas were leaving the synagogue, the people invited them to speak further about these things on the next Sabbath.

Acts 13:40–42 NIV

On one occasion, Paul and Barnabas journeyed into Antioch and attended the Sabbath synagogue service. The synagogue ruler, noticing two traveling visitors, asked Paul if he had a word of instruction. Without hesitation, Paul declared the gospel, telling the people that the Messiah had come and paid for their sin.

Just as we tend to go back for more when a meal is really delicious, the people couldn't get enough. They asked Paul to return the following Sabbath because they wanted to hear more of this great news.

The danger of being a Christian for a long time, however, is that the Good News becomes too familiar. We lose the wonder of the amazing reality that God put on flesh and became one of us to shoulder our sin and remove it as far as the east is from the west.

Revisit the marvelous reality of the gospel right now. Really *dwell* on the life of Jesus—His birth, sinless life, death, and resurrection. As you do, you'll want more. More of the God of the gospel.

Lord, as I think through the gospel right now, I am both delighted and amazed. Help me to never get over this marvelous thing You have done.

Sweet Spirit

And he who searches our hearts knows the mind of the Spirit,
because the Spirit intercedes for God's people in accordance with the will of God.
Romans 8:27 NIV

The Orthodox priest John of Krondstadt said, "When you say a prayer, the Holy Spirit is in every word of it, and like a Holy Fire, penetrates each word." What powerful possibilities there are when the Spirit of all-powerful God is enlisted on our behalf!

One of the promises of Jesus to His disciples and to all His followers was the gift of the Holy Spirit, and one of the works of the Holy Spirit is to search our hearts and intercede for us. In the Greek, one of the meanings of *intercede* is "to confer with, to embrace." Imagine: the Holy Spirit working together with a person's soul—guiding the mind and heart in the direction of God's will. He searches each heart, embracing and encompassing the deepest weaknesses and needs, and then confers with God to communicate what humanity's words cannot express. As John Bunyan said, "We know not the matter of the things for which we should pray, neither the object to whom we pray, nor the medium by or through whom we pray; none of these things know we, but by the help and assistance of the Spirit."

Truly, ours is a kind and caring, all-powerful heavenly Father.

Dear God, let the words of my mouth and the meditations of my heart be bathed in the Holy Spirit and offered in praise of You.

Enduring Faith

Through him we have also obtained access by faith into this grace in which we stand, and we rejoice in hope of the glory of God. Not only that, we rejoice in our sufferings, knowing that suffering produces endurance.

Romans 5:2–3 ESV

Trying out for the varsity team as a tenth grader, young Michael was told that he just wasn't good enough. Hurt by being cut from the team, the teenager determined to make the team the following year. Practicing relentlessly in all of his spare time, Michael developed the kind of skills that would not only allow him to make the squad the following year but eventually become the star of that team. Were it not for the disappointing rejection he suffered as a high school sophomore, Michael Jordan might never have discovered the inner determination and endurance needed to become one of the greatest professional athletes the world has ever seen.

Following God requires much endurance. But the endurance we need is supplied by God as a gift. In fact, the same grace that *places* us in Christ *keeps* us in Christ. And God, in His wisdom, knows the heartaches and trials that will produce a holy endurance in us.

God takes the ugly and turns it into the beautiful, and in the end we are blessed by it.

Lord, I'm amazed at how You redeem the hardships and difficulties in my life to make me more like Jesus.

Different Is Good

The sun isn't like the moon, the moon isn't like the stars, and each star is different.

1 Corinthians 15:41 cev

Homogenization. That word is usually associated with milk. But it also means "making something uniform or similar." You could say "making something fit in." All around us—in our families, schools, churches, and even the culture at large—there are forces constantly trying to fit us into predetermined roles or molds. But God's creation clearly reveals an opposite perspective.

God appears to not only appreciate variety but to emphasize it. The sun, moon, and stars are in no way homogenized. Each one gives glory to the Creator by being unique. The same holds true for humanity. Yes, we have similarities, but we are also each different from everyone else.

God created every element of nature to reflect the vastness of His own image and character. The more we learn to value and respect the variety within creation, the more familiar we become with the One who designed it all from the beginning.

Creator God, Your message is clear: different is good, very good.

Tangled in Grace

Each time he said, "My grace is all you need. My power works best in weakness."
So now I am glad to boast about my weaknesses,
so that the power of Christ can work through me.

2 Corinthians 12:9 NLT

On a December day in 2005, some people spotted and rescued a two-month-old bottle-nose dolphin that had become tangled in the ropes of a crab trap off the coast of Florida. The dolphin was taken to a nearby sea lab for treatment, but her tail eventually flaked off due to the trauma of being entangled in the ropes. Amazingly, a team of experts rallied together and developed a prosthetic tail for the dolphin, Winter. The advancements in prosthesis design that were discovered in helping Winter are now being used to provide better prosthetic limbs to American war veterans. Who would've ever thought that so much good would come from this dolphin's misfortune?

With God there are no impossibilities. What some would see as futility, God sees as an opportunity to display His strength and dispense His grace. He can redeem the most hopeless and desperate of situations to reveal His wisdom and might.

With God on your side, you are never entangled in impossibility or isolation. The Lord will meet you in places of weakness and lavish you with His grace and power. How marvelous!

Father, Your gracious favor is amazing. I realize that even in my times of weakness, You are with me.

Grappled to God

Having predestinated us unto the adoption of children by Jesus Christ to himself, according to the good pleasure of his will, to the praise of the glory of his grace, wherein he hath made us accepted in the beloved.

Ephesians 1:5–6 KJV

"The friends thou hast, and their adoption tried, grapple them to thy soul with hoops of steel," says Polonius in William Shakespeare's *Hamlet*. "Hoops of steel" is powerful imagery. Not only is steel an almost indestructible metal, but Shakespeare uses the plural "hoops" to show the level of commitment to those we "adopt" as friends.

We all want to feel secure, no matter our age, and we constantly search for a sense of belonging. Well, look no more. In the wonder of God's redemptive work in Jesus Christ, adoption is available to all who accept it by faith. There is no condition of acceptance. By God's immeasurable grace, we are all free to come to Him as His beloved children. Each of us is invited to call Him Father and to find in Him the love and identity we have sought all our lives.

By His pleasure and the act of His will, God has freely adopted all who believe through Jesus Christ. Praise Him and thank Him for welcoming us into His beloved family.

O God, I praise You for the abundant grace You lavished upon humanity by redeeming us through Jesus Christ.

Peace That Passes Understanding

Do not be anxious about anything, but in every situation, by prayer and petition, with thanksgiving, present your requests to God. And the peace of God, which transcends all understanding, will guard your hearts and your minds in Christ Jesus.

Philippians 4:6–7 NIV

Christian singer Amy Grant has been quoted as saying, "I'm not anxious to be anywhere other than where I am right now." What a poignant reminder to stay focused in the present moment and to realize that being anxious does nothing to change the condition of any situation—except perhaps to make it worse.

Sometimes, when situations look dire, it feels counterintuitive to believe that a thing like God's peace is possible. But the peace of God transcends what our hearts might be feeling and our minds might understand. Through the redemptive work of Jesus and communion with God, we are given a peace that passes all human understanding whatever the circumstances.

The word "petition" in the Greek carries with it the earnestness of begging as well as meaning "to bind oneself to the request." There is a beautiful mystery in our bond to the petition and God's bond to His response. The miraculous power of God's peace arises in our souls when combined with thanksgiving. So today, begin your prayers by praising God simply for who He is—the supernatural source of all peace.

God, may the miraculous peace of Your presence always reside in my heart and mind.

Easter People

But the Lord is faithful, and he will strengthen you and protect you from the evil one.

2 Thessalonians 3:3 niv

The day Christ died was horribly tragic for His followers. From the perspective of the centuries since, it was the beginning of the wonderful events of Easter, but for them it was the blackest day in history. Their Savior had been betrayed, beaten, crucified, and buried. It appeared that Satan had indeed won. It was black. It was bleak. It was "a Good Friday world," as author Barbara Johnson described it.

But God was faithful. The massive, earth-shaking events that took place on Easter morning changed the world forever. Evil was stomped under the feet of Christ. Death was the vanquished foe. It was an eternal revolution with precise ramifications.

Satan was defeated then, and he's defeated today. He still prowls the earth, stirring up trouble, delightedly inspiring blasphemy and despair, hoping the saints will be fooled and remain stuck in his Good Friday world. But there is protection: The Sovereign Lord with His unlimited, miraculous power has promised to guard and strengthen. A benevolent Holy Spirit continues to work His will in incomprehensible ways.

Extraordinary resources are available through an unshakably steadfast God. Focus on His faithfulness. Be an Easter people in this Good Friday world.

Almighty God, You are trustworthy and never fail. My hope is in You.

Our Kind Priest

For we do not have a high priest who is unable to empathize with our weaknesses, but we have one who has been tempted in every way, just as we are—yet he did not sin.

Hebrews 4:15 niv

The idea of a merciful and compassionate high priest was new and powerfully appealing to the Jewish Christians of the first century. No such priestly attributes are found in the Old Testament, and in New Testament times, the Sadducee priests were notoriously unfeeling and cruel. In addition, these new Christians were being persecuted socially and physically at every turn by both Jews and Romans. So imagine how they felt at hearing, "Listen—Jesus understands. He was tempted just like we are. He walked in our shoes, and He knows exactly how it feels to go through the battles that we face. But here's the good news: *He knows exactly how to help.* He feels our pain, but He is God."

It's still true today. Jesus is in a unique High Priest position where He remains exalted, holy, and faithful to God and yet is merciful in an everyday, understanding way toward His people who are feeling the pull of sin. He intercedes, reconciles, strengthens, encourages, loves—every day…all the time. How great is the Lord!

Lord Jesus, You are the most compassionate and wise High Priest, and I glorify Your name!

Great Plans

It won't be long before this generous God who has great plans for us in Christ—eternal and glorious plans they are!—will have you put together and on your feet for good. He gets the last word; yes, he does.

1 Peter 5:11 msg

The school year is finally over, and summer has arrived. That's when every kid loves to hear the wonderful words, "We're going on vacation!" All the homework and early mornings and school lunches fade into memory, and the countdown begins. Half the fun is anticipating the unknown until it is revealed what the trip will hold. There are so many details for parents to take care of—hotels, car tune-up, what do we do with the dog?—but the payoff is amazing. The happy smiles of their little ones say it all.

It's impossible to imagine what our generous, big-hearted God has planned for us. We know the timeline: eternity. We know He's infinitely creative, so though our minds can't conceive of the variety, detail, brilliance, and delight that lie in store, we can anticipate the wonder. Time to begin the countdown. Soon it will all be unveiled.

He's in control, He has the last word, and it's going to be glorious.

Lord, You are so amazing! I can't wait to see what You have planned.

June 30

O Love of God

This is love: not that we loved God, but that he loved us and sent his Son as an atoning sacrifice for our sins.

1 John 4:10 niv

An Aramaic refrain was written in Germany in the eleventh-century, then penciled onto a wall of an insane asylum centuries later, and fashioned into a hymn during a break from hard manual labor in 1917.

To write the love of God above,
Would drain the ocean dry.
Nor could the scroll contain the whole,
Though stretched from sky to sky.

The broad, sacrificial love of God for mankind is poetic in its imagery—it dips into the abyss of hell, stretches into the highest heaven, extends to the cross. His benevolent love is worthy of the noblest poem. His surprising and immeasurable love is given freely and cannot be matched, cannot be changed, and *will not* be withdrawn.

Let us sing of His great love:

O love of God, how rich and pure!
How measureless and strong!
It shall forevermore endure
The saints' and angels' song.

Lord God, Your love is magnificent. I sing of Your sacrifice, Your sovereignty, and Your glory.

A Detailed God

Do not use dishonest standards when measuring length, weight or quantity.
Use honest scales and honest weights, an honest ephah and an honest hin.
I am the LORD your God, who brought you out of Egypt.
Keep all my decrees and all my laws and follow them. I am the LORD.

LEVITICUS 19:35–37 NIV

The great architect from the mid-twentieth century, Mies van der Roh, coined the phrase "God is in the details." This seemed to describe not only van der Roh's understanding of the creative process but also a deep appreciation for God's involvement.

The Creator's participation in the minute details of our lives is amazing. The Levitical laws of the Old Testament were not instituted as a heavy-handed way to control human behavior but were one way for God to demonstrate His care for His people.

His heart is an honest one. How could we trust Him otherwise?

For people of faith, an honest, caring heart will always reflect the standards of the Father. If we pay attention to details in dealing with family, friends, and business associates, people will glimpse something important: the kindness and consideration of God.

Lord, I'm amazed that You choose to be in the details of my day, and now I choose to reflect Your glory in my life.

Our Great Provider

When you have eaten and are satisfied, you shall bless the LORD your God for the good land He has given you.

DEUTERONOMY 8:10 NASB

As we get older, there's a different kind of excitement at Christmas- time. For children, their joy comes from receiving that favorite gift. But as we grow older, we find more delight in *giving* that present. There is just something gratifying about offering a good gift to someone who matters to you.

When the Israelites were getting ready to enter the land God had promised them, He had Moses remind the people of past blessings. Moses recounted the miraculous ways that God fed and clothed the people. He reminded them of the precious Law that God had given them. And then Moses delivered a word about what was yet to come: more blessings. God was not done showering His people with good gifts.

God is a good God. That is why He has blessed you with so many good gifts. Amazingly, He is not done giving out good things. Be grateful for what God has done for you in days past. And be filled with wonder at the fact that even now He is choosing that perfect gift for today and tomorrow and the day after that—all because you matter to Him.

God of wonder, You have been so good to me. I am humbled to know that You still have good things in store for me.

The Quickening

God, your God, will cut away the thick calluses on your heart and your children's hearts, freeing you to love God, your God, with your whole heart and soul and live, really live.

Deuteronomy 30:6 msg

Guitarist Brian "Head" Welch's metal band, Korn, sold more than 35 million albums worldwide. He had the world's idea of a dream life—and thick calluses on his heart. But in time, something changed. It started with a softening—an invitation to church. Then came the quickening, then enlightenment, and then purity.

"I hit rock bottom," he has said. "I sunk to the lowest gutter I could ever think of. I prayed Matthew 11:28—'*I'm* weary. *I'm* burdened. *I* need rest for my soul. Search me right now. Search my heart.' And *instantly*, I got the love from God coming into me, and then it came out of me. It was so powerful. It changed me. My dream came true way more than I dreamt about."

He experienced a callus-cutting that regenerates, renews, and frees a person to really live. "And then," said Welch, "you're exactly where you need to be. The question about life is answered."

How does God do it—reach into the heart, cut away the burden and weariness, and put in love? Only He is able. He is the Liberator who frees the whole heart to love Him.

Compassionate God, You are able to make me free. Thank You.

Perfect Welcome

Ascribe to the LORD the glory due his name; bring an offering and come before him. Worship the LORD in the splendor of his holiness.

1 CHRONICLES 16:29 NIV

Holy. It's a word we hear and use a good bit in church life, but not one upon which we often stop and dwell. The word "holiness" means a state of moral perfection. Moral *perfection*! Holiness involves a complete absence of sin in both motive and action.

God is perfectly holy. He does no wrong because there is no wrong to be found in Him. You would think that a morally perfect being would be completely unapproachable, that it would be impossible for us to interact with Him. Yet King David, when confronted with the perfection and holiness of God, came before Him, not just with reverent fear but also with singing and offerings. And we are invited to join David in song before a holy God.

Who can fathom a God who is both holy and approachable? Who can comprehend a God who is altogether other, yet willing to be among us? Stand in His presence today with joy, knowing you are welcome there. Come before Him and worship Him in the splendor of His holiness.

Lord, You are altogether beyond my comprehension, and I am amazed at Your holiness.

Praise from the Seas

Praise the LORD from the earth, you great sea creatures and all ocean depths.

PSALM 148:7 NIV

Scientists at one time assumed there was no life in the deep sea. With light unable to penetrate to those depths, they reasoned, any life at the ocean floor would depend upon falling organic matter from the upper zone for survival. When explorations to these tremendous depths began in 1960—descending deeper into the earth than Mount Kilimanjaro rises above it—discoveries began to prove otherwise. Oceanic life was abundant, even at its deepest points. It has been said that we know more about the moon's surface than we know about our own ocean floors, but what we have seen reveals amazing life forms and species that expand the boundaries of our imaginations.

It is easy for humans to walk the earth and assume it is all here just for us. But creatures like the flashlight fish and the giant tubeworm have been living in the depths of the ocean for centuries. We are just now learning of their existence, but the Creator has always known. He made those creatures just as He made us, and their beauty and magnificence bring Him glory. May we find in their fabulous design the signature of the Divine Artist and praise His name.

The land and the oceans are Your handiwork, O God. Praise Your name!

His Mysterious Ways

God never forgot his sacred promise to his servant Abraham.

PSALM 105:42 CEV

God moves in mysterious ways, His wonders to perform." Some people believe this sentence to be in the Bible, but it's not. It is the first line from the last hymn ever written by William Cowper. He had decided to commit suicide, but a thick fog prevented his taxi from reaching the Thames River. When the driver stopped to let Cowper out, the desperate man discovered he was back in front of his home. God had moved in His mysterious way to save Cowper's life.

God worked His wonders in mysterious ways through a baby born to an elderly woman long past her childbearing years as well. The Lord never forgot His promise to Abraham—though it was more than twenty-five years in coming.

The birth of a son to a hundred-year-old woman would not have made for an obvious plan to most of us, but that's the point. God works according to His own methods and within His own time frame to accomplish His purposes. God's ways are perfect, and He will use whatever means necessary to make good on His promises.

Lord, You keep Your promises. You never forget, and You are always faithful.

Controversial Mercy

But the Lord will redeem those who serve him.
Everyone who trusts in him will be freely pardoned.

Psalm 34:22 NLT

Article II, Section 2 of the United States Constitution gives the president "power to grant reprieves and pardons for offenses against the United States." With a stroke of his pen, the man who lives in the White House can make legal trouble simply disappear.

As you can imagine, giving one man such power has been controversial from the beginning. Recipients of pardons have ranged from former President Nixon to Vietnam draft dodgers to George Steinbrenner and Peter Yarrow of Peter, Paul, and Mary.

To be pardoned means that the offender is no longer held and treated as guilty. That person is immediately freed from the legal consequences of their offense. Remarkably, our God promises to likewise pardon all those who trust in Him. The wrongdoing fades from focus, and our astonishingly merciful God gets the glory. All thanksgiving and praise belongs to Him.

Pardon to all who trust in You. Hallelujah, what a Savior!

Love That Lifts

I learned God-worship when my pride was shattered.
Heart-shattered lives ready for love don't for a moment escape God's notice.
Psalm 51:17 msg

In 2012, a documentary about three underprivileged student-athletes transcending inner-city Memphis shocked Hollywood and won an Oscar. The stars of *Undefeated* were underdogs in every way. America is an underdog culture. Her people cheer the loudest for the war veteran skiing on prosthetic legs, the small-town soprano with an unpolished voice and a dream, the lowly beagle vying for Best of Show.

Underdog status is hard-won, usually signaled by broken hearts, little pride, and even less hope. Perhaps that is why God is so ready to love and use those who are overlooked.

Consider the shepherd boy who would be king, wielding only a slingshot and five smooth stones. Or the outcast prostitute with a brilliant red rope who helped bring down a city. Or the unwed pregnant teenager who bore a Savior. God roots for the shattered because they need Him—they need His compassionate love in difficult circumstances against very poor odds. They're more willing to ask for it, receive it, and humbly praise Him for it, recognizing that real strength comes from God, and that human limitations and inadequacies provide opportunities for His power to shine. The glory is all His.

Matchless God, please help me to have a heart of humility—ready for love, ready to praise.

Starry, Starry Night

"So—who is like me? Who holds a candle to me?" says The Holy.
"Look at the night skies: Who do you think made all this?"

ISAIAH 40:25 MSG

If you look out your window tonight, you can see upwards of five thousand stars. Those are just the ones that are visible out of the billions that are actually out there in our galaxy. You can see them because stars are enormous balls of plasma producing their own light and energy through nuclear fusion.

"The sun is but a morning star," wrote Thoreau. Our daytime star and more than a hundred times the size of Earth, the sun has an average temperature of 5500 degrees Celsius. If it comes any closer, it will boil away our water, destroy our atmosphere, and end all terrestrial life.

Here's the thing: the sun—an "ordinary" star—came out of God's mouth, according to the Psalms. He breathed it out! How massive is The Holy to have a mouth that breathes out stars? And not just stars, but the galaxies—125 billion and counting—plus the heavens and the hosts!

And then, in an extraordinary move, this majestic God leaned down and, using that same mouth, breathed into Adam…tiny, human Adam.

God breathes out stars. And He breathed out you. There is none like Him.

God of the Universe, You are my Morning Star, wonderfully and powerfully creative. I stand in awe of You.

Living Proof

O, that you would rend the heavens and come down,
that the mountains would tremble before you!
Isaiah 64:1 NIV

Paul Simon once described faith as "an island in the setting sun," but added that "proof, yes, proof is the bottom line for everyone."

The prophet Isaiah wanted proof—he wanted to hear God speak. More than seven hundred years had passed since Mount Sinai's summit erupted in fire. Lightning flashed, the ground shifted, the air was supercharged with electricity...and Moses emerged with two stone tablets. God came down. God had spoken.

But not in Isaiah's lifetime. And Isaiah desperately wanted God—*begged* God—to show His mighty power, to demonstrate His glory, to *do something* in the land of Judah. His people wanted a visible display. They longed for proof.

Isaiah's lament is also ours. When circumstances feel out of control today, we lament: "Show Yourself...prove You are real." We scream it. We cry it. We whisper it in the dark. But God chooses how and when to reveal Himself. His is a plan of faithfulness—of living within the gap of proof and promise. He is a gracious God with a gracious purpose, and He has fully revealed Himself through His Son, Jesus Christ. He continues to speak to His people through His Holy Spirit. If you want proof, just listen.

Merciful God, Your plans are mysterious and perfect. I am amazed by Your power and presence.

A Royal Affair

They will tell of the glory of your kingdom and speak of your might, so that all men may know of your mighty acts and the glorious splendor of your kingdom.

Psalm 145:11–12 NIV

On April 29, 2011, much of the world paused to watch a wedding. Televised globally, the wedding of Prince William and Kate Middleton was a sight to see. With all the pomp and splendor expected of a royal wedding, the world simply wanted a glimpse of England's prince marrying a "commoner." Over five thousand street parties were held throughout the United Kingdom to mark the royal wedding, and an estimated one million people lined the route between Westminster Abbey and Buckingham Palace. Over 36 million Brits caught a peek of the nuptials on television, while another 70 million viewers tuned in on the YouTube Royal Channel. In fact, people around the world were fascinated by this gala event.

Deep inside the heart of mankind is an attraction and fascination with royalty. And this explains, in part, why God is so worthy of our attention. The Bible speaks repeatedly of God as King, and not just any king—the King of all kings. If every earthly king past, present, and future could get but the smallest glimpse of God, they would stand dumbfounded at His majesty. They would see that His kingdom is not of this earth, that His rule is infinite in scope, and that His wealth is immeasurable. They would cry out, "He is *the* King."

My God and my King, there is none like You. I bow my heart before You and confess that You are my Lord.

Burning with Praise

And they called back and forth one to the other,
"Holy, Holy, Holy is God-of-the-Angel-Armies. His bright glory fills the whole earth."

Isaiah 6:3 MSG

Celestial beings have been demoted in popular culture. They rest on earthly mantels, looking sleepy and peaceful. They perch in gardens, luring butterflies and finches. Around Valentine's Day, they're chubby babies who fly around firing arrows tipped in love.

But in the Bible, they are terrifying.

What Isaiah describes are Seraphim literally, "burning ones." Fiery, six-winged creatures flying around God's throne, crying out "Holy, Holy, Holy" in antiphonal praise. One group calls out, and the others respond, and it goes back and forth, over and over again. And their voices make everything shake and fill the temple with smoke.

These are no garden babies. These creatures burn in love for God—passionate about His holiness, public in their adoration, united in their message, answering one another, agreeing with enthusiasm. They can't stop themselves. They are literally *on fire for God.*

You have the same God. He is so pure, so perfect...never giving you a reason to be embarrassed by Him. His name is holy; His reputation is holy. He is holy in His laws, His wisdom, His power, His influence, His goodness. What a joy to have such a God! So go ahead: boast in Him. Holy is His name!

Lord of hosts, help me to be on fire for You, passionately...publicly.

Point of Origin

He made the earth by his power; he founded the world by his wisdom and stretched out the heavens by his understanding. When he thunders, the waters in the heavens roar; he makes clouds rise from the ends of the earth. He sends lightning with the rain and brings out the wind from his storehouses.

Jeremiah 51:15–16 NIV

When you think about "the wind from his storehouses," does anything come to mind? For those who study such things, a list does exist. Some of the names may ring a bell, while others may not at all. The longest-known and most dependable of the earth's winds are the harmattan of Algeria, the sirocco of Calabria, the trades of Martinique, the katabatics of Antarctica, the simoon of Iran, the onshores of the Atacama, and the Namib.

What about kinds of lightning? Did you know there is more than one kind? There's cloud-to-sky, cloud-to-ground, intracloud, and intercloud.

Did you know that all of these—the lightning types and the earth's winds—have a single point of origin?

They do. It is the Lord, the One who powerfully made and wisely founded the earth and who crafted the heavens with His understanding. Magnify His name, for He is above all and over all. He is too wonderful to comprehend!

immortal Father, the aspects of nature that take my breath away all originate with You. I praise Your name.

Ever-flowing Resource

The One who builds His upper chambers in the heavens and has founded His vaulted dome over the earth, He who calls for the waters of the sea and pours them out on the face of the earth, The LORD is His name.

AMOS 9:6 NASB

Aristotle had a theory that streams and rivers were regenerated from underground sources, with almost no impact from the rain. It wasn't until the late sixteenth century that his theory got an overhaul. The science employed by Pierre Perrault, Edme Mriotte, and Edmund Halley (yes, the same man who is known for his study of comets) revealed the flaw in Aristotle's idea and gave us the description of the earth's water system, known as the hydrologic cycle. Rain falls, pushing water into streams both underground and above the surface. The rivers run to the sea, the sun evaporates the water into the clouds, and rain falls. What a beautiful plan designed by the God of wonders to keep His creation alive and flourishing.

Our world is alive with manifestations of God. He "calls for the waters of the sea and pours them out on the face of the earth." The magnificent mind of the Creator fashioned a system that regenerates itself and makes life on earth possible, and that is just one of His great ideas. Praise Him, for He alone is capable of such splendid works.

Dear God, Your majesty reaches to the highest heavens and Your glory extends to the ends of the earth.

First Things First

But seek first his kingdom and his righteousness,
and all these things will be given to you as well.

MATTHEW 6:33 NIV

Those fictional heroes of pop culture—Indiana Jones, Luke Skywalker, and Superman—all had one thing in common: focus. Whenever they were on a mission, they identified their goal, and nothing could distract them from that single target. They always put first things first.

As followers of Jesus Christ, we are on a mission, seeking His will for our lives. When we seek the kingdom of God with a "first things first" mind-set, everything else we need is given to us as well. The beautiful mystery is that the God we seek has the same desire for relationship with us. And Jesus's words in Matthew 6 reveal that very arrangement—that promise of communion.

God asks us to seek Him first so He can supply all of our needs. The sooner we come to Him, the sooner He begins to work everything according to His will and His glory. Our God is a God of love, of mercy and grace. When we put Him first in our lives, all of who He is becomes available in every aspect of our existence. Only He is big enough to give us everything we need.

Why would we ever look anywhere else?

Lord, You are the first priority of my life. You are all I need.

Cosmic Shout-Out

I tell you, whoever publicly acknowledges me before others, the Son of Man will also acknowledge before the angels of God.

Luke 12:8 NIV

Seven-time NFL Pro Bowler John Randle was only two minutes into his acceptance speech at the Professional Football Hall of Fame ceremony when he stopped and mentioned a coach from his early years at a community college. He thanked the coach for helping and encouraging him at a time of uncertainty. It was a touching shout-out.

Jesus promised a heavenly shout-out in Luke 12:8, and He added weight to this future celestial event by identifying himself as the "Son of Man"—a title Jesus took from the Old Testament prophet Daniel, with new and enhanced meaning.

As Son of Man, Jesus connected fully with our humanity and our suffering. His sacrificial death provided the perfect ransom for sin. But here is the wonder of it all: this Son of Man, who completely identifies with us, was not a mortal being but the divine Messiah who reigns over heaven and earth. How incredible! The Lord of the ages, who angels heed when He speaks, will celebrate His triumphant return with acknowledgment of all the redeemed—a great cosmic shout-out!

Dear Lord, we proclaim Your greatness throughout the earth and joYously await the day of Your return.

The Miracle of Second Birth

Flesh gives birth to flesh, but the Spirit gives birth to spirit.

John 3:6 NIV

The biological mechanisms by which pregnancy takes place make conception a marvelous thing to consider. Life begins when one microscopic sperm cell from a man takes a perfectly unobstructed path during a specific window of time and fertilizes one tiny egg inside a woman's Fallopian tubes. The newly formed embryo is then transported into the woman's uterus, demanding precise movements inside her that she cannot dictate. Then, the woman's womb must be receptive to the embryo that has worked so hard to arrive there.

When all of this has happened with immaculate precision, a child is conceived. And that is just the beginning. After all of this comes nine equally amazing months of pregnancy, then the birth!

The Bible says that those who believe in the name of the Son of God will experience spiritual birth. Jesus did more than we could imagine to make new birth possible, some of which we know and some of which we do not. But Jesus did all the work, then preserved in writing what was necessary for us to believe. And in believing, we have life—wonderful spiritual life in Christ.

God, You alone deserve all the glory for my spiritual birth. I stand in holy wonder at all You've done.

July 18

Simple Equation

Those who know my commands and obey them are the ones who love me, and my Father will love those who love me. I will love them and will show myself to them.

John 14:21 NCV

Most people know the traffic laws. To help us out, specific speed limits are posted at regular intervals. But seeing and knowing are only half the equation. The other half is actually *obeying* the laws. And that's where a dividing line occurs between those who know and those who know *and* obey.

Jesus is quite clear in John 14 that the ones who love Him not only *know* His commands but *obey* them. Jesus also clearly indicates that those who love Him are the ones the Father loves. It's really not a complicated equation. The love Jesus is speaking of here is the committed love of relationship. Jesus is offering in these verses the promise of intimacy and revelation to those who hear, know, and obey His teachings.

How incredible that our gracious Father offers us a way to show—in a concrete way—that we love His Son, and then pours His perfect love back on us! His grace is wonderful.

Praise You, mighty Lord, for Your clear path to the Father's love.

Our Uncontainable God

The God who made the world and everything in it is the Lord of heaven and earth and does not live in temples built by human hands. And he is not served by human hands, as if he needed anything. Rather, he himself gives everyone life and breath and everything else.

Acts 17:24–25 NIV

For centuries there has been an ongoing debate over God versus science, as if they were mutually exclusive. Three hundred years before Jesus, the Epicureans held that matter was eternal and that the world was formed by a fortuitous concourse of atoms. And as recently as this decade, physicists have formulated the M-theory, to describe the behavior of fundamental particles and force, and to even account for the very birth of the universe.

There is nothing new under the sun when it comes to the debate. If the Lord of the heavens and the earth could be put in a test tube—or a temple—then He would not be God.

Why do we think we can contain God? It's possible to harness the wind for power or the sun's rays for energy, but we cannot isolate, control, or make God dependent on our definition of Him.

We are finite creatures. We cannot explain God, but we can marvel at the wonder of His great and astonishing power. A power that leaves man's understanding in the dust.

God of the universe, You are beyond understanding and Your ways are past finding out. Your glory is beyond measure.

In Plain Sight

For what can be known about God is plain to them, because God has shown it to them. For his invisible attributes, namely, his eternal power and divine nature, have been clearly perceived, ever since the creation of the world, in the things that have been made. So they are without excuse.

ROMANS 1:19–20 ESV

In 1987, a children's book titled *Where's Wally?* was published in England (later published in North America as *Where's Waldo?*). The book featured double-page illustrations of people doing a variety of things at a given location. The goal for the reader was to locate Wally. Since he wore a red-and-white striped shirt and hat, along with big black-rimmed glasses, you would think Wally would be easy to locate. But the illustrator included several decoys within the already jumbled pages, making it a challenge to find him.

Thankfully, God has not set up the world in a way that makes Him hard to find. As a matter of fact, all one has to do to see God's character is to look out the window. Though He is invisible, God has not hidden Himself.

Look around your world today. Let your eyes rest on the things not made by human hands—the very pages of God's artistry. As you stare at these things, try and imagine the One who made them. As you do, you will find your heart being filled with a renewed sense of wonder.

The works of Your hand give me a small glimpse of Your might and character. And what I see leaves me speechless.

The Great Reconciler

Therefore, accept each other just as Christ has accepted you so that God will be given glory.

Romans 15:7 NLT

In 1993, Deo Ntiyankundiye, a Tutsi officer in the Burundian National Police Force, had a shot at killing the feared Hutu soldier known as "Mbawa" (the nickname of Antoine Harushimana). The sort of Hutu-Tutsi tensions typified in this near-fatal encounter exploded in neighboring Rwanda in 1994, resulting in a tragic genocide. Burundi, on Rwanda's southern border, has a similar tribal mix, and while it has avoided genocide, civil conflict over many decades has resulted in thousands of dead. Could two men who had nearly killed one another find forgiveness and friendship?

After years of fighting against each other and seeking to avenge wrongs done to them, both Deo and Antoine were transformed through their encounters with Jesus Christ. Today, having grasped the implications of their faith, not only have they been healed from bitterness by forgiving one another as well as others who caused them pain, but they now work together in ministry.

This kind of supernatural reconciliation shines in a world of darkness, silently declaring that it is only possible through the piercing, heart-transforming, overwhelming love of God. Just ask Deo and Antoine: God gets all the glory.

O God, nothing is impossible with You. Even hearts full of hatred can melt under the force of Your love.

Pension Crisis

Work hard for sin your whole life and your pension is death.
But God's gift is real life, eternal life, delivered by Jesus, our Master.

Romans 6:23 msg

The world is in a pension crisis.

Pensioners are buying in to the view that sin is delightful. Wise. Sophisticated. And that righteousness—decency, morality, virtue—is stupid. Wasteful. Obnoxious.

Since a pension is something earned, then paid in regular installments, pensioners are getting their sin-penalty payments on a regular schedule. And the cycle will continue: sin, penalty, sin, penalty—each pensioner doomed to receive exactly what he's earned—unto death.

Delightful? Wise? Not from God's point of view. Not when the gift of salvation is there for the receiving.

Salvation is a gift that gives in perpetuity: deliverance from sin—grace—on a regular basis unto eternity. Stupid? Wasteful? Or just outrageously generous?

Can it be that our Father is so big-hearted and magnanimous that He would give us real life forever through His Son? Thank Him, for indeed He is that full of love for us and that generous with His amazing grace.

Gracious God, I don't deserve it, but thank You for Your eternal gift.

Illumination

For God, who said, "Let there be light in the darkness,"
has made this light shine in our hearts so we could know the glory of God
that is seen in the face of Jesus Christ.

2 Corinthians 4:6 NLT

To the one feeling around in the darkness when thunderstorms knock out all electricity, light is not to be taken for granted. At that moment, it is seen for the miracle it is, and—for a moment, anyway—valued as a lifesaver. Light keeps the right path in sight and chases fear out of the corners.

Light is everywhere in the Bible—figuratively, as an emblem of knowledge, purity, and truth; and literally, as electromagnetic radiation created by the great Fountain of Light. In every instance, the light pours from the same source of power and divinity, beauty and holiness, integrity and certainty: the one true God.

The Father not only created first light, He actually illuminates the human heart with a light that "shines"—it does not blind; it does not burn. It is a splendid, cheerful, alluring glow. And all the more so because it reflects the glory of God in the face of His Son.

Everything is made clear by the light of Jesus. Even the darkness flees in His presence.

Glorious God, the light shines at Your command and all the world is illuminated...my heart glows in You.

The Top-Nine List

But the Holy Spirit produces this kind of fruit in our lives: love, joy, peace, patience, kindness, goodness, faithfulness, gentleness, and self-control. There is no law against these things!

Galatians 5:22 NLT

A novel came out in the 90s about a quirky guy who made Top Five lists of everything important in shaping his life: books, films, music, memorable split-ups. It was a way for him to analyze his life and document its progress at the same time. By the end of the book, the process of creating the lists changed him.

Paul was a list maker too. Earlier in his letter to the Galatians, he made a Top Fifteen list of "Deeds of the Flesh." It was pretty inclusive, and might have been discouraging if he hadn't followed it up with his Top Nine "Fruit" of excellent, Christlike qualities essential for crucifying those fleshly deeds.

Lists worked for Paul because he was able to outline qualities that everyone can agree on: lists defining love, generating good thoughts, promoting compassionate daily living—qualities the Holy Spirit lovingly creates to exalt God's divine purposes.

In this list we are able to recognize the trademarks of the Holy Spirit, the very evidence of His presence in our lives. The results are supernatural. God, whose character is excellent and evident, is put on display when the believer produces the Spirit's fruit.

Holy Spirit, Your guidance is perfect and energizing. Do Your fruitful work in my life today!

Glorious, Perfect, and Wise

I have not stopped giving thanks for you, remembering you in my prayers. I keep asking that the God of our Lord Jesus Christ, the glorious Father, may give you the Spirit of wisdom and revelation, so that you may know him better.

Ephesians 1:16–17 NIV

The story goes that Saint Augustine was taking a stroll along the seashore while meditating on the Trinity. When he came upon a child pouring seawater into a hole in the sand, he asked, "What are you doing?" The child looked up and said, "I am emptying the sea into this hole." "Oh, you will never succeed," Augustine replied. "I will succeed sooner than you will understand the Trinity," the young lad retorted.

Trinity comes from the Latin *trinitas,* "three." The doctrine is not explicitly taught in the Bible, but the foundations of the concept are spread throughout the New Testament. Jesus discusses His relationship with the Father and His promise to send the Holy Spirit to His followers multiple times in the Gospel of John.

Paul and the other New Testament writers assumed the relationship of the Godhead to be true and didn't waste time disputing the concept. They encouraged belief in the Father, the Son, and the Holy Spirit, and taught that through constant prayer and the Spirit's empowerment, we would deepen our understanding of the mystery of the Godhead: our perfect Redeemer, Jesus; our wise Comforter, the Holy Spirit; our glorious Father, God.

O glorious Father, give us Your Spirit of wisdom and revelation so that we may know You better.

Without Fault

Even before he made the world, God loved us and chose us in Christ to be holy and without fault in his eyes.

Ephesians 1:4 NLT

You know the ads that include a really dramatic before-and-after shot of their product? Ads for cleaning products in particular seem to do this. They will provide images that make their product look almost magical. With just a single swipe, the most disgustingly stained surface suddenly sparkles and shines like never before!

These commercials would lead you to think that the featured cleaning product will make your surfaces better than new. Sure, they can make surfaces cleaner. But perfect? No product is *that* good.

Consider this, though: when God removes a person's sin, He leaves them spotless.

The Bible states that God's work of redemption leaves us holy and without fault in His eyes. Think about those words: "without fault in His eyes." The God who sees every nook and cranny—the God whose standards are not of this world—finds us to be perfectly clean.

How could people so deeply stained by sin be made perfectly holy? This only happens by the hand of a miracle-working God. He loved us before He made the world, and He sent His only Son to redeem our sin-stained lives. Nothing could be more miraculous!

Lord, You are able to make me perfectly clean. Please make me without fault in Your eyes.

All Grown Up

And I am sure of this, that he who began a good work in you will bring it to completion at the day of Jesus Christ.

Philippians 1:6 ESV

Whether it's the first time a baby rolls over, crawls, take steps, or says "Mama" or "Dada," moms and dads want to be there for those milestone moments. But parents don't enjoy those moments of growth just because they're fun to watch; they enjoy them because growth is critical.

The Bible says that God does something marvelous with the spiritual development of His children. Through the work of His Spirit, God gives His people spiritual birth. Then that same Spirit produces growth. Destructive thought processes and behaviors are sanctified, and the believer develops more and more into the likeness of Jesus.

But the best is yet to come! One day Jesus will return and gather His people from all corners of the earth. All wrongs will be made right, and God will complete His people, perfecting everything about them, making them like Jesus the Son.

Stop for a moment and reflect upon the growth you've experienced. Then take some time to anticipate what is yet to come.

Lord, You do wonderful works in Your people. Through the power of Your Holy Spirit, may Your will be done in my life.

The Message Is the Mission

And pray for us, too, that God may open a door for our message, so that we may proclaim the mystery of Christ, for which I am in chains.

Colossians 4:3 niv

"We find that after years of struggle, we do not take a trip," said author John Steinbeck; "a trip takes us."

A trip indeed "took" the apostle Paul—hundreds of miles over many, many years. He was heartily welcomed, met with a Roman governor, and drew large crowds. He was thrown out of one city and fled another. He was stoned and left for dead. Imprisoned, he was still eager to spread the mysterious plan of Jesus. He was compelled by God's powerful and appealing message…and determined to deliver it.

Churches take missionary trips in stride now, but to the early saints in AD 44, a trip to proclaim the gospel of Christ was unimaginable. It was a new and dangerous idea. Yet despite difficult trials and horrendous persecution, God was equipping Paul and the other disciples to spread the gospel, and they gave God all the glory.

He is amazing this way. Only He can give the tools and the resources and prepare the way. Only His Spirit can keep the fires of the message alive. He is faithful and true and opening doors every day.

Merciful God, Your gospel is irresistible. Use me to throw open doors of faith.

Profound Truth

This truth gives them confidence that they have eternal life, which God—who does not lie—promised them before the world began.

Titus 1:2 NLT

"So help me God." These words are often used at the end of an oath to add credibility. Why? Because if a statement is made and sealed before holy God, it is true. God Himself is the very standard of truth.

The apostle Paul says that eternal life was promised to us before the beginning of time by God Himself. And God does not lie.

God's nature is to speak the truth and there is no situation where He would do otherwise. His promise of life eternal provides the foundation for our faith. His divine truth raises our hope and faith, helping us to endure the troubles of everyday life. It keeps our minds and hearts focused on heavenly things, drawing us ever closer to Him.

Realize that God had eternal life in mind for His children before He began creating the world. Isn't His redemptive work amazing?

Dear God, You promised us the hope of eternal life from the beginning of time. Your plans are wondrous.

Soaked in Joy

You have loved righteousness and hated wickedness; therefore God, your God, has set you above your companions by anointing you with the oil of joy.

Hebrews 1:9 niv

In ancient times, shepherds would rub oil into the wool of their sheep. Lice and other insects would often get into a sheep's wool, burrow into the animal's ears, and cause serious disease or death. Rubbing oil on the sheep would make its wool slick, which would make the lice and insects slip off the sheep. In time, the rubbing of oil became symbolic for blessing and protection. People would be anointed with it to symbolize a variety of sacred meanings. This anointing was meaningful to both the one being anointed and the one doing the anointing.

The Bible says that God anoints His people with oil. This in and of itself is a meaningful thing, because a person would never anoint someone for whom they had disrespect or disdain. So for God to anoint His people is a rich expression of affirmation and love. And what kind of oil does God spread over us? He anoints us with the oil of joy.

God gives us His blessing and protection, which fills us with joy. He makes us happy! What a thoughtful and wonderful God we have, that He Himself would honor us with this beautiful gift.

Lord, You are a wonderful blessing. Anoint me now with the oil of joy.

The Future Is Now

What a God we have! And how fortunate we are to have him, this Father of our Master Jesus! Because Jesus was raised from the dead, we've been given a brand-new life and have everything to live for, including a future in heaven—and the future starts now!

1 Peter 1:3–4 MSG

"We talk about heaven being so far away," said Dwight L. Moody. "It is within speaking distance to those who belong there."

We don't always think of it this way, but the future starts now. *Now.* It's not speculative. It's not an empty promise. It's a daily, powerful, *living* hope that became active at the moment of Christ's resurrection.

God loves His people and has given us life. When the world seemed cold and broken, our faithful God sent the promised Savior to redeem it. When Jesus left for His heavenly throne, He sent the compassionate Holy Spirit to restore it. The Holy Spirit whispered His Word to His scribes to constantly renew it.

The Father is in the business of redeeming, restoring, renewing *everything* until it is healed and whole. It's proof of His abiding love.

Yes—a future in God's brilliant heaven is worth living for. But the future is now. Here. On the fading earth that is your home. You have everything to live for in the world God created...in a world that matters. Embrace the hope. Live it now.

Loving God, I embrace Your powerful, living hope.

The Last Laugh

Is anything too hard for the LORD? I will return to you at the appointed time next year and Sarah will have a son.

GENESIS 18:14 NIV

Missionary adventurer Jim Elliot was following God's plan to evangelize the Auca Indians in Ecuador. But four years in, warriors slaughtered him and four fellow missionaries. It seemed this mission was too hard for the Lord.

Thousands of years earlier, a retired, childless couple got the news from God that they would have a baby. The mother-to-be laughed; it was physically impossible. So Abraham and Sarah sought their own means to bear a child through a surrogate mother.

Many times human wisdom and forethought fail. Plans fall through. Dreams collapse. It can all seem impossible. But in the beginning, God spoke and it was done. God commanded and it stood fast. Nothing is too hard for Him. Not creating a baby in the womb of an old woman. Not continuing a ministry in a hostile country following a tragic death. Not for the God of miracles.

Jim Elliot's wife and others continued working among the Auca Indians, and their ministry changed thousands of lives. Abraham and Sarah had the impossible baby—a child of the covenant, the beginning of a great and powerful nation. Nothing—*nothing*—is too hard for the Lord.

Sovereign Lord, You are the God of the impossible. Help me to trust Your ways.

Gracious Guide

In all the travels of the Israelites, whenever the cloud lifted from above the tabernacle, they would set out; but if the cloud did not lift, they did not set out—until the day it lifted. So the cloud of the LORD was over the tabernacle by day, and fire was in the cloud by night.

EXODUS 40:36–38 NIV

After a collapse at the gold and copper mines in New South Wales, Australia, in November 1999, there was only one way to rescue the fifty-seven miners trapped below: the rescuers used rope as a guide through the debris and moved them all to safety. It wasn't possible to see the path ahead; the only option was to believe in the carefully placed rope and move one step at a time.

The Israelites finally learned that lesson. The only way to stay out of trouble was to follow the message in the cloud of the Lord. If it had lifted, it was time to move. Otherwise, stay put, be patient, and wait on God. He showed His faithfulness to them by visible signs during the day and through the night, and it was up to them to be obedient.

This same God, who had the power to form a cloud over the tabernacle and fill it with fire at night, is still our strong Deliverer. He speaks, He beckons, He commands, and sometimes He communicates through silence, but always He is our Guide. In all these ways He leads us along His path and displays His glory in our lives.

Father, I thank You that even now You are my Guide. I am overwhelmed that the Master of the universe is mindful of me.

There Is None Else

Know this well, then. Take it to heart right now: GOD is in Heaven above;
GOD is on Earth below. He's the only God there is.

DEUTERONOMY 4:39 MSG

"I finally gave in," wrote C. S. Lewis in *Surprised by Joy*, "and admitted that God was God." That was a hard admission for Lewis—an atheist from age fifteen, "very angry with God for not existing," a dabbler in the occult and theism. But once sold out to Christianity, Lewis became an outspoken and prolific writer on the sovereignty of God.

He took it to heart, then converted it to page: Aslan, the Great Lion in *The Chronicles of Narnia* who is both temporal and spiritual, both a children's guide and "not a tame lion"; the "Old One" in *The Space Trilogy* who rules from Deep Heaven; Charity, the Universal Love in *The Four Loves*, both glorifying and reflecting the nature of God.

Just like Moses, Lewis urged the people of God to consider who God *is*—Lord of heaven and earth, actively and proactively involved; what He's *done*—created the universe, delivered His people from bondage, revealed His covenant of love; and what He *requires*—honor, glory, reverence.

Man is prone to forgetfulness. So this is a plea to remember, to acknowledge His holiness, to remember His goodness, to profess that God is God. There is none else.

Lord of all, help me to hold fast in my heart that You are God, that no one and nothing else is above You.

A Commanding Voice

The voice of the LORD is over the waters; the God of glory thunders, the LORD thunders over the mighty waters. The voice of the LORD is powerful; the voice of the LORD is majestic.

PSALM 29:3–4 NIV

Anyone who spends any amount of time observing nature will eventually end up asking, "I wonder how *that* works?" Take a river, for example. It's a steady flow of water always moving toward another body of water. And why does a river do this? Water within a river is generally collected from precipitation that makes its way into the river's channel, as well as from other sources such as groundwater recharge, underground springs, or melted ice. Wherever the water comes from, it's a fascinating natural phenomenon.

Watching a seemingly endless supply of water flow day after day, the psalmist David no doubt found himself mystified by this natural wonder, and his thoughts in Psalm 29 centered not on *what* made it flow but *who* made it flow. Sitting by that river, perhaps he thought of the day when God created water and separated it from the land, or of his ancestors' deliverance from Egypt through the sea and into the Promised Land. Or of the coming Messiah, who would walk on water and command its waves to be stilled.

Look around today at nature's wonders. Our God is over them all.

God, Your greatness is a wonder to behold. Move me to meditate on You.

Binder of the Broken Heart

The LORD is close to the brokenhearted and saves those who are crushed in spirit.

PSALM 34:18 NIV

George Matheson's lyrics have comforted multitudes:

O joy, that seekest me through pain.
I cannot close my heart to Thee
I trace the rainbow through the rain
and feel the promise is not vain

The composer of the beautiful hymn "O Love That Will Not Let Me Go" said this about the writing of the song: "Something had happened to me which…caused me the most severe mental suffering. The hymn was the fruit of that suffering…this came like a dayspring from on high." He never did publicly describe the cause of the suffering, but those who knew him assumed it was heartbreak: because Matheson was blind, his fiancée decided she couldn't go through life as his wife and ended their engagement.

Healing comes from the Lord. It is His nature to heal, and He mercifully made it part of our nature to accept that healing and walk on in strength. Spirits can be crushed and hearts will be broken—it is the human experience. Sometimes we can feel that God is very far away. But Scripture says He is close. In time, His wonderful compassion will bind every wound.

Healer of my soul, I need Your tender mercy to heal me.

The Heart to Help

And call for help when you're in trouble—I'll help you, and you'll honor me.

Psalm 50:15 MSG

Before the telegraph was invented by Guglielmo Marconi in the closing years of the nineteenth century, ships at sea were completely isolated from shore and from other sailing vessels. A ship could vanish from the high seas and go unnoticed until it failed to arrive at port. After ship-to-shore communications were perfected, sailing vessels equipped with telegraphs were no longer isolated.

In March 1899 the *East Goodwin Lightship*, moving along the southeastern English coast, was rammed in a fog in the early morning hours by the *SS RF Matthews*. An SOS was transmitted to a shore station and help was dispatched. It was the first use of a wireless telegraph in communicating the need for assistance by a ship in distress.

Centuries before wireless communication, a songwriter named Asaph penned a psalm about another, more personal kind of emergency: *if you're in trouble, call on the Lord for help*. The petitioner was not isolated anymore. God was always in range, and He promised to not only hear but to help. He wouldn't be limited by distance or restricted to human effort. The Father would employ the full resources of His omnipotence to send whatever is needed for rescue. And He does.

Lord, You are the God who hears and the God who helps. I depend on You.

Unshakeable

Cast your cares on the Lord and he will sustain you; he will never let the righteous be shaken.

Psalm 55:22 NIV

Are anxieties weighing you down? Are you overwhelmed by your worries? Trying to solve everything on your own is exhausting, and it's not what God wants you to do. God wants you to turn your cares over to Him, just as it states in today's verse.

I experienced this firsthand recently, so I know it's not always easy to do. We want to be in control of every situation, even those beyond our reach, which adds to our stress level.

Fears do not have to hold us captive. We can choose to step forward in faith, even if it's a baby step. We can breathe in His peace as we breathe out our anxieties. God will be there to provide the strength we need to handle whatever we encounter. When we put our trust and hope in the Lord, He will not let anything stand in the way of His purpose for our lives.

In Psalm 55:22, David wanted to run, but instead he turned to God. Let's be like David and wait on God. He will not let His followers be shaken.

Lord, I will not be shaken by my circumstances because my feet are firmly planted in Your Word.

Arrayed in Holy Majesty

Your troops will be willing on your day of battle. Arrayed in holy majesty, from the womb of the dawn you will receive the dew of your youth.

Psalm 110:3 NIV

If we were invited by a president or a king to attend an official gathering, the first question to come to mind would probably be, "What am I going to wear?" We've all seen those red-carpet events where stars stroll before the cameras in their designer clothes. But when Jesus extends His scepter to grant us an audience, we won't have to scurry to our closet or call a stylist. The Priest-King will array us in holiness…His holiness.

Before the great flood, the earth was watered each morning with dew. The beauty of the psalmist's "dew of your youth" metaphor is its freshness and purity. Even when we are young, fresh, and pure, we consecrate ourselves to the Lord's service. Dressed in His holiness, we are willing servants of the Lord our God, ready to do battle in the service of our amazing King.

O Lord, clothe me in Your righteous holiness and lift up my head to praise You.

A Toast to God

What can I give back to God for the blessings he's poured out on me?
I'll lift high the cup of salvation—a toast to God! I'll pray in the name of God.

Psalm 116:12–13 msg

Perhaps nothing inspires spontaneous joy like a wedding. The air is electric with love and hope, music floods the gathering place, and the mixed fragrance of candles and cut flowers drifts through satin and silk. Guests burst into applause, hug indiscriminately, wipe away happy tears.

And they toast. They raise glasses and pour out their hearts in front of friends and strangers. They just can't help themselves.

That's what the writer does in Psalm 116. He can't help himself.

The Hebrew "cup of salvation" is one of thanksgiving. It's ceremonial—like a wedding toast—and marks a time to remember. The gift table—the bounty and happiness and mercy God in His excellent goodness has heaped on His children—is remembered. And since the psalmist has no way to repay the Lord's kindness, since God is in need of nothing, the writer raises his glass and tastes the love in the blessing.

It's a good moment and a reminder that God loves love—unashamed, spontaneous, public love. Here's to God, the generous Giver of every good thing!

God of Love, You have provided every blessing, every mercy, every kindness.

Just One

I, yes I, am God. I'm the only Savior there is.

Isaiah 43:11 MSG

Automobiles. Telephones. Computers. The Internet. Electric cars. And not just things, but people with names like Ford, Edison, Kennedy, King. Every invention or name on the list could have been followed by a singular phrase: "…will save the world."

People have been grasping for something or someone ever since the fruit was plucked in that garden long, long ago. And each time our faith is placed in the things of this earth, our hopes are dreadfully disappointed.

There is only One who can and truly will save the world—the same One who created all things, knows all things, and by whose power all things move and have their being. This One is the great I AM, the only true God revealed in the birth, life, death, and resurrection of Jesus. As the classic Gaither song reminds us, "Kings and kingdoms will all pass away/But there's something about *that* name."

I look to You, not just as Savior but as Lord and Provider.

August 11

The Roar of Creation

Sing for joy, O heavens, for the LORD has done this; shout aloud, O earth beneath.
Burst into song, you mountains, you forests and all your trees,
for the LORD has redeemed Jacob, he displays his glory in Israel.

ISAIAH 44:23 NIV

A great battle ensues at the end of *Prince Caspian,* book four of C. S. Lewis' Chronicles of Narnia. And at a pivotal moment, the evil Telmarines blanch white in terror, fling down their weapons, and run. Why? Because the trees—the Awakened Trees—have *come to life.* And they *roared.*

"Have you ever stood at the edge of a great wood," asks Lewis the narrator, "on a high ridge when a wild southwester broke over it in full fury on an autumn evening? Imagine that sound." Aslan woke the trees…and God does the same when He reveals His glory.

Isaiah is being poetic when he calls on the earth, the mountains, forests, and trees to exult. And yet, it's not beyond imagination that joy in the Lord's wondrous power can make inanimate objects roar in praise. God is great. Why wouldn't nature rejoice?

"When we were here," mourns young Lucy on her way to find Prince Caspian, "the trees danced." And they will dance again…for the glory of the Lord.

Redeeming God, Your power is so great that nature itself sings Your praise. May my life ever praise You as well.

Arise and Shine

Arise, shine, for your light has come, and the glory of the LORD rises upon you.
See, darkness covers the earth and thick darkness is over the peoples,
but the LORD rises upon you and his glory appears over you.

ISAIAH 60:1–2 NIV

In the early summer of 2001, eight cave explorers hoping for an exciting adventure entered a twisting network of tunnels in the Doubs Gorge on the Swiss border of France. But the adventure turned into a nightmare when water gushed into their cave, trapping them in the pitch-black darkness until their rescue three days later. Finally, they stumbled forth from the cave, never happier to see the sunshine—a most welcome burst of light.

Just before Jesus performed a miracle of healing on a blind beggar in the Gospels, He referred to Himself as "the light of the world" and then rubbed some mud over the beggar's eyes. Jesus told the man to go wash off in the Pool of Siloam, and suddenly the beggar could see. Jesus was indeed the Light of the world, and He was doing individually what He would soon do for all humanity.

The black fog of sin once covered the earth, blinding us to the wonder of God's miraculous power. But like the welcome light of day after the darkness of an underground cave, the light of Jesus Christ dispelled the darkness and brilliantly beacons hope today. Arise! Shine! Light has come.

Dear Lord, Your light has burst upon the earth. I long for Your glory to shine through me.

Forever God

But the LORD is the true God; he is the living God, the eternal King. When he is angry, the earth trembles; the nations cannot endure his wrath.

JEREMIAH 10:10 NIV

Baal was the name of the fertility god worshiped in ancient Canaan. Baal, along with Ishtar—the Babylonian goddess of love and war—inspired cults and practices that were disgusting to God and His servants, including Jeremiah. Throughout Scripture, from Genesis to Revelation, God makes it clear that while there might be other gods out there—always man-made and always unreliable—He is the one true and living God, not a counterfeit. Jeremiah's calling was to proclaim the eternal God to all who would hear.

Of course, there was more to the message. Our God is not only a living God; He is life itself for all of creation. He is the everlasting King who has dominion over the earth and all its inhabitants past, present, and future. He is the God of heaven and earth, before whom all other gods must hide.

O Lord, You are the one living God and we worship You, the eternal King.

Hearing and Being Heard

Thus says the Lord who made the earth, the Lord who formed it to establish it, the Lord is His name, "Call to Me and I will answer you, and I will tell you great and mighty things, which you do not know."

Jeremiah 33:2–3 NASB

Experts teach us that good communication involves two fundamentals: hearing and being heard. Professional counselors spend countless hours every year teaching people how to communicate to enhance both their relationships and their lives. Fortunately, we never have to worry about God's willingness to talk with us. In fact, because of His love for us, God participates in every part of the communication process.

God instructed us, through the prophet Jeremiah, to call out to Him and to listen to Him. In other words, God reminded us that He *listens* to us and that He *speaks* to us. And we are better as a result of this dialogue with God. We come to know and understand what we did not know before.

How incredible it is to be able to communicate with the One who laid the earth's foundation. That God would actually listen and speak to us, His creation, is a wonderful reality that only draws us closer to Him.

Lord, tell me Your great and mighty things, and I will listen.

Over All the Starry Sky

He who made the Pleiades and Orion, who turns midnight into dawn and darkens day into night, who calls for the waters of the sea and pours them out over the face of the land—the L*ORD* *is his name.*

AMOS 5:8 NIV

The Pleiades is one of the closest clusters of stars to our planet, and is therefore the most visible to the naked eye. It held a prominent place in many ancient cultures, evidenced in the early texts from what is now Japan, Egypt, India, Pakistan, and the Celtic lands. The Pleiades was probably part of the idol-worshiping religions of Amos' world. When the prophet exclaimed that the Lord made the Pleiades, he was declaring Yahweh's position in the universe—contrary to the beliefs of the pagans around him.

God is the Creator of the stars of the heavens.
He makes the sun rise and set.
He controls the storms that rise up out of the ocean and cover the land.
His name is the Lord, and He is the force behind everything seen and unseen.
Give Him the glory due His name.

God, the universe is a reflection of Your glory. May I bring You glory by reflecting Your goodness.

August 16

Quiet

In quietness and confidence shall be your strength.

Isaiah 30:15 NKJV

In our busy, media-driven, noisy world, we often forget the benefits of quietness. In the Bible, quietness is associated with blessing, rest, security, peace, holiness, ease, assurance, gentleness, and righteousness. It is held in contrast to strife, foolish arguments, wickedness, fear, rash actions, and trouble.

Some of us, when we feel weak and needy, respond with bluster and busyness. We talk too much. We fret. We go on the defensive and become argumentative. We rally the troops and give pep talks. But God's Word points to a better route.

According to Isaiah 30:15, quietness is a source of strength. Choosing to rest instead of stirring things up, choosing to be confident instead of worrying is the true path to strength. This is a deliberate, even an unnatural, response in time of crisis or high demand, but it is the path that makes us look like Jesus.

This attitude of quietness is not just for emergencies, though; it is our strength for daily living. If you find yourself in turmoil, uneasy, insecure, weak—just meet with the Lord to rejoice in His love and strength, and your heart will receive His quietness. Shh.

Dear Lord, help me to find strength today in the quietness and confidence that You provide.

Strong Love

Love the Lord your God with all your heart and with all your soul and with all your mind and with all your strength.

Mark 12:30 NIV

In 1960, Mrs. Maxwell Rogers was sitting in the kitchen of her home in Tampa, Florida, when a neighbor rushed in saying that Rogers' teenage son, Charles, was trapped underneath his car. Charles had put the family vehicle up on a jack to work on the universal joints when the car became unbalanced and fell on him. Mrs. Rogers rushed out to the car and somehow managed to lift a corner of the 3,600-pound Ford Ranch Wagon enough to allow a neighbor to pull Charles out from underneath. Mrs. Rogers cracked several of her vertebrae in the process—a price she willingly paid to save the son she loved so dearly.

When love is strong, the expression of that love will reflect its strength. Like a mother summoning a strength she didn't even know was possible, we should love God with every fiber of our being. He is worthy of such love, worthy of our best, worthy of all we have.

God, You are deserving of more love than I could ever express. Set my sights on honoring You.

Lamb of God

The next day John saw Jesus coming toward him, and said, "Behold! The Lamb of God, who takes away the sin of the world!"

John 1:29 NKJV

In 375, Augustine wrote, "Why a lamb in his passion? Because he underwent death without being guilty of any iniquity. Why a lamb in his resurrection? Because his innocence is everlasting."

The Old Testament concept of a scapegoat was a beast that was sacrificed for the sins of the people without knowing or choosing it. The Lamb of God was just the opposite: Jesus was never confused about Himself; the world needed saving and He chose to be the One to save it. Jesus made the conscious decision to obey the will of the Father and lay down His life for the sins of the world.

John the Baptist looked straight into Jesus's face, clearly identified Him as the Son of God, and stated what His mission was on the earth. John called all humans—then and now—to sit up straight, lean in, and pay attention as he pointed to the Lamb of God and announced to the world the greatest wonder of all: God's redemptive work through His Son was about to begin.

Praise You, O Lamb of God, for taking away the sins of the world.

Closest of Friends

When he heard this, Jesus said, "This sickness will not end in death. No, it is for God's glory so that God's Son may be glorified through it."

John 11:4 niv

Gayle King. Lem Billings. Guy Pelley. These aren't household names. But the names of their best friends are. As close friends to people like Oprah Winfrey, Princes William and Harry, and John F. Kennedy, these individuals have a different perspective when it comes to the faces the rest of us only recognize. To them, Winfrey, Kennedy, and the princes aren't just famous people, they are friends who have cared for them.

Jesus had a close personal friend named Lazarus. Jesus often visited Lazarus and his sisters in their small hometown of Bethany. On one occasion, however, it appeared that Jesus wasn't there for His friend. Having received word that Lazarus was deathly sick, Jesus didn't show up until days after Lazarus had died. But when Jesus did arrive, it was clear that He cared deeply for His friend. After weeping, Jesus raised Lazarus from the dead. What appeared at first to be indifference was in fact Jesus demonstrating a radical love and exhibition of His glory. And this is what God does in our lives. Though He may seem to be uninvolved, He has a plan and is going to work all things together for His glory *and* your good. This is what Jesus does for His friends.

God, I trust Your sovereign plan and am amazed that You would befriend someone like me.

August 20

Far and Near

From one man he made every nation of men, that they should inhabit the whole earth; and he determined the times set for them and the exact places where they should live. God did this so that men would seek him and perhaps reach out for him and find him, though he is not far from each one of us.

Acts 17:26–27 NIV

Imagine having to craft a penny using nothing but simple tools and your hands. Think about how long it would take you to make it look just right, with all the details on the front and back of that coin. Now imagine making one hundred pennies, or even more! Consider this: one billion pennies, stacked one on top of the other, would reach approximately a thousand miles into the sky. The thought of making that many pennies by hand is absurd, right?

The Bible paints a picture of God delicately making the first human being on the sixth day of creation. Then He made another. Then another. And another. It is estimated that more than 7 billion people are living right this moment. Seven *billion*! And countless others have lived before now and will be born in the future.

When you consider the sheer number of people God has made—a much bigger and more complex task than creating pennies—you begin to get just a glimpse of how infinitely powerful and resourceful God is. It's even more astounding to realize that this great big God draws near to us as we seek Him.

Lord, the depth and breadth of Your creative hand astounds me. I'm further astounded when I realize how near You are.

Taking a Bullet

Each of us should please our neighbors for their good, to build them up.
For even Christ did not please himself but, as it is written:
"The insults of those who insult you have fallen on me."

Romans 15:2–3 niv

Every March 30, Timothy McCarthy looks at the calendar and remembers what happened on that date in 1981. President Ronald Reagan had just delivered a luncheon address inside a Washington, DC, hotel and was making his way outside to a limousine. Then, amid a crowd of cheerful onlookers, the sound of gunfire erupted. After missing the president on his first three shots, John Hinckley Jr. had a clear shot, so he fired a fourth time. However, Timothy McCarthy selflessly positioned himself in front of Reagan, taking the bullet and suffering harm for the good of the president.

There is no greater expression of love than absorbing pain for the well-being of others. Jesus inspires us in this regard. He put on the ultimate display of love on Calvary's hill when, on a Friday afternoon, the sinless King of heaven positioned Himself to take the wrath and pain that was due the rest of us. The insults hurled toward Jesus should have landed on us. But they didn't, because in awesome sacrificial love, the Savior stretched Himself out in our place, suffering harm so that we could live forever.

Jesus, the way You gave Yourself up on the cross, absorbing the insults that I deserve, causes me to fall before You and bless Your name.

Just As We Are

For there is no difference between us and them in this. Since we've compiled this long and sorry record as sinners (both us and them) and proved that we are utterly incapable of living the glorious lives God wills for us, God did it for us. Out of sheer generosity he put us in right standing with himself. A pure gift. He got us out of the mess we're in and restored us to where he always wanted us to be. And he did it by means of Jesus Christ.

Romans 3:23–24 MSG

Evangelist Billy Graham says he was saved in a revival meeting where "Just as I Am" was playing. A young woman named Charlotte Elliott had written the song almost a century earlier. She was in distress at the time, wondering if her faith was merely a collection of emotions. Her distress reached a breaking point, and she sat down with pen and paper to remind herself of the certainties of God. She quickly wrote out the formula of her faith, acknowledging: *Just as I am without one plea/ But that Thy blood was shed for me.*

God's amazing love accepts us no matter what mess we're in. His grace and mercy are poured out on us at the instant we open our hearts to receive Him. He is the origin of mercy. He is the definition of grace.

I come with nothing, O Lamb of God, and yet You love me. How amazing.

August 23

Living Sacrifice

Therefore, I urge you, brothers and sisters, in view of God's mercy, to offer your bodies as a living sacrifice, holy and pleasing to God—this is your true and proper worship.

ROMANS 12:1 NIV

Albert Einstein said, "Only a life lived for others is worth living." For the believer, the only meaningful, eternal way to serve others is to dedicate that service to God, day by day, for a lifetime.

In the ceremonies of the Jewish religion, an animal without flaw was offered as a sacrifice, and when the act was finished, the animal was dead. It couldn't be sacrificed again. How different is a living sacrifice! We offer the best we have—our gifts and talents, our dedicated minds, our resources and riches—to the Lord with each new day.

Ours is not a service of death, but a vigorous and active involvement. In fact, our lives are one long act of giving ourselves back to God, freely, voluntarily. He is holy and deserves our everlasting praise, our worshipful service.

God, only by Your tender mercies and through Your miraculous power can I continually worship You as a living sacrifice.

August 24

Better Than the Rest

God alone made it possible for you to be in Christ Jesus.
For our benefit God made Christ to be wisdom itself.
He is the one who made us acceptable to God.
He made us pure and holy, and he gave himself to purchase our freedom.

1 Corinthians 1:30 NLT

Ancient Corinth was a bustling city. One of the crown jewels of Asia Minor, the city was populated by native Greeks, Jews, Roman citizens who had migrated from Italy, and people from many other locales. Part of Corinth's appeal was what the city promised. A place of great wealth, Corinth was the epicenter for the worship of the Greek goddess Artemis. Artemis offered affluence and divine knowledge to those who would worship her and make substantial offerings. In other words, the people who journeyed to Corinth could earn and purchase Artemis's acceptance.

The apostle Paul wrote to the Christians in that city and reminded them that life in Christ was altogether different from what Artemis offered. Jesus does not simply promise spiritual wisdom, wealth, and purity. As the actual source of it all, He delivers it. And unlike Artemis, Jesus is not just waiting for those who work their way to Him. To the contrary, Jesus *came to us* and purchased our freedom through His own blood, through His sacrifice for us. Quite simply, there is none like Him!

I am blessed that You took the initiative, Jesus. You alone gave us our freedom.

August 25

Power to Spare

Now to him who is able to do immeasurably more than all we ask or imagine, according to his power that is at work within us, to him be glory in the church and in Christ Jesus throughout all generations, for ever and ever! Amen.

Ephesians 3:20–21 NIV

The GE90, a turbofan aircraft engine built by General Electric, is so powerful it can lift a Boeing 777 weighing 656,000 pounds into the air and keep it there for almost twenty-three hours. The thrust generated by the ten-foot fan is the most intense in the world. Anytime a flight crew and passengers get on an airplane powered by that gigantic engine, they can be assured of its ability to perform. It has proven itself over the past twenty years, and if there are any doubts, one need only look to its history.

Infinitely greater power is at work within every believer. The greatest gift, the biggest answer to prayer, blessings beyond what is described in books or even in the Bible, are easily within the realm of God's superabundant power. He has blessed us over and beyond our hopes, but because of who He is, we can still ask for more. After all, we have a history with Him. He is exceedingly, magnificently able to exceed every request through His infinite power.

Lord, my imagination fails and my prayers fall short of all You want to give me. How can I ever thank You?

August 26

God Is All and in All

There is one body and one Spirit, just as you were called to one hope when you were called; one Lord, one faith, one baptism; one God and Father of all, who is over all and through all and in all.

Ephesians 4:4–6 niv

Leo Tolstoy wrote in his diary, "God is that infinite All of which man knows himself to be a finite part." What a beautiful mystery that God *is* all and is *in* all. The collection of "ones" in Ephesians 4:4-6 is a singular description of the unity of the Godhead in direct relation to all creation, and specifically to those who accept the redemptive grace and mercy of God through Jesus Christ.

God is present in everything. By His miraculous power, all things are sustained, from the unseeable cosmos to invisible atoms. God has made us. His power runs through us. He works through us. He is alive in us. He transforms us and uses every willing heart to work His will in the world.

As great and wonderful as God's creation is, the work of grace is by far His greatest gift. Without the atoning sacrifice of Jesus, all the wonder of creation would mean nothing. Though we may be only a finite part of this wonder of God, as Tolstoy said, we are a *living* part, fully energized by the Spirit of God to give Him praise and honor in *all* things.

O Lord, God of us all, I worship You for making me a part of Your kingdom.

Extravagant Generosity

You can be sure that God will take care of everything you need,
his generosity exceeding even yours in the glory that pours from Jesus.
PHILIPPIANS 4:19 MSG

Nothing is ever lost by generosity. Big-hearted givers are in the habit of giving freely without expecting anything in return—not even a thank you.

But Paul penned a dilly of a note to the Philippians, didn't he? The gratitude he expressed for their generosity in his time of need has gone on to become absolutely beloved by millions of people in upwards of two thousand languages.

Paul made sure his readers understood that God—the richest, most generous, most gracious benefactor—took note of their generosity and would use it for His glory. The Philippians' benevolence illustrated God's own perfection, His unmatched goodness in supplying riches of grace and mercy...and supplying them *abundantly*.

Pastor Grant C. Richison has said, "We cannot outgive God. He has a bigger shovel."

God extravagantly shares His overflowing resources in glory and on earth. He is infinitely wealthy, incomprehensibly generous, inexhaustibly faithful. And He has a really big shovel.

God, You are so good, so benevolent. I smile to think of Your generosity.

Home Run

For everything God created is good, and nothing is to be rejected if it is received with thanksgiving, because it is consecrated by the word of God and prayer.

1 Timothy 4:4–5 NIV

Ty Cobb was the best hitter in the history of Major League Baseball, at least statistically speaking. Cobb was eighteen years old when he broke into the big leagues with the Detroit Tigers, and he played the next twenty-two years with the team. Having established nearly one hundred individual records in the Major Leagues, Cobb still holds the all-time career batting average of .366.

What's interesting about Cobb's career batting average is this: he failed to get a base hit over 60 percent of the time. In a league that has existed since 1875, the best batter in the history of the league produced nearly two bad at-bats for every one good one. Imagine how impressed we would be if anyone ever came along who had twice as many successful at-bats as unsuccessful ones! They would have to be superhuman!

Isn't it awe-inspiring that God has never once produced a bad result? Think about that. *Every single thing* God has ever done has been good. Never one mistake. Never one bad move. Never one pop fly or strikeout. The Lord is perfect! He never fails.

Lord, everything You have ever done is good. I thank You for all You have done in my life, because I know You never make mistakes.

Out of Nothing

By faith we understand that the universe was formed at God's command, so that what is seen was not made out of what was visible.

HEBREWS 11:3 NIV

Colin Gunton, the British theologian, once wrote that "God is not to be likened, let us say, to a potter who makes a pot from the clay which is to hand; he is, rather, like one who makes both the clay and the pot." From nothing, God created what pleased Him.

In December 2011, NASA announced that its satellite Voyager 1, launched in 1977, had entered a new region between the Milky Way and the area called interstellar space. It was stuck there, "plying the celestial seas in a region similar to Earth's doldrums," but was expected to move on soon. It is already 11 billion miles from the sun, with no estimate of an end to its journey. Yet God knows every inch of that trip.

A million bacteria squirming on the head of a pin, five hundred thousand protozoa floating in a bucket of seawater, phytoplankton by the billions, and hummingbirds no bigger than a bumblebee—God spoke their tiny forms into existence.

The scope of our world stretches larger than our imaginations. All we see (and don't see) is the handiwork of a Being grand enough to make it reality. The greatness of the Creator is marvelous to contemplate.

God, I cannot even begin to fathom You. You fill me with wonder!

Once for All Time

Everyone has to die once, then face the consequences. Christ's death was also a one-time event, but it was a sacrifice that took care of sins forever. And so, when he next appears, the outcome for those eager to greet him is, precisely, salvation.

Hebrews 9:28 msg

The Old Testament rules for offerings and sacrifices were many-layered and complicated. There were burnt offerings, grain and drink offerings, peace offerings, and purification offerings and though they are foreign to our culture, they are deeply significant to the theology of the Bible. Through them we gain some understanding of the vast chasm between God and humankind, and see the plan laid out for our salvation. Christ, both holy and human, did *once* what the priests in the old covenant could not do through their endless annual sacrifices: bear your sin.

Christ was offered once. *One time*, the Father watched His holy, blameless Son suffer the torment of the Roman cross—the dying pangs, the struggle to breathe, the cold sweats. Once was enough. Christ would not repeat it, and it paid for sin forever.

He did not die to leave salvation to chance, relying on the sacrifice of wheat or oxen. His once-and-forever payment was magnificently permanent. He will not fail to save you and bring you into His Father's glory.

Holy Father, Your sacrifice of Your Son was beyond comprehension and full of mercy. Thank You for the gift of salvation.

Our Defender

My dear children, I write this to you so that you will not sin. But if anybody does sin, we have one who speaks to the Father in our defense—Jesus Christ, the Righteous One.

1 John 2:1 niv

One of the first legal dramas on television was *Perry Mason.* The wise attorney solved one challenging courtroom case after another with stories of infinite variety and twists. But one fact remained the same week after week: with Perry Mason on your side, you would not lose. With a passion for truth and justice and a talent for cleverly representing his clients, Mason defined what it is to be an advocate. He was determined to defend.

The ministry of Christ took on another dimension after His ascension. Jesus became not only our Savior but also our Defender. This is a marvel of our mysterious God. Sin still traps and entangles believers. Jesus Christ, in His humanity, experienced life and death here on earth, and that qualifies Him not only to help us navigate our daily experiences but to stand before God as our perfect and wise Defender. Thank Him today for so wondrously standing in your stead.

I am indebted to You, Lord, for the help and comfort You provide through the atoning sacrifice of Your Son.

September 1

But God...

"You meant to hurt me, but God turned your evil into good to save the lives of many people, which is being done. So don't be afraid. I will take care of you and your children." So Joseph comforted his brothers and spoke kind words to them.

GENESIS 50:20–21 NCV

Theodicy—the theological word for the question: how can a good, almighty, and all-knowing God permit evil? It's the conundrum people have wrestled with for generations. And with the advent of social media, the evil is often as close as our computer monitors. Poet William Stafford wrote, "The darkness around us is deep." How do we live in light of such dark?

The story of Joseph and his brothers reminds us of the great adversative phrase "but God." This reality stands in direct opposition to the evil that seems to swallow us. It's a truth that grounds us, even in our hurt, with the faith and hope that there is One who walks in the darkness with us. One who not only can but does turn evil into good. One who desires to see hearts saved and lives redeemed.

Yes, the darkness is deep indeed—*but God* is for us. If this is true, then who or what can stand against us? How great is our God!

Thank You, Father, that You turn evil into good.

Secret Things

The secret things belong to the LORD our God, but the things revealed belong to us and to our children forever, that we may follow all the words of this law.

DEUTERONOMY 29:29 NIV

How many times have you thought, *I really didn't need to know that*? How many things have you wished you could un-see, un-hear, un-comprehend? How often do you think Eve wanted to un-bite that piece of fruit in the garden?

If you're a parent, you've probably doled out innumerable pieces of need-to-know information to your kids and felt pretty wise about it. How much more wise are the revelations our Father gives us to live by? Not only is God infinite and omniscient, He holds the power to reveal. God has His "secrets"—reasons for why things happen, what causes them… mysteries too profound for anyone but Him—but He also wants His children to know Him. He wants us to know how to follow Him.

That's why He has revealed one astounding thing: His great love for you. He has never tried to keep it a secret. He shouted it from great heights, displayed it in a rainbow, dictated it to scribes, and sent it in the form of a carpenter's son.

Praise to our God, who chooses to reveal Himself to us. Only He has the ability to unveil the path of righteousness to every generation.

O God, You have revealed Yourself to us in Your Word. I seek to know You more.

A Voice on Fire

And you said, "Behold, the Lord our God has shown us his glory and greatness, and we have heard his voice out of the midst of the fire. This day we have seen God speak with man, and man still live."

Deuteronomy 5:24 ESV

The Mann Gulch fire of 1949 raged in the Helena National Forest of Montana. The blaze claimed the lives of thirteen firemen, twelve of them members of an elite smoke-jumper team. As the jumpers found themselves trying to outrun the flames, crew foreman "Wag" Dodge did an unthinkable thing: he lit a second fire. This second fire burned an area of grass down to the ground, creating a safe place to lie down in while the first fire burned all around it. Dodge then called out to his men, a voice within the fire. Little did the men know that heeding his voice could have made the difference between life and death. Wag Dodge was one of three survivors.

The grandeur of our God is often experienced in unthinkable fashion, like a voice calling out of the fire. His desire, however, is not to consume but to save—to ensure life more abundant and free. He can be heard, calling us to a safe place, speaking directly to us. God's merciful voice holds the key to our rescue and to the salvation of the world.

Your voice, O Lord, is my true light and salvation.

September 4

Waiting for God

In you I trust, O my God. Do not let me be put to shame, nor let my enemies triumph over me.
No one whose hope is in you will ever be put to shame,
but they will be put to shame who are treacherous without excuse.

Psalm 25:2–3 NIV84

Slowly dying in Ravensbrück concentration camp in Germany, Betsie ten Boom told her sister Corrie, "There is no pit so deep that God's love is not deeper still." Corrie constantly marveled at her sister's determination to find the best in every situation, no matter how grim, and in every person, no matter how brutal. How could anyone doomed to that notorious camp—known for its torturous medical experiments, hangings, starvation, beatings, and random shootings—find hope?

Much like David in Psalm 25, Betsie called upon the infinite goodness and mercy of God. She did not ask that her enemies—the cruel guards and medical tormentors—be slain. She prayed for them. Where she saw suffering, she interceded and sought God's compassion. Where the world saw vicious darkness, she petitioned God to shed His glorious light.

That is the mystery and wonder of God. He promises that He will come to those who wait. He brings comfort to the brokenhearted, strength to the weak, and deliverance to the downtrodden. He is the God of hope.

You know my enemies and my weaknesses, God. Only Your infinite goodness will bring relief.

Sacrifice of Praise

Whoever sacrifices a thank offering honors Me, and whoever orders his conduct, I will show him the salvation of God.

Psalm 50:23 HCSB

In the last years of King David's life, a plague struck Israel. In order to halt the plague, David was instructed by the prophet Gad to "build an altar to the Lord on the threshing floor of Araunah the Jebusite." When David arrived at the threshing floor, Araunah offered the king not only the floor but all the articles necessary for the sacrifice at no cost to David. But David's response was immediate: "No, I insist on paying you for it. I will not sacrifice to the Lord my God burnt offerings that cost me nothing" (2 Samuel 24:24).

Sacrifice costs us something. While praising God might not seem to be a costly sacrifice, it is nonetheless the best sacrifice one can offer God. Praise comes from the heart and requires focus, physical energy, and time spent in God's presence. When we spend time with Him, we begin to experience the joy of God's goodness. God is genuinely honored when praise comes from a grateful heart.

O Lord, let me honor You with the sacrifice of a grateful heart.

God to the Rescue

Help us, O God of our salvation! Help us for the glory of your name. Save us and forgive our sins for the honor of your name.

PSALM 79:9 NLT

"Rescue me from their ravages," cried David, who was barely one step ahead of Saul, "my precious life from these lions" (Psalm 35:17 NIV).

The Israelites certainly pled for Yahweh's help as the Egyptian army chased them across the Red Sea. Daniel probably had a similar prayer as King Darius ordered him to the lions. And in 2012, Argentinean Analia Bouguet sobbed in grief as doctors handed her a death certificate just twenty minutes after her tiny daughter was stillborn.

But doesn't God—your loving, generous God—love to rescue?

When the waters destroyed Pharoah's invincible army, Miriam took up a tambourine and exalted God. Darius decreed at Daniel's rescue, "He is the living God…he rescues and he saves." Analia fell to her knees in the hospital morgue where she'd come to say good-bye, only to find her baby alive. "I'm a believer," she told an Argentinean news agency. "All of this was a miracle from God." The story went viral.

It is the same forever as it has always been: God rescues because of His love for us, and He rescues as only He can. At our most desperate, we can look to Him, the hope of the hopeless.

You are the Great Rescuer…always, forever. I entrust myself into Your hands.

What a Wonderful World

What a wildly wonderful world, God! You made it all, with Wisdom at your side, made earth overflow with your wonderful creations.

Psalm 104:24 msg

Are you familiar with the narwhal? Imagine something like a whale outfitted with a horn much like a unicorn. Adult males average sixteen feet long and weigh upwards of 3,300 pounds. The males are distinguished by an ivory tusk that pierces the upper lip on the left side and extends forward as much as ten feet. But beyond that we know more about the rings of Saturn than we do the narwhal. It is a creature both wild and wonderful, like something out of a dream. And who created the narwhal? Our wild and wonderful God. From the obscure depths of the Bering Sea to the peak of Everest and into the shadows of cypress swamps, our world is overflowing with the wonderful creations of our wildly expressive God. He is the Source of all that was and is and will be. His world reflects the range, the variety, the spectrum of His creativity.

What a wildly wonderful God!

O God, You created all that is. Let me never doubt Your ability to move in me.

The Beauty of Remembrance

Full of splendor and majesty is his work, and his righteousness endures forever. He has caused his wondrous works to be remembered; the LORD is gracious and merciful.

PSALM 111:3–4 ESV

On September 11, 2011, the "Reflecting Absence" memorial opened on sixteen hallowed acres of New York City. Two water-falls spilling into acre-sized pools, four hundred white oaks, three thousand names stencil-cut into bronze parapets, and the Survival Tree—the last thing alive to leave Ground Zero. By year's end, a million visitors had already passed through the memorial, staring into the pools, sitting under the trees, making paper impressions of particular names.

People wanted to remember.

People needed to remember.

Memorials are important because human recall can be short and fickle. But God's memory is long. He sent you rainbows by which to remember His deliverance. He gave you a wooden cross for remembering His extraordinary sacrifice. He carved ten rules into stone to help you remember His steadfast righteousness. And He writes personal memorials every day on the tablet of your heart—lasting testimonies of His enduring love.

Look around. God builds memorials every day to display all that He's done. Reflect on them. And remember.

Lord God, remind me of Your deliverance...help me to remember.

Besieged by God's Love

You hem me in behind and before, and you lay your hand upon me.
Such knowledge is too wonderful for me, too lofty for me to attain.

Psalm 139:5–6 NIV

Miracles are a retelling in small letters of the very same story which is written across the whole world in letters too large for some of us to see," wrote C.S. Lewis. From stories in Scripture to modern-day collections of "miracle" books, we read accounts of personal testimonies to God's intervention in a person's life. What they all have in common is what Lewis referred to as the "same story," reminding us that the Author of these miracles is God and His greatest miracle is the gift of Jesus.

The Hebrew word translated "hem" in Psalm 139:5 means "to press upon, to compress." Its common reference was that of besieging a city with troops in war; to surround a city so there was no way of escape. How wonderful it is to imagine our God on every side of us, protecting us from our enemies in every direction.

The knowledge of God's omniscience and omnipresence is too much for the human mind to contain. But it is a miracle nonetheless—the everyday miracle of God's mysterious presence in the lives of His children.

What an encouragement that You surround me with Your love!

Look and Listen

Ears that hear and eyes that see—the LORD has made them both.

PROVERBS 20:12 NIV

The ear and the eye are awesome examples of God's meticulous creativity. The ear gathers sound waves—everything from bird songs to human language—and converts them into nerve impulses that allow the brain to identify each sound. The eye has a similar function: it collects and regulates light, focusing it to form an image and then transmitting these signals to the brain.

Sight and hearing are gifts from God, and while the eyes and ears are wonders of the physical body, there is a deeper meaning to their purpose. Scripture admonishes us to use the "inner" or spiritual aspect of perception: an ear that hears the Word of God and perceives its lessons; an eye that sees the works of God and glorifies Him as the Creator. The "waves" of the voice of the Spirit, and the "signal" of His discernment and direction reach us at a supernatural level. Everything we hear and see is a gift from the loving Lord of creation.

You alone give the gift of sight and the miracle of hearing. Help me to use these blessings as You intended.

September 11

Chief End

They are my people—I created each of them to bring honor to me.

Isaiah 43:7 CEV

Of the questions in the Westminster Shorter Catechism, the most famous is surely, "What is the chief end of man?" The answer to this question is equally memorable: "Man's chief end is to glorify God, and to enjoy him forever."

A variation on this famous query could be something like this: "What is the chief end of God?" Based on the words of Isaiah and the Westminster Catechism (not to mention the whole witness of Scripture), the answer is rather straightforward: "To receive glory and honor from His creation."

All things have been created to give homage to their Creator. This understanding imbues life with a sense of meaning rather than aimlessness. It also reveals the fundamental definition of the word *enjoy*: honoring God and giving Him the glory that is due to Him.

Our lives are not our own; they are God's. And He created each of us to live for Him. Is He getting the glory from your life?

You created everything on purpose, O God. Guide me to honor and enjoy You this day.

God Has View

"My thoughts are nothing like your thoughts," says the Lord.
"And my ways are far beyond anything you could imagine.
For just as the heavens are higher than the earth, so my ways are higher than your ways and my thoughts higher than your thoughts."

Isaiah 55:8–9 NLT

Madeleine L'Engle is best known for her classic book *A Wrinkle in Time*. But it is her lesser-known nonfiction book *Walking on Water* that contains the framework for her thought. In it, she writes: "I have a point of view. You have a point of view. God has view."

We often adamantly insist that we have all the angles covered, we've researched every option, we've made projections with verifiable data. But the truth is that even on our best days, we see through a glass darkly.

God, however, is not like us. He is not limited in what He can see and do. God sees full scope and far range, from an unhindered perspective. His view is not hampered by a cluttered past or the baggage of sin or the clouds of fear. We cannot even imagine what is known to Him in a glance. But we can ask and we can seek, and in Him we shall find.

Our vision is limited by what we can see from the field. God sees from the press box, above and beyond.

Because You have view, O Lord, I can rest knowing You are above all.

Perfect Cycle

Is it not to share your food with the hungry and to provide the poor wanderer with shelter—when you see the naked, to clothe him, and not to turn away from your own flesh and blood? Then your light will break forth like the dawn, and your healing will quickly appear; then your righteousness will go before you, and the glory of the L*ORD will be your rear guard.*

ISAIAH 58:7–8 NIV

During the winter holidays each year, there are outreach programs in almost every city for those in the community who are struggling to get by. Items are collected and organized, and distribution tables are set up so that as each mom or dad arrives, volunteers can receive their request and pull together the supplies to meet that need. It's a practical, direct exchange, and without it, many families would have to suffer.

The volunteers don't own the food or the clothing. They're just responsible for handing it out. And that's what Isaiah really meant in chapter 58 with the term "share": the reality is that no matter what we have, we are merely in charge of the distribution, just like the outreach volunteers. Whatever we have, God gave us. It is His beautiful heart that provides our food, our money, our clothes, while His Spirit directs the delivery through us to those who need it.

There is compassion in the Father's ways. He pours out His resources for us, and we divide and share them. He then promises to multiply our blessings...and the cycle starts all over again. What have you handed out today?

Your provision is bountiful, O God. Keep my heart set on extending Your blessings to those who cross my path.

September 14

In God Alone

"Let the one who boasts boast about this: that they have the understanding to know me, that I am the LORD, who exercises kindness, justice and righteousness on earth, for in these I delight," declares the LORD.

JEREMIAH 9:24 NIV

We live in a self-promoting world. We are taught to load our résumés with our most favorable attributes and accomplishments and take every opportunity to toot our own horn. But God asks us to do the opposite. Instead of boasting about our exploits and successes, God invites us to boast in Him.

"Boasting" in the sense that Jeremiah mentioned means to glory in something. The Hebrew term borders on "raving" or "madness." When you begin to experience the presence of God, His goodness and His miraculous power, it is hard not to be a little "mad," much like being in love.

We see this in the apostle Paul's life. Despite all his outstanding credentials, Paul wrote, "May I never boast except in the cross of our Lord Jesus Christ." When we taste God's kindness, justice, and righteousness on the earth, it is not meant for us alone. We are charged with shouting it from the rooftops so that others will know how great God is.

All my accomplishments are because of You, Lord. Help me to remember this and proclaim it.

God of the Waters

Why don't you honor me? Why aren't you in awe before me?
Yes, me, who made the shorelines to contain the ocean waters.

Jeremiah 5:22 MSG

The wave that barreled out of the Indian Ocean in 2004 slammed into fourteen countries and killed more than 230,000 people. Two years later, eight hundred were missing or dead from the giant, invading waves south of Java Island. In 2011, Japan watched walls of water trigger hydrogen explosions and nuclear meltdown, and twenty thousand people went missing or dead.

What a fearsome, terrible thing a tsunami can be. Beginning in the depths of the ocean floor and rolling for thousands of miles up to hundreds of feet in the air, it is an awesome reminder of the power of the ocean and the interaction of the earth and its currents.

The Lord of all the earth carved the bowls that hold every sea. He poured the ocean water and set the tides to turn with a power beyond our imagining. Don't doubt for a moment that He is big enough to control whatever is coming your way this day.

Lord God, wash over me like a wave and connect me with Your power.

In the Least of These

"And when did we ever see you sick or in prison and come to you?" Then the King will say, "I'm telling the solemn truth: Whenever you did one of these things to someone overlooked or ignored, that was me—you did it to me."

MATTHEW 25:39–40 MSG

In 1994 some 3,500 Congressional and international power brokers from over 100 countries gathered at the National Prayer Breakfast in Washington, DC. They assemble annually to "meet Jesus, man to man," and that year, tiny Mother Teresa of Calcutta had a huge word for these influential leaders.

"Love, to be true, has to hurt," she said. "It hurt Jesus to love us. Jesus makes Himself the hungry one, the naked one, the homeless one, the unwanted one." She asked those attendees to give to "the least of these" until it hurt, because as Jesus taught, to deny love to the obscure, the poor, the despised and afflicted is to deny God.

Jesus's unrestrained grace and goodness is available to *every* sufferer. This is His revolutionary plan—that He who is highly exalted is miraculously present in those who are the least honored. Honor Him whose heart has no limits. Love others until it hurts.

In all my actions, Jesus, I long to exalt You and to lift up those who are suffering.

September 17

Stand Out

But love your enemies, do good to them, and lend to them without expecting to get anything back. Then your reward will be great, and you will be children of the Most High, because he is kind to the ungrateful and wicked.

Luke 6:35 NIV

Do you want to be unique? There are countless marketing and self-help gurus ready and willing to give you a fast lesson: "Ten Ways to Stand Out in a Crowd"; "Be the New You"; "How to Shine in the Marketplace."

Jesus shows us a different way to stand out—not from the crowd, but to God. When confronted by an enemy or faced with the distasteful reality of an unappreciative person, do the opposite of what most people would do: be quick to show mercy and always ready to help. There's no better way to reflect the Father. After all, who of us can say we have not sometimes been ungrateful in spite of God's goodness?

We can love others because we have been the recipients of undeserved love. God's compassion and mercy are without limits—even to those who are ungrateful and who live as if He did not exist. He is the One who supplies the grace to conduct ourselves as children of the Most High.

You have been merciful to me. I want to reflect Your heart, Father.

They Believed in Him

"Now fill your pitchers and take them to the host," Jesus said, and they did.
This act in Cana of Galilee was the first sign Jesus gave,
the first glimpse of his glory. And his disciples believed in him.

John 2:8, 11 msg

A handful of disciples accompanied Jesus to the wedding in Cana and witnessed the awkward moment when the wine ran out. When Jesus's mother asked Him to help, He turned 180 gallons of ordinary water into exquisite wine, without fanfare. And they believed in Him.

Jesus revealed His power over natural laws, His benevolence, His delight in doing good and, just like that, introduced a new era of joy and hope. Gone was the age of legalism. Now was the time for personal touch.

It was a sign—a public mark of power and grace and divine goodness. And it was so affirming, so life-changing that the disciples believed, literally, *into* Jesus. They wholeheartedly transferred their trust from themselves to their Redeemer. And then went out and conquered the world.

What a glorious moment. What a Savior.

Lord Jesus, with Your power and glory, You make the ordinary extraordinary. I celebrate You.

September 19

In the Beginning

Everything was created through him; nothing—not one thing!—
came into being without him.

John 1:3 msg

The Word was there at the beginning, as John tells us in the first sentence of his Gospel. Even before the beginning, outside of time and space—before the laws of physics, biology, and geology, before creation—there was great purpose and unlimited power, and *Logos* was there. The Word not yet made man, but present with the Father.

From the Word came creation—the unfolding of God's will in infinite detail. God communicated His will through the Word. And in that creation was *Imago Dei*, the "image of God," man—the one for whom God would unfold His revelation and redemption.

From the beginning, everything was created through Him, created for Him...everything done for love. The heart of all that would ever exist in the universe could be found in the Love that set it into motion with the words, "Let there be light."

Without God, there is nothing. But with Him is eternal purpose, from beginning to end.

From beginning to end, You are enough.

Source of Salvation

Salvation is found in no one else, for there is no other name under heaven given to mankind by which we must be saved.

Acts 4:12 NIV

We need look no further than Jesus when it comes to the truth.

None of the great teachers in history made a personal claim to *be* the truth. Not Moses, Buddha, Confucius, or Mohammed. Whenever any ruler in history declared himself a god and insisted on being worshiped, that delusion was quickly dispelled at his death. Jesus Christ was and is the only One who can and did claim to be God. Even now, as Watchman Nee put it, "God will answer all our questions in one way and one way only, namely, by showing us more of his Son."

In Jesus are all the answers we need; in Him is our salvation—He is, in every aspect, our Way, our Life, our Truth.

The word "salvation" means "to be preserved in a state of safety." When looking for a place of refuge, when needing answers beyond your own understanding, when seeking transformation that lasts, look no further: Jesus saves.

For the gift of salvation through Your Son, Jesus Christ, I offer You my all.

Perfect and Righteous

But if you see that the job is too big for you, that it's something only God can do, and you trust him to do it—you could never do it for yourself no matter how hard and long you worked—well, that trusting-him-to-do-it is what gets you set right with God, by God. Sheer gift.

Romans 4:5 msg

Abraham is mentioned more than 230 times in the Bible, and at some point in every narrative, the word *faith* shows up. He wasn't perfect—he had colossal failures in patience and obedience. He got kicked out of Egypt for lying about his marriage, and nearly destroyed his family with a substitute wife and heir. *Righteous* would not be the first word stamped on Abraham's application to heaven, were it not for Jesus.

Abraham *did* have belief, however—a deep, abiding belief. He didn't die with his hand on the door latch of eternity: he walked through on faith. And God, in His enduring kindness, accepted Abraham despite his failure and sin, calling him righteous for that simple belief. A sheer gift from God.

Obviously the job of being righteous is too big for any human being. Only our perfect Redeemer is able to set us right with Himself.

Help me to trust You for all those things I cannot do for myself.

Authoritative Orders

Who is he who condemns? It is Christ who died, and furthermore is also risen, who is even at the right hand of God, who also makes intercession for us.

Romans 8:34 NKJV

Napoleon's horse had gotten away from him. A private in Napoleon's army, seeing the horse escaping, hopped on his own horse and chased it down. Upon the return of the steed, Napoleon looked at the man with a sense of satisfaction and said to him, "Well done, Captain." And according to the story, no one dared question this man's new rank. After all, Napoleon himself had bestowed it upon him.

The reality is that those of us who are in Christ are no longer subject to sin's judgment. Our sin was condemned on the cross in Christ Jesus. There is a spiritual enemy who would seek to belittle us and accuse us according to our past. But the One who has declared our sins eternally forgiven is his Superior, and He has elevated us to a new rank.

Christ died, rose from the dead, and is now enthroned in heaven. If He declares you justified before God, no one—not even Satan—can argue with that.

Lord, You declare my sins forgiven as a pure act of grace. Help me to walk in Your grace.

September 23

God's Great Patience

What if God, although choosing to show his wrath and make his power known, bore with great patience the objects of his wrath—prepared for destruction? What if he did this to make the riches of his glory known to the objects of his mercy, whom he prepared in advance for glory...?

Romans 9:22–24 NIV

Most of us would probably agree with C. S. Lewis' remark that "There are only two kinds of people in the end: those who say to God, 'Thy will be done,' and those to whom God says, in the end, 'Thy will be done.'" In these sobering words, we recognize how holy and divine God is. Yet throughout the Bible, we also hear of His longsuffering ways. Although He does not tolerate sin, He is patient with our struggles against it, being "gracious and compassionate, slow to anger and rich in love" (Psalm 145:8 NIV).

If we were being honest, though, the majority of us would have to admit that we long for God to be quicker to anger—especially when it seems that the bad guys are winning. What are we to do then?

Trust. Remember, God is not only patient with His own children, but sometimes He endures the other guys. As hard as that is to grasp, God can be trusted to work patiently in His own time—in ways we cannot comprehend and with thoughts we cannot fathom—to reveal His glory and His power to all of creation. The objects of His wrath and the objects of His mercy will all be set right—in due time.

Give me the faith, God, to be grateful for Your mercy and compassion toward us all. And thank You for Your patience with me.

Whatever

So whether you eat or drink, or whatever you do, do it all for the glory of God.

1 Corinthians 10:31 nlt

The young man pushed and shoved his way through the crowd with little concern for who or what was in his way, rushing to who knows where. He knocked some shopping bags out of a lady's hands with barely a glance.

It's hard not to judge a moment like that, especially when his T-shirt had one word emblazoned on it in all capital letters: Whatever.

Jesus is constantly redeeming our attitudes and behaviors. A T-shirt that no doubt was meant to express a clear statement of indifference might suddenly mean something entirely different when the wearer is devoted to God. As we come to know and follow Jesus as Lord and Savior, the *whatever* of apathy becomes the *whatever* of submission. Our actions begin to reflect the character of Christ, and the Holy Spirit indwells and empowers our lives, our actions, our decisions.

With God's purposes in mind, that same T-shirt means, "Whatever I'm doing, I'm doing for His glory!"

In whatever I do, may I commit myself to You, Father. You alone are worthy.

Be Who You Is

God has made us what we are, and in our union with Christ Jesus he has created us for a life of good deeds, which he has already prepared for us to do.

Ephesians 2:10 GNT

Mother Teresa loved to say, "The only success is faithfulness." Brennan Manning used to quote an old-time preacher who told him, "Brennan, be who you is, 'cause if you ain't who you is, then you is who you ain't."

God has made each of us what and who we are. And wrapped in the redemptive love of His Son, Jesus, each of us has been created for a life of service and ministry, and for a particular service and ministry that God has specifically intended for us to do.

Every time you use the specific gifts and abilities He has given you, you reveal His imprint. His fingerprints are everywhere in your life, to His glory. So don't try to be anyone besides who you are because the Great I AM loves for you to be you.

His genius is evident in every person ever born, and one beautiful way to pay homage to that unprecedented creativity is to walk the path and do the work He has prepared just for you.

I can be who You want me to be because of Your creative love, O Lord.

September 26

Fast Forgiveness

Be gentle with one another, sensitive. Forgive one another as quickly and thoroughly as God in Christ forgave you.

Ephesians 4:32 MSG

Writer Stephen King is often quoted as saying, "The road to hell is paved with adverbs." He sees this particular figure of speech as a crutch and adds, "The adverb is not your friend."

While even the apostle Paul probably would have agreed that it is a good thing to be able to write clear sentences without frills, he waves away King's advice as he writes of the forgiveness we experience through God in Christ. Paul describes it with some very important adverbs: *quickly* and *thoroughly*. Far from being crutches, these words are transcendent descriptions of the love of God. He does not hesitate or partially forgive. His is a love that is immediate and complete.

Each of us can experience freedom from the bitterness of festering unforgiveness by following His example and emulating His love. It's a love that forgives—quickly, thoroughly, and over and over again.

I want to live a life full of love like Yours. Thank You, Father, for Your forgiveness.

The God of Contentment

I can do everything through him who gives me strength.

Philippians 4:13 NIV

The world had rarely watched an athlete as closely as they did the quarterback for the University of Florida. At least, that's what the Internet seemed to indicate on Saturday nights. Every Saturday for his games, Tim Tebow would don a black strip with a Bible verse reference written in white underneath his eyes. Whichever Scripture reference Tebow wore would be the most heavily searched on Internet engines over the next twenty-four hours. A Bible verse that Tebow wore frequently was Philippians 4:13.

While many fans interpreted this verse to be about winning a game, it was, of course, composed in the middle of a much more serious circumstance. These words were written by the apostle Paul while he was in prison for his faith. Hungry and isolated, Paul declared that he was content. He had learned the secret of relying on Christ, who filled him with the supernatural power to remain strong.

The strength that God provides is a beautiful testimony to His love. Whether our bank account is full or pitifully sparse, whether we dine on filet mignon or macaroni, His grace makes contentment and peace possible.

Lord, You are able to bring peace in any circumstance. Show me how to trust You in good times and in hard times too.

Our Righteous Judge

Now there is in store for me the crown of righteousness, which the Lord, the righteous Judge, will award to me on that day—and not only to me, but also to all who have longed for his appearing.

2 Timothy 4:8 niv

Millions of Americans take notice whenever an industry's annual awards are presented—whether it's the ESPYs for athletics, the Grammys or Oscars for entertainment, fashion's Best-Dressed list, or the Gallup organization's Most Admired list. We are a culture that likes to award those who stand out.

But there is one award that we can all receive without the burden of competing with or excelling against our peers. It is given by Jesus Christ to all who love Him and long for His return—and given because of *Him*, not because of anything we did to earn it.

This honor is a righteous crown from a righteous Judge. The word *righteous* in both cases means the same thing: "made holy and innocent by justification." God's redemptive work through Jesus is an equal-opportunity rewards system—available for all who believe. Only Jesus could make us holy in the sight of God, so only Jesus can hand out a "crown of righteousness."

How incomprehensible is His perfect judgment, and how merciful is His heart.

Dear Lord, You are my righteousness. You are my salvation and reward.

Fading Never

And again to the Son, You, Master, started it all, laid earth's foundations, then crafted the stars in the sky. Earth and sky will wear out, but not you; they become threadbare like an old coat; You'll fold them up like a worn-out cloak, and lay them away on the shelf. But you'll stay the same, year after year; you'll never fade, you'll never wear out.

Hebrews 1:10–12 MSG

Planned obsolescence. It's a business strategy in which the eventual obsolescence of the product is built in from its conception. This is done so that in the future, the consumer will be motivated to purchase new products and services that the manufacturer brings out as replacements for the old ones. Examples include ink-jet printer cartridges, batteries, most fashion items, and according to Scripture, the earth and the sky as well. They are going to eventually wear out.

But not God. Unchanging and ever-relevant, there is no chance of Him becoming obsolete. He was before all things; He will exist after everything about this world has passed away. There's no need to replace Him either—He simply can't be improved upon.

The God above all other gods, the Creator of Heaven and Earth, He is the Lord—always in season—and He will never fade.

Everything will fade away except for You. Help me live with that mind-set.

September 30

Our Strength in Suffering

Be glad for the chance to suffer as Christ suffered.
It will prepare you for even greater happiness when he makes his glorious return.
Count it a blessing when you suffer for being a Christian.
This shows that God's glorious Spirit is with you.

1 Peter 4:13–14 CEV

The refrain of the old hymn says, "Count your many blessings, name them one by one." When this was sung in small churches years ago, sometimes there would be pauses in the church service as members of the congregation would stand up and share about something that God had done. But rarely did you hear suffering or hardship or pain counted in the testimonies; successes, victories, and triumphs were always viewed as the blessings.

What Peter does in these verses is turn our usual approach to blessings on its head. He tells us to count our sufferings—one by one if needed—and see them as evidence of the presence of God's Spirit with us; in other words, as blessings. The wonder of the work of the Comforter is that He gives strength when despair comes, and peace when there's trouble. His amazing presence is obvious in times of distress. Only He can give us the mind of Christ, the joy of the Lord, and the calm assurance that our suffering will be exchanged for eternal happiness upon Christ's glorious return.

Your sustaining presence in the midst of my suffering gives me peace.

Who Is Like God?

Who is like unto thee, O Lord, among the gods?
Who is like thee, glorious in holiness, fearful in praises, doing wonders?
Thou stretchedst out thy right hand, the earth swallowed them.

Exodus 15:11–12 KJV

The gods of Egypt were many. Each tribe worshiped its own deity, represented by an animal: the Frog, the Bull, the Falcon, the Cat—the list was long. The children of Israel survived in the middle of this religion of idols for *four hundred years*! Then, in a wondrous miracle, God sent ten plagues against the Egyptians to confound those gods.

More miracles followed. The children of promise were guided through the desert, and when they arrived at the Red Sea, God parted the waters so they could cross to the other side and escape Pharaoh's pursuing army.

Finally free! The Israelites could not help but give praise to God. The music and lyrics burst out of them with an exuberance that could not be contained. God had done wonders. He had literally suspended the laws of nature on their behalf—the laws He had created and established—and now the Egyptian army lay forever silent at the bottom of the sea. Who is like our God? The Red Sea tells the story.

I worship You, God, for Your deliverance in times of need.

October 2

God's Wellness Plan

Keep the Lord's regulations and his commandments.
I'm commanding them to you today for your well-being and for the well-being of your children after you, so that you may extend your time on the fertile land that the LORD your God is giving you forever.

DEUTERONOMY 4:40 (CEB)

The latest health-and-wellness statistics reveal that the global market in this category has surpassed the $600 billion mark for the first time. The United States remains the world's biggest market for health foods and beverages, at $153 billion in retail value—accounting for one-quarter of global sales. The largest category, close to 40 percent of US sales, is that of general *well-being*. What financial extremes we go to, hoping to ensure our health!

It's amazing to think that our heavenly Father, full of wisdom and love, made a great plan for this very thing. He has shown the way that is good for us and our children, if we will only follow His direction. First John 5:3 tells us that "his commandments are not burdensome," for they are rooted in none other than the love revealed to us in Jesus's life, death, and resurrection. Keeping His commandments means daily abiding in His love, for a wellness this world cannot give—a health of mind, body, and soul.

Lord, Your plan for my well-being is tried, tested, and true. How can I thank You?

The Glory of His Holiness

Glory in his holy name; let the hearts of those who seek the Lord rejoice.

1 Chronicles 16:10 NIV

There are quests that have engaged scientists and adventurers for centuries. They seem to hold endless fascination, though they are hopeless: for instance, the search for the Philosopher's Stone that supposedly can turn anything to gold, or for the Elixir of Life that is rumored to impart immortality.

There is, however, a quest that makes the heart rejoice. Seeking the Lord is not a journey with a dead end. In the original Hebrew, the term for "seek" is an active word: "to search out, to strive after, to desire." And when we seek Him, the Bible promises we will find Him.

There is a twofold result for those hearts who "search out" God: they are gradually drawn into His holiness, and then they are changed by it—a transforming process that is cause for rejoicing. This is a transcendent work of God, not something we can do for ourselves. Are you on the quest yet?

Lord, strengthen my heart as I seek after You, and transform me by Your holiness.

The Path

Now you've got my feet on the life path, all radiant from the shining of your face. Ever since you took my hand, I'm on the right way.

PSALM 16:11 MSG

Like the traveler in Robert Frost's famous poem, every person takes a road in life, encounters a divergence, ponders the consequences, and calmly makes a choice—the right choice...the wisest one.

At least, that's the poetic metaphor.

The reality is that people spend a lot of time at that fork in the road, paralyzed by crisis, questioning choice and fate, delayed by indecision. And that's where God steps in.

The all-wise Counselor, the Chief Shepherd, is happy to offer His hand to the lone traveler, pointing out the excellence of His way, the beauty of His Word, the pureness of faith, the bright light of His glory.

In God is every wise path, every season of good judgment and guidance. His Word is sure, His statutes uncompromising. Read them for His never-failing direction and wisdom.

Great Counselor, please take my hand and guide me.

October 5

Honor and Praise

Since you are my rock and my fortress, for the sake of your name lead and guide me.
Free me from the trap that is set for me, for you are my refuge.
Into your hands I commit my spirit; redeem me, O LORD, the God of truth.

PSALM 31:3–5 NIV

Soldiers are routinely honored for their bravery on the battlefield. Schoolteachers are honored for their years of commitment to the education of our children. And there are those special times when mothers and fathers are honored by their children for their sacrifice over the years. The psalmist reminds us that God is due honor as well.

God's protective hand keeps us safe through tests and trials. God leads and guides us and promises never to forsake us. In His faithfulness, He has rescued us from sin and death. He is our mighty fortress, the Rock that cannot be moved. Glory to His name! We can trust Him …with everything.

I want to please You today, God. I give You this day.

October 6

Sold Out

All the nations you have made will come and worship before you, Lord;
they will bring glory to your name.
For you are great and you do wondrous things; you alone are God.

Psalm 86:9–10 NIV

Who doesn't love to be part of a sold-out event? There's nothing like the buzz in a crowded room full of people who are waiting to experience a once-in-a-lifetime moment together.

On an eternal scale, there will come a day when the ultimate sold-out event will occur: all the nations God has made will gather to worship His name. There the worship will not be compulsory, but will spring from the unified hearts of every participant.

In the original Hebrew the word for "glory" means "to shine clearly with the intent to celebrate what is revealed." When the nations gather, it will be obvious who they have come to celebrate and why. The nations will rejoice in the greatness of God and His awesome works. The peoples will not just praise God for His past actions, but for what He is doing now, and what He will continue to do.

Make no mistake: no other god will receive such praise. The only object of our worship will be the God of all creation. He will not share the stage with a pantheon of gods. In Him alone will the nations exult.

There is no one greater than You, and I rejoice in Your goodness today.

October 7

A Father's Compassion

Just as a father has compassion on his children, so the LORD has compassion on those who fear him; for He Himself knows our frame; He is mindful that we are but dust.

PSALM 103:13–14 NASB

Jesus began his famous prayer, "Our Father in heaven." He was not praying to an idol or mythological god; He was praying to the God He knew to be true and appealing to God's great compassion for His people.

The Hebrew word that David uses in this psalm to state the intrinsic frailty of our humanity comes from the same verb that is used for the potter's craft. The Father knows we came from dust and that we are fragile and breakable. We are the ones who forget what weak creatures we really are. We want to ignore God and depend on ourselves. We look in a thousand directions for clever ways to circumvent Him. But God is always there and always—every time—compassionate. Though we reject Him, still He extends tenderness toward us.

This compassion is a constant: we constantly need it, and God is constantly giving it. No one but Him would do such a thing for "dust" like us.

God of glory, remember me in my brokenness and extend to me Your wonderful compassion.

Fiery Strength

May the glory of the LORD endure forever; may the LORD rejoice in his works— he who looks at the earth, and it trembles, who touches the mountains, and they smoke.

PSALM 104:31–32 NIV

There are currently about 1,500 active volcanoes in the world. Their amazing power is caused by the friction between tectonic plates. When these giant slices of the earth's surface collide, they generate such a tremendous amount of heat that rock melts into magma, which rises to the surface as lava. From the "Ring of Fire"—an arc of volcanoes in the Pacific Ocean—to the volatile mountains of fire in Iceland, they can erupt without much warning, stunning the world with their geysers of ash and rivers of lava. The smoke alone from a volcano can reach several thousand feet into the atmosphere and spread outward in a blanket that turns day into night.

What an astounding spectacle! And what a picture of the mighty God we worship!

He is fierceness and power, beauty and complexity—all in one. From the shattering force of a volcano to the delicacy of a lily, our Creator has made a world of intricate design, and He sits in awesome majesty over all His works. His glory will endure forever!

How can I forget Your power and strength? Your magnificent creation displays it every day.

Eyes of Truth

For a man's ways are in full view of the LORD, and he examines all his paths.

PROVERBS 5:21 NIV

Everyone squirms at the thought of having their mind read. It is unsettling enough that our actions are constantly being recorded in this world of video surveillance. Even Hollywood stars, who make their living in front of a camera, like to have a life away from the public eye. So who would be anything but uncomfortable if their thoughts were on display for all to the world to see and judge?

Though it is possible for our inner world to remain private where other people are concerned, the Lord cuts through all that. He sees us as we are, with our secrets and destructive habits and sin. All our intentions are examined by Him, all our thoughts are known.

Our choice? To humbly fall before Him and offer every part of ourselves to His transforming grace—or to continue living in a darkness that only He can dispel.

When we surrender to the Light, the miracle of grace is perfectly realized: His mercy is there for us in spite of our blemishes. There is no greater love!

You love me enough to examine my paths. Your mercy is awesome.

A Global Choir

From the ends of the earth we hear songs, "Glory to the Righteous One."

Isaiah 24:16 NASB

At the beginning of Jesus's ministry, there were only a few disciples following Him. Before long, two turned into twelve. As Jesus traveled about, teaching with authority and performing miracles, His band of twelve became a hundred, which soon became several hundred. Before long, His followers were literally singing His praises.

Eventually Jesus would be crucified and resurrected. And in the wake of His resurrection, the number of believers in Israel grew exponentially. After His ascension, more and more people committed themselves to Jesus and His gospel—Jews and Gentiles alike.

Today, Jesus's followers number well beyond a billion and span the globe. And those who follow Him point to undeniable evidence as their reason—the transformation of their hearts. That our heavenly Father can take a heart of stone and turn it into a heart of flesh is nothing short of a miracle. Believers all over the planet are singing the same lyric: *Jesus changed my heart.*

Think about how Jesus has changed your life, and as you do, let your heart burst forth in worship, singing glory to the Righteous One.

Lord, I cannot help but sing Your praises. What You have done in my heart causes me to worship You.

Follow the Leader

Who sent his glorious arm of power to be at Moses' right hand,
who divided the waters before them, to gain for himself everlasting renown,
who led them through the depths? Like a horse in open country, they did not stumble;
like cattle that go down to the plain, they were given rest by the Spirit of the LORD.
This is how you guided your people to make for yourself a glorious name.

ISAIAH 63:12–14 NIV

"I have a dream." Fifty years later, we hear those words and immediately remember Martin Luther King Jr. guiding our nation through the tumultuous days of the civil rights movement. Or we read "Four score and seven years ago" and envision Abraham Lincoln calling our country back to unity.

Knowing we need good leaders, we look for traits we admire, trust a few persuasive qualities, and commit ourselves to follow. Still, as God warned the people of Israel when they demanded a king like all the surrounding nations had, it is foolish to ever place our full trust in man.

It is God, first and last, that we can rely on to lead us. When God led Abraham from one part of the world to another, He took great care to see that Abraham and his family were provided for. On a much larger scale, God led Israel from Egypt to the Promised Land. And He will lead us on the journey of our lives.

As individuals and a nation, Almighty God will lead the way through every situation in life. Follow the perfect leader. Follow God.

Where You lead, Lord, I will follow.

Mighty Home-Maker

But it is God whose power made the earth,
whose wisdom gave shape to the world, who crafted the cosmos.

Jeremiah 10:12 MSG

We live on a unique and lovingly crafted planet. Our heavenly Father set our universe in motion, and were it not for a perfectly balanced ecosystem, we would not be able to live on this mysterious home we call Earth.

Venus is a volcanic wasteland; Mercury and Mars have no atmosphere; Neptune and Uranus are freezing; Jupiter and Saturn are covered with gas. Earth is the only known planet just the right distance from the sun, with a large amount of water and varied land masses with temperate climates. Only Earth is capable of—in fact, *ideal* for—sustaining life. And only a genius Creator could have designed it that way.

God, however, in His infinite wisdom, didn't just design a planet; He prepared a *home.* He ingeniously arranged the Earth with everything humanity needs to make it a *dwelling place*—mountains, hills, meadows, forests, and fields, with lakes and rivers and seas intermingled. Then, He brilliantly spread a tent-like atmosphere over everything to protect it from solar damage.

Enjoy your home. It is proof of God's singular and incomparable wisdom.

I count myself blessed to be able to dwell on Your earth. Make me a good steward of it.

God of Glory

Then the cherubim lifted up their wings with the wheels beside them, and the glory of the God of Israel hovered over them.

EZEKIEL 11:22 NASB

The first job of cherubim was to guard the tree of life in Eden. Images of them bookended the lid of the Ark of the Covenant, their outstretched wings forming what was called the "mercy seat." They were believed to be the protectors of the sacred objects contained in the Ark and a visible pedestal for the invisible throne of God. In traditional Christian angelology, cherubim are angels of the second-highest order.

Few humans in history have ever laid eyes on such creatures. They are among the mysteries of God that exceed our imaginations. Still, the cherubim reveal another evidence of God's creativity and authority. Every king selects a chosen few to be a part of the retinue that goes with him wherever he goes. Such an entourage is part of a king's glory—part of God's glory. We serve the King of Glory!

I submit to Your authority, O God, and join Your angels in serving You.

Backstage with God

*When you help someone out, don't think about how it looks.
Just do it—quietly and unobtrusively. That is the way your God,
who conceived you in love, working behind the scenes, helps you out.*

Matthew 6:3–4 msg

Being a stagehand is not a glamorous job. It usually involves working nights and weekends for little if any pay, and no recognition. It's an unsung, behind-the-scenes vocation if ever there was one.

So why would anyone want to be a stagehand? To be part of that theatrical environment. To help set the scene, realize a vision, showcase someone who can wow the audience every time. If you're a really good stagehand, you might get to overhear an audience member say, "How did they *do* that?"

That's what a wildly creative God does for His people. He works backstage to get the details right—scenery, lights, sound, props, rigging, special effects—so that when you take the stage of life, you'll be able to fulfill the dreams He has called you to.

God set the world in motion and conceived us in love. The work God does in our lives—and the way we are to live with each other—is not simply a performance for applause, but an extension of His grace and compassion. An act of love. Our amazing God is working behind the scenes every day of our lives.

Father, You back me up with Your quiet strength and tender mercy. Help me fulfill Your plans for me.

Grand and Glorious

And then they'll see the Son of Man enter in grand style,
his Arrival filling the sky—no one will miss it!

Mark 13:26 MSG

It is said that Queen Victoria, deeply moved after hearing a sermon about the magnificent return of Jesus, told the speaker, "Dean Farrar, I should like to be living when Jesus comes, so that I could lay the crown of England at his feet."

When we contemplate such a magnificent event, it is easy to imagine why even the regent of a great power like England would be humbled and amazed.

Scripture tells us Jesus's entrance will be on a grand scale like nothing the world has witnessed. He will enter as the King of kings, with His splendor filling the sky. The heavens will declare His glory, and the world will see Him for who He is: our mighty God. What a day that will be! Are you ready?

Jesus, I anxiously await Your return. Prepare my heart so that I may help others be ready.

The Calmed Storm

He got up and rebuked the wind and the raging waters; the storm subsided, and all was calm. "Where is your faith?" he asked his disciples. In fear and amazement they asked one another, "Who is this? He commands even the winds and the water, and they obey him."

Luke 8:24–25 NIV

Recent headlines near the Sea of Galilee looked like this: "Weekend storms wreck $30 million in crops"; "Storm disrupts air traffic, brings down trees." But back then—in the final year of Jesus's life—the headline could've read: "Renowned teacher saves experienced fisherman."

Yes…experienced. In fact, several disciples on deck that day were commercial fisherman. They knew their way around a boat, knew how to handle high seas, and didn't foolishly cast off from shore with fierce clouds rolling in. But then, as now, gale-force winds swooped through the western ravines without warning, hit the shallow water, and whipped up violent, terrifying waves as high as twenty feet.

The storm was sudden and fierce—just like traumas in life: a cancer diagnosis, the death of a child, a lost career, a divorce. When you're hit with life-changing news, it's easier to understand why the disciples were frantic that day, and why they thought their Master had lost control.

Faith in a sovereign, powerful God can feel risky during a crisis—until we remember who He is. The Creator who called light out of darkness and threw the stars into space can calm every storm of your life.

I remember that You are Lord, and I thank You for Your supernatural peace in the middle of life's storms.

The Light of the World

The true light that gives light to every man was coming into the world.

John 1:9 niv

Twilight. The French call it *l'heure bleue*—the "blue hour"—that brief and magical interlude when it's neither day nor night, when the sky is neither completely lit nor completely dark. It is the ambience of painters and photographers. But that diffused light also obscures reality. It's vague, dim, uncertain. You can misread the signs and turn down the wrong street—a dangerous street. You can easily be deceived.

The apostle John lived in the twilight years after Jesus's death. Jerusalem had fallen to the Romans. Uncertainty was rampant. But Christ struck a match that would not go out. So John began an 823,000-word argument that Jesus is the true light—the eminent and excellent light that pierced the darkness from the beginning of time, the light that eradicates ambiguity and ignorance and deception. The only light.

Jesus borrows His shining glory from neither dusk nor dawn, neither man nor angel. He is the Light of the world. Bask in Him.

How wonderful is Your light that shines through the darkness of this world. Make me a reflection of Your radiance.

Mission: Love

Righteous Father, the world has never known you, but I have known you, and these disciples know that you sent me on this mission.

JOHN 17:25 MSG

Jesus prayed a fervent prayer. At its heart, it was a desire to connect the Father, His Father, to the world. This was His mission. Such a mission had never been undertaken on this earth, and it would require pure love—extraordinarily gracious love, sacrificial love, the laying-down-of-one's-life love. It was a mission made possible only by heaven's hand.

God the Father designed the plan and Jesus fulfilled it.

The wonder of God's love was in every step of that journey, all the way to the cross. Christ's resurrection birthed the new mission for the next batch of missionaries, the disciples, who took the message to the world.

God showed His love and His longing for connection through Jesus and His earth-shaking mission to Planet Earth. Praise Him for His awesome purposes.

Father God, let me be a daily missionary of Your purpose.

October 19

Lord of the Harvest

But he never left them without evidence of himself and his goodness.
For instance, he sends you rain and good crops and gives you food and joyful hearts.

Acts 14:17 NLT

In the Aramaic translation of the Hebrew Bible, God holds four keys of life and death—powerful emblems gripped in His hand and never trusted to angel or seraph: keys of provision, the grave, the barren womb, and the rain.

The rain seems out of place on this key ring, until you consider that man cannot control or cause rain—particularly *regulated* rain that, in proper quantities and intervals, makes flowers bloom for bees to pollinate the crops that need water to grow and feed Earth's *seven billion people*.

Plentiful harvests and meals on the table are all from the Father's hand. He is so wondrously good that He doesn't just nourish our bodies but feeds our souls with contentment and our hearts with joy. All of these things are undeniable proof of His goodness. He is the Source of all excellent gifts.

Bountiful God, Your never-ending goodness is irresistible.

From Ages Past

Now to him who is able to establish you in accordance with my gospel, the message I proclaim about Jesus Christ, in keeping with the revelation of the mystery hidden for long ages past, but now revealed and made known through the prophetic writings by the command of the eternal God, so that all the Gentiles might come to the obedience that comes from faith—to the only wise God be glory forever through Jesus Christ! Amen.

Romans 16:25–27 NIV

Martin Luther wrote in the preface to his commentary on the book of Romans: "This letter is truly the most important piece in the New Testament. It is purest Gospel. It is well worth a Christian's while not only to memorize it word for word but also to occupy himself with it daily, as though it were the daily bread of the soul." In part, it was Luther's understanding of the book of Romans that inspired him to write his *Ninety-Five Theses*, which launched the Reformation that altered the theological landscape of the Western world forever.

Paul ends his letter with an exuberant expression of praise for God the Father. His doxology is a summation of a great mystery "hidden for long ages," now unfolding. He celebrates the eternal God who directed the writing of the Scriptures so that faith in Him through Jesus Christ might be advanced all over the world for every generation until the return of Christ.

Until You return, Jesus, show me ways to advance Your kingdom.

October 21

Even That

Since he did not spare even his own Son but gave him up for us all, won't he also give us everything else?

Romans 8:32 NLT

Search the Internet for the phrase "willing to do anything" reveals a spectrum of people—from professional athletes to political parties to bored college students—publicly claiming their willingness to do anything to achieve a particular result. Even in the case of bored collegians, there is usually a line they won't cross; not always, mind you, but usually.

God the Father publicly displayed His willingness to go to the extreme of giving even His own Son so that we might live. That's a line not many fathers would even begin to consider crossing, but God did. For us to then doubt His willingness to provide for us in all things not only belittles Jesus's sacrifice on the cross, it indicates a diminished trust in God's great love—a love willing to even do that.

His powerful sacrifice echoes from His being into our hearts: He is love.

Your willingness to give even Your own Son amazes me. Yours is a love like no other.

The Good Times Are Coming

That's why I don't think there's any comparison
between the present hard times and the coming good times.
Romans 8:18 msg

The old hymn writer described them as "seasons of distress and grief." We often call them "hard times."

The hard times are no respecter of persons; they befall everyone. And if you're not currently experiencing them, just wait awhile and the weather will change. The difficulties come at us financially, emotionally, physically, and spiritually. Sometimes the weight of this fallen world is enough to subject us to the worst kind of sickness: despair.

The faithful follower of Jesus Christ is not some oblivious Pollyanna but rather a seasoned veteran of the joys and sorrows of life—someone who's seen both sunshine and storms. But the saints who persevere cling to a hope unseen but promised by the One who always keeps His word: *Don't despair. Hold on to Me. The good times are coming. I promise. I am the Lord.*

David sang this song, and it is still true: "Those who know Your name will trust in You, for You, Lord, have never forsaken those who seek You" (Psalm 9:10 niv).

Our forever-faithful God deserves all our hope and trust.

I am placing all my hopes in You, O God. You are the great I AM.

October 23

One God, One Lord

For even if there are so-called gods, whether in heaven or on earth (as indeed there are many "gods" and many "lords"), yet for us there is but one God, the Father, from whom all things came and for whom we live; and there is but one Lord, Jesus Christ, through whom all things came and through whom we live.

1 Corinthians 8:5–6 NIV

When Moses descended Mount Sinai after forty days with God, he held two tablets of stone upon which were inscribed the Ten Commandments for the people as dictated by God Himself. The first: "You shall have no other gods before me" (Exodus 20:3).

"Before me" is literally translated in the Hebrew as "before my face, in my presence, beside me, except me." God is the Creator of all humanity, and He expects first place in our lives. The truth is, no other god—no other source, no other love, no other passion—will ever be who God is. All things come from Him. He is life itself.

Worshiping multiple gods is unacceptable. The focus of our lives is to be on God alone. When Jesus said the greatest commandment was to love the Lord your God with all your heart, mind, and soul, it was in support of the First Commandment. If our love and devotion is centered on God alone, then the "gods" and "lords" and "idols" that take up space in this world have no chance. These objects cannot stand beside God as equals. God has no equal.

My desire is for You to be first in my life, above all other things.

October 24

How Freedom Grows

It is absolutely clear that God has called you to a free life. Just make sure that you don't use this freedom as an excuse to do whatever you want to do and destroy your freedom. Rather, use your freedom to serve one another in love; that's how freedom grows.

Galatians 5:13 msg

Paul gives us a gardening tip of sorts in Galatians 5:13. He's not talking about roses or hollyhocks, but something integral to the kingdom of God—*freedom*. God has called each and every one of us to a free life—free from sin and fear, and alive to the light of hope and resurrection. But if that freedom becomes shortsighted license (an excuse to live only for one's self), then growth is stunted and the flower of freedom will most likely wilt and possibly even die.

Tending the garden to produce a bumper crop of freedom means daily serving one another in love. We'd like to think it's much more scientific than that, but it's not. God has revealed to us in nature the elements necessary for plants to thrive, and we can see the parallels in our relationships with each other and with God. Setting aside our personal agendas and allowing God to love others through us are the sunlight, water, and nutrients that spiritual freedom needs to be ever green.

This is how the Father rains His sweet and wondrous love on us: He liberates us and then gives us perfect instructions for living a full life.

Help us to serve one another, Lord, as You have loved and served us.

An Eye-Opener

I pray also that the eyes of your heart may be enlightened in order that you may know the hope to which he has called you, the riches of his glorious inheritance in the saints, and his incomparably great power for us who believe.

Ephesians 1:18–19 NIV

The human eye is fascinating to say the least. Made up of rods, cones, and many other delicate and microscopic parts, this complicated human organ can process changing light conditions almost instantly and focus light rays that come from varying distances. The eye converts all of this light to impulses and conveys to the brain the various details of one's surroundings. It's really quite amazing. In fact, the human eye is so complicated that doctors have yet to figure out how to perform a complete eye transplant from one person to another.

The Bible says that God's Spirit gives us spiritual sight. As complicated and complex as the human eye is, the spiritual eye is far more miraculous. And God has the knowledge and power to make both the spiritual and physical eyes work.

Consider the greatness of God. He understands every part of our physical and spiritual lives. There is nothing He does not see or understand. To Him, all things are simple.

God, open my eyes to the things You want me to see.

October 26

Reverent Submission

Submit to one another out of reverence for Christ.

Ephesians 5:21 NIV

Revelation is the first step to holiness, and consecration is the second. A day must come in our lives, as definite as the day of our conversion, when we give up all right to ourselves and submit to the absolute Lordship of Jesus Christ." These powerful words by Watchman Nee reveal the profound choice of submission. Make no mistake; submission is a choice in our relationship with Christ.

The word for *submit* in the Greek means "to put oneself in an inferior position or condition, to be subordinate." This concept turns today's cultural mind-set on its head. We are of the opinion that we have rights, that we deserve something; we have an entitlement mentality, which means we rarely express gratitude. But out of reverence to Christ, we have the freedom to submit to Him—and to one another.

Jesus lived the attitude of a servant, taking the time to meet the needs of those He met, feeding the crowds who gathered to hear His message, washing the feet of His disciples in His last hours with them. And how do we tangibly show that we revere and respect Him as Lord?

Do as He did. By submitting to God and serving one another, we are lifting our lives in worship to our Maker and Sustainer.

Grant me a grateful heart for everything You provide, and may I dedicate it to Your use in the name of Your Son, Jesus.

The Kingdom of Light

Being strengthened with all power according to his glorious might so that you may have great endurance and patience, and giving joyful thanks to the Father, who has qualified you to share in the inheritance of his holy people in the kingdom of light.

Colossians 1:11–12 NIV

Light describes the kingdom of God. God, who presides over it, "is light, and in him is no darkness at all" (1 John 1:5 NIV); Christ is "the light of man," "the true light," and "the light of the world." The angels of that divine kingdom are "angels of light." The citizens of that kingdom are "the children of light." And in the New Jerusalem, "the glory of God gives it light, and the Lamb is its lamp" (Revelation 21:23 NIV).

That's what we inherit as His holy people. *That's* why we ask Jesus to strengthen us with His glorious might so that we will patiently endure until we are together in heaven with Him. And *that's* why we sing and praise and lift our hands in thanks to the Father.

He has written us into the will. We will inherit the kingdom.

Father, help me to walk in Your light.

How Refreshing

Your love has given me great joy and encouragement,
because you, brother, have refreshed the hearts of the saints.

Philemon 7 NIV

A tall glass of cold water after mowing the lawn. A dip in the lake on a sweltering summer afternoon. A long shower after cleaning out the attic all day. Refreshing. Each of us have felt the relief they bring.

Somehow the simple joys can be the perfect answer to our momentary need. How sweet it is to pour that glass of water for another thirsty worker. To offer refreshment to someone else is to share in the great connection of being human.

There are times when our spirits are dry too. We get discouraged or bitter or sad, and it seems impossible to reach for the help we need. That's when the wonder of God's plan can be seen so plainly: God recharges His people through each other. When one believer extends an encouraging word or pitches in to help another, the result is beautiful. The disheartened one is invigorated to take the next step, the discouraged one refreshed—like a parched desert traveler after a drink from a well.

The Lord has given us one another. It's how He works. It's how we work best too.

God, You provide spiritual refreshment to and through Your people. Work through me to bring refreshment to others.

Behind It All

Jesus has been found worthy of greater honor than Moses, just as the builder of a house has greater honor than the house itself. For every house is built by someone, but God is the builder of everything.

Hebrews 3:3–4 NIV

Frank Lloyd Wright spent more than seventy years creating designs that revolutionized the art and architecture of the twentieth century. Many innovations we see in buildings today are products of his imagination. All in all, he designed 1,141 works—including museums, houses, offices, churches, schools, libraries, bridges, and many other types of buildings. Of that total, 532 resulted in completed works, 409 of which still stand.

But who built or created Wright? Who is behind the imaginative genius that crafted so many works of art and left a challenging legacy for future generations? The supreme Architect behind all that was and is and is to come is God, the Master Builder. This is His world, and all its majesty, both natural and man-made, can be traced back to His divine imagination and creative genius.

God is behind it all. His signature adorns everything that is beautiful, inspiring, or uplifting to the senses, soul, and spirit—whether the human artist knows it or not.

This is Your world. Help me not to forget that everything within that is good comes from You.

Our Heavenly Destiny

But you have come to Mount Zion, to the city of the living God, the heavenly Jerusalem.
You have come to thousands upon thousands of angels in joyful assembly,
to the church of the firstborn, whose names are written in heaven.

HEBREWS 12:22–23 NIV

It is only natural for believers to think about heaven and what it might be like. Scripture does not offer an abundance of detail, but we are assured that it will be glorious. The twelfth-century monk, Saint Bernard, wrote:

Jerusalem the golden, with milk and honey blest,
Beneath thy contemplation sink heart and voice oppressed.
I know not, O I know not what joys await us there,
What radiance of glory, what light beyond compare.

Jesus said that God was not the "God of the dead, but of the living" (Matthew 22:23 NIV). The plan of our living God always was for His children to be present with Him for eternity.

Because of the atoning sacrifice of Jesus Christ, we get a glimpse of the future destination of all believers. We shall be welcomed by the living God into His glorious city that is populated with angels and the spirits of those who have gone before us. There, in that celestial city, our wonderful Savior will be seated at the right hand of God. There will be no more tears. Joy will abound. And all will be well.

You have assured my future and redeemed my past. What more can I ask for?

October 31

Greater Than Gold

In all this you greatly rejoice, though now for a little while you may have had to suffer grief in all kinds of trials. These have come so that the proven genuineness of your faith—of greater worth than gold, which perishes even though refined by fire—may result in praise, glory and honor when Jesus Christ is revealed.

1 Peter 1:6–7 NIV

For a child, the phrase "in a little while" or "in a minute" can cause eye-rolling, sighing, and sometimes an outright tantrum. From a child's perspective, waiting a minute to go outside or play with their friends or watch a favorite television show feels like forever.

That's often how it is with suffering and grief in our lives too. Everyone experiences difficulty, and most of the time it feels like the treatments will never end or the sadness will never lift or the financial strain will never go away. That's from our perspective. From God's timeless perspective, however, it is only for a little while.

During those times, our faith is being purified. Yes, it is a time of waiting, but if we'll just trust the Lord, that "little while" will be transformed into a precious gift—a faith that has been refined by the fire. Such faith is more precious than gold, the work of a God who never lets anything go to waste.

Thank You, Lord, for purifying seasons. They are all in Your eternal hands.

November 1

A Step Back

And now, do not be distressed and do not be angry with yourselves for selling me here, because it was to save lives that God sent me ahead of you.

Genesis 45:5 NIV

Maybe you've seen Van Gogh's painting *Still Life: Vase with Twelve Sunflowers*. Did you know that when you stand inches from the canvas, all you see are colorful clumps of paint? But step back a little, and the distance gives you a perspective that changes everything. In fact, step back ten feet, and somehow all those separate strokes come together, and the painting now looks like the masterpiece it is.

That's kind of like our lives, isn't it? Consider Joseph's story. Because of his brothers' hatred, Joseph ended up in Egypt. Yet through his imprisonment in Egypt, Joseph found himself in the royal palace, where he rose to the rank of second-in-command. And because of Joseph's work as a royal adviser, the storehouses of Egypt were established, enabling the land to survive a famine that otherwise would have taken both Joseph's life and the lives of those he loved.

If you're experiencing some dark moments these days, understand this: God may be sending you ahead so that you can soon play an unexpectedly important role in someone's life. Be amazed by that possibility and by the wise, loving provision of a God who is always at work in you, creating a masterpiece.

Lord, I marvel at the way You choreograph history—including my own. Give me patience and peace while You do Your work.

The Creator of All

Look, the highest heavens and the earth and everything in it all belong to the LORD your God.

DEUTERONOMY 10:14 NLT

In Dante's classic allegory *The Divine Comedy*, he chronicled his journey in Paradise and his passage through nine spheres of heavens. He wrote this about the ninth sphere: "This heaven has no other where than this: the mind of God, in which are kindled both the love that turns it and the force it rains. As in a circle, light and love enclose it,...only He who encloses understands."

What a rich expression of the indescribable quality of the heavens!

Offering a different take on the heavens is the American National Center for Atmospheric Research, which has scientifically analyzed the distinct layers of earth's atmospheric stratification and determined each layer's specific characteristics. It is a study that has put all that humans know about the heavens into analytical form.

But neither the language of poets nor the language of scientists can explain the wonder of God's creation, beginning with the earth's atmosphere and extending to the planetary system and beyond. Poetry and science merely point out the immensity of an endless progression of space, too vast to comprehend yet functioning like clockwork. And all of it established by an awesome Creator.

Dear God, I marvel at the miracle, the scope, the intricacy of Your creation. I can only respond with awe and praise—and You are worthy of both.

I'll Be There

But will God really dwell on earth? The heavens, even the highest heaven, cannot contain you. How much less this temple I have built!

1 Kings 8:27 NIV

At some point, every parent wishes they could be in more than one place at the same time. Inevitably, one child's soccer game will conflict with another child's piano recital, both of which are being held at the same time as the meeting at church—all at different places in different parts of town.

Every parent's wish is God's reality. We can't imagine what it would be like for the boundaries of time and place to evaporate; to be unlimited and "always present." Yet God lives it every day. What is impossible for us is simply a part of who He is.

The good news is that we are the beneficiaries of His omnipresence. Because He is everywhere at all times, He is always with us. In fact, the phrase "I am with you always" is repeated twenty-two times in His Word. He wants His people to know and rest in that truth. Are you finding comfort in His presence right now?

Your constant presence is an indescribable blessing. What peace and hope I find in the truth that You are Emmanuel—"God with us"!

Rambunctious Praise!

Shout with joy to God, all the earth! Sing the glory of his name;
make his praise glorious! Say to God, "How awesome are your deeds!
So great is your power that your enemies cringe before you."

Psalm 66:1–3 niv

Getting someone's attention in a city park, wanting the dog to come back with the ball, calling the kids in for supper, celebrating the last-second touchdown—all of these are good reasons to shout. Certain situations just call for "volume." The greatest reason for upping the decibels, however, is worship.

Our enthusiastic adoration makes the Father happy. And with our words of praise, we say to our souls: "Praise the Lord, everyone in this room, this city, this country, this world! Get loud, oceans and wind, wolves and nightingales! Laugh with joy, for your God does awesome things!"

Soft words are lovely and a whispered prayer is sacred. Yet another appropriate way to approach the King of kings and Lord of lords is with joyful shouts of praise. May they be a life-giving part of your repertoire as you celebrate the Almighty!

God of wonders, the list of reasons to praise You is endless. Accept my shouts of praise as an offering of worship.

Every One

Every creature in the forest is mine, the wild animals on all the mountains.
I know every mountain bird by name; the scampering field mice are my friends.

Psalm 50:10–11 MSG

Consider the staggering statement of Psalm 50:10-11. Our amazing God declares that every creature is His and that He knows them—each one of them—by name.

It is not hyperbole in the least, for our God is not given to exaggeration.

Be even more amazed when you learn that zoologists have records of twenty thousand species of fish, six thousand species of reptiles, nine thousand species of birds, one thousand species of amphibians, and fifteen thousand species of mammals. A million insect species have been identified, and entomologists estimate that there could be another million waiting to be discovered. It takes platoons of scientists to keep track of the number of creatures on the earth. Yet God, in His omnipotence, not only tracks each species but each individual animal within each species, and He cares for them one by one.

So next time you read a passage like Psalm 50 that praises the immensity of our Creator-God, let the words drive you to your knees in humbled awe. The Lord Almighty knows His creatures, each and every one by name—including you. Great is the Lord!

Great are You, Lord, and greatly to be praised! You are an incredible God!

Blessed Boundaries

You are good and Your works are good; give me knowledge of your rules.

PSALM 119:68 BBE

America has long been described as the "land of the free." We are a country of pioneers and self-made men, of the American Dream fulfilled and the freedom of thought and speech. So, understandably, we Americans are suspicious of boundaries. Regulations and rules make us nervous—that is, until we consider life without them. No traffic laws? No safety requirements for airlines? No referees at ballgames? Maybe rules do have their place after all.

Our good God appreciates the value of rules: He has issued commands for His glory and for our benefit. He has presented guidelines to live by that will lead us to good places and keep us from falling into traps. We have His precepts, His laws, His darkness-shattering truth to prevent us from getting lost along the way.

As you read your Bible today, let the very fact that you hold God's Word in your hands be a tangible reminder that He is good—and good to you! He has not left you to wander or stumble through life. God's rules and guidelines are blessed boundaries indeed!

Thank You that You have made Your life-giving ways known to me. Enable me to walk in Your ways, enjoying fellowship with You.

God-Made

The rich and the poor have this in common: the Lord made them both.

Proverbs 22:2 CEV

"Self-made men are the men…who are what they are, without the aid of any favoring conditions by which other men usually rise in the world and achieve great results." Those words are from an 1859 lecture by slave-turned-social-reformer-and-orator Frederick Douglass entitled "Self-Made Men." His message became the basis for much of the so-called American Dream: an unknown man of humble origins works hard, gets an education, and moves beyond his inherited social position to a level of success he never imagined.

It's the kind of rags-to-riches story that Hollywood loves. Yet as compelling as this storyline is, the writer of Proverbs presents another bracing truth for all who might consider themselves self-made men or women: whether we are educated or not, born with a silver spoon or a plastic fork in our hand, each one of us is the Lord's. We are all God-made—in His image and for His purpose—for an eternal covenant relationship with Him that is characterized by rich, life-giving communion. You're not "Made in China" or "Manufactured in the USA"; you've been lovingly handcrafted by Heaven itself!

In the fact that I am God-made, not self-made, please help me find freedom to enjoy both the gift of life and my relationship with You.

Hidden Design

As you do not know the path of the wind, or how the body is formed in a mother's womb, so you cannot understand the work of God, the Maker of all things.

Ecclesiastes 11:5 NIV

When a woman is expecting, her pregnancy eventually becomes obvious. But initially nothing on the outside reveals the miracle that is happening inside her body: the hidden cells that are multiplying, the organs that are forming, the systems that are developing. Totally unseen by the outside world, a human being is being knit together by the Almighty according to His amazing design. For forty weeks, life is tucked away inside the mother's womb. Then one day the child emerges, takes those first breaths, and issues those first cries of life that bring joy to a parent's heart.

Scientists continue to make new discoveries about the process of *in utero* development, but they will never understand all the mysteries of how life is formed. Still, just as we anticipate that day when the long-awaited infant will be born, we can be sure that God's plans for our spiritual growth and transformation will come to fruition in His perfect time. He is quietly, secretly, faithfully working to form our character to be more like Christ's.

Lord God, I don't always see Your hand at work, but I know from Your Word that I can trust You to do Your work in me.

Majesty

And the LORD will cause his majestic voice to be heard and the descending blow of his arm to be seen, in furious anger and a flame of devouring fire, with a cloudburst and storm and hailstones.

ISAIAH 30:30 ESV

Much is made of the prophet Elijah hearing the "still, small voice" of God (1 Kings 19). And why not? There's a lot to be said for the importance of listening intently. We live busy lives in a noisy world, and we don't want to miss God's whisper. This is, however, only one facet of God's voice.

As the prophet Isaiah proclaimed, God also raises His voice in the storm and displays His majesty in fire, rain, wind, and hail. The thundering voice of God is unmistakable. His glory devours the enemy. His power moves mountains, splits the skies, and divides the waters. His mighty displays of strength and sovereignty demand our attention and our worship.

When God decides to be heard, nothing can mute the splendor of His voice. Whether He thunders or whispers, make sure you're attuned to hearing Him today.

God, Your wondrous creation speaks of Your majesty and might. May I hear in its testimony Your voice calling me to worship and obey.

Everlasting

Have you never heard? Have you never understood? The LORD is the everlasting God, the Creator of all the earth. He never grows weak or weary. No one can measure the depths of his understanding.

ISAIAH 40:28 NLT

According to his official website, he ended his boxing career in 1940 with an astounding record of 60-7-8, and fifty of his wins were knockouts. He has even been called the perfect boxer, combining agility and quickness and pure power, a master at bobbing and weaving. Jack Dempsey was indeed one of the greatest champions in boxing history.

Dempsey was also one of the original clients of Everlast equipment, using it in his training as well as in his professional matches. The marketing strategy was clear: consumers would see that using Everlast would ensure "everlasting" athletic success. What the marketers didn't factor in was that no man's success lasts forever. As good as Dempsey was, he eventually grew too weak to withstand the skills of a boxer named Gene Tunney. The same happens to all of us, no matter our area of endeavor.

Thankfully, the Lord our God is not like us. He never grows weak or weary. No one can outlast Him. He never has and He never will meet His match. And His great faithfulness endures to all generations.

The Lord our God is truly everlasting, a trustworthy champion for His people—past, present, and future.

You are truly everlasting, O God! What a comfort that Your presence will never fade, and Your love will never end.

November 11

God of Covenant

I, the Lord, *have called You for a righteous purpose, and I will hold You by Your hand. I will keep You and appoint You to be a covenant for the people and a light to the nations.*

Isaiah 42:6 HCSB

Covenant. A foundational principle of the Old and New Testaments, this rich word from the ancient world carries with it the concepts of promise, adoption, sacrifice, blessings, and family. According to Sandra L. Richter in her insightful book *The Epic of Eden*, "For all of history our God has *chosen* to be identified by this singular event—the God who rescues slaves from their bondage and claims them as his own." In other words, the God of the Bible is a covenant God, and He chooses to speak in the language of covenant.

What is especially significant is that the Holy God covenants with forgiven-but-still-sinning souls like us. By the wonder of God's righteousness manifest in Jesus Christ, we are made righteous. This is not an arrangement we humans could have initiated; it is not a bargain we could have struck with God. Only Jesus could bridge the gap and establish an eternal agreement between God and His people.

Long before Jesus was born in Bethlehem, Yahweh appointed His Son to be the sacrifice who would cement His everlasting covenant and be the light for the nations for all time. What a privilege it is to be one of God's covenant people!

Covenant God, thank You for pledging Yourself to sinful people—for eternity. Help me to live a life worthy of Your covenant people.

Hope for the Hopeless

For nothing is impossible with God.

LUKE 1:37 NIV

When God is about to do something great, He starts with a difficulty," said author and evangelist Armin Gesswein. "When He is about to do something truly magnificent, He starts with an impossibility."

Can donkeys talk? See Numbers 22:21-39. Can a government employee survive a night amid hungry lions? Read Daniel 6. Can a virgin have a child? That story is in Luke 1 and 2.

The Bible is full of such "impossible" happenings. All of these events were witnessed and well documented at the time they happened, yet some people find these accounts too incredible to believe.

So, what about the two-year-old boy who fell twelve feet from a window and landed on concrete? The prognosis: severe brain damage, broken neck, he'll never walk again. Seven hours later, he was fine because, as he put it, "angels catched me."

Or the Boy Scout who was found unharmed after four days in the Utah wilderness?

Or the brain scan that suddenly, inexplicably, came back clear of tumors? All of these events were witnessed and well documented too.

God is able to do what we could never imagine, because He specializes in the impossible. Always has, always will.

Nothing is impossible with You! Let that truth grow my faith and revolutionize my prayers.

No Expiration Date

Sky and earth will wear out; my words won't wear out.

LUKE 21:33 MSG

Ever tried to keep a house clean? Entropy works against you. Ever tried to keep plants alive? Again, entropy interferes. Webster's defines *entropy* as "a process of running down or a trend to disorder." The earth we live on is in a state of entropy: it is, simply put, wearing out. For instance, though world energy consumption has been projected to increase by 59 percent in the two decades leading up to 2020, our energy supplies are falling behind. On another front, *National Geographic* reports that swaths of forests the size of Panama are being lost each year.

Such widely accepted statistics shouldn't surprise readers of Scripture. Throughout time, God has reminded human beings again and again that everything He makes is expendable: "The heavens vanish like smoke, the earth will wear out like a garment" (Isaiah 51:6); "Then I saw a new heaven and a new earth, for the old heaven and the old earth had passed away" (Revelation 21:1).

Is anything an exception to this finite existence? Jesus said yes. As the immutable, everlasting, omniscient Son of God, Jesus taught that no matter what happens *in* the world or *to* the world, His words—God's truth—will last forever. And two thousand years after Jesus spoke those words, you're reading them. May that fact encourage you to trust Jesus and His never-changing, eternal Word.

I am humbled at Your Word and the everlasting truth it contains. Motivate me to read and learn and live that Truth every day of my life.

The Spring of Life

Jesus answered, "Everyone who drinks this water will be thirsty again, but whoever drinks the water I give them will never thirst. Indeed, the water I give them will become in them a spring of water welling up to eternal life."

John 4:13–14 NIV

In the arid countryside of Samaria, people valued and protected their local well. It was not only a source of refreshment but the source of life for the people living in the area. Often a well was also a destination point for travelers.

The water in the well had to be brought up by a bucket, and water would have to be drawn day after day after day. Jesus, however, offered the woman at the well—and by extension, all the rest of us—His living water. The kind that will forever quench our thirst.

Every believer is given the presence of the Holy Spirit. And the Spirit will exist in our lives as a bubbling spring of mercy, grace, comfort, and peace. Just as water enables our physical bodies to function and thrive, so the Spirit of God provides the nourishment our souls need to live abundantly.

That's why Jesus invites His people to receive the Holy Spirit and live in His power. This invitation points to an important spiritual reality: accept this invitation to drink of God's supernatural power. It is the only water that keeps us alive in this life and the life to come.

My thirst can only be quenched by Your living water, Lord. Draw me close to You.

A Determined Love

Now when they had come and gathered the church together,
they reported all that God had done with them,
and that He had opened the door of faith to the Gentiles.

Acts 14:27 NKJV

On January 20, 2012, a fifty-five-year-old New Yorker fell inside his second-floor apartment and was unable to get up. When firefighters realized that obstructions inside the apartment would prevent them from going inside and getting the injured man down the stairs, they got creative. Propping a ladder against the second floor of the apartment building, they used a chainsaw to create a hole big enough to remove the man. Then, with ropes and a stretcher, they lowered him to safety—in effect, creating a new door.

In reporting to the church about his recent missionary journey, the apostle Paul credited the Lord for opening the door of faith to the Gentiles. The door wasn't physical, of course; it was spiritual.

In the same way that God Himself opens doors of faith so that people from every walk of life might be saved, He also made a way to reconcile each of us to Himself. He orchestrated events, relationships, and conversations so that you would open your eyes and soften your heart to declaring Jesus as Savior and Lord. Like those determined firefighters, God opened doors so you would be rescued.

Thank You, dear Father, for opening my eyes and my heart to Your love.

Forsaking Never

Who shall separate us from the love of Christ? shall tribulation, or distress, or persecution, or famine, or nakedness, or peril, or sword?

Romans 8:35 KJV

Pilot Nate Saint had decided he wanted to do something great for God. So he enlisted as a missionary and, with four other missionaries, flew into the remote areas of Ecuador to take the gospel to the Auca Indians.

Despite encouraging signs that a relationship could be established and the gospel shared with the Aucas, Saint and his colleagues were killed on January 8, 1956, by the very tribesmen they sought to evangelize. How did the families of these missionaries respond? Saint's sister and the wives of the other men who died that day continued the work, and the Auca Indian tribe—now the Waorani—came to know the Lord.

Though Saint and his companions lost their lives that day deep inside the jungle, they died knowing that no tribesman, no weapon, no earthly power could separate them from the love of God. And they wanted the Aucas to have this assurance as well.

Following Jesus is the only earthly endeavor with eternal value. When you understand that—when you clearly experience the transforming impact of His love in your life—going to extreme measures to share that truth with others is a natural response.

God's power can not only soften the heart of any enemy but enable His followers to face any challenge. His love will never let His people go.

Though Your ways are mysterious, I rest in Your great love and faithfulness.

The Conquest Is the Lord's

The world is unprincipled. It's dog-eat-dog out there! The world doesn't fight fair.
But we don't live or fight our battles that way—never have and never will.
The tools of our trade aren't for marketing or manipulation,
but they are for demolishing that entire massively corrupt culture.

2 Corinthians 10:3–4 MSG

It's been about thirty years since Francis Schaeffer made the following observation, yet it's just as true—if not more so—today: "We as Bible-believing evangelical Christians are locked in a battle. This is not a friendly, gentleman's discussion. It is a life and death conflict between the spiritual hosts of wickedness and those who claim the name of Christ."

Because the battle continues to rage, those Christ followers who join in the battle will encounter longstanding strongholds of evil entrenched, protected, and defended by entire communities. Christian leaders especially must brace themselves to stand their ground on the frontlines where the fighting is most intense.

Whatever your battle position—whether you're in the thick of the fighting, working from the war room, or back at base camp, supporting the war effort—remember that the army you belong to marches under the banner of the glorious Redeemer. God's mighty weapons are truth, love, righteousness, and faith—and those weapons are massively effective. Furthermore, the wise and powerful King of heaven developed the battle plan, and it is impossible for Him to fail. The conquest is the Lord's. The powers of evil will be defeated by the God of peace. And the glory is already His.

Mighty God, the enemy is devious and determined. Yet You stand against him. I celebrate that the victory is Yours.

The Master's Own Child

And because you Gentiles have become his children, God has sent the Spirit of his Son into your hearts, and now you can call God your dear Father. Now you are no longer a slave but God's own child. And since you are his child, everything he has belongs to you.

GALATIANS 4:6–7 NLT

He never took a formal golf lesson. He learned the game as a kid by hitting Wiffle balls around his home in the Florida panhandle. So no one was more elated than Bubba Watson when he won the 2012 Masters Golf Tournament and donned the coveted green jacket. It was a whirlwind week for other reasons, though. Just before tournament play began, Watson and his wife became the proud parents of a newly adopted son. And as the golfer with the unconventional swing made the traditional media blitz that Masters champions do, it became evident—in every interview, article, and tweet—that the primary thing on Bubba Watson's mind was not his new green jacket but his new son.

Our heavenly Father has us on His mind too. In fact, that has always been true. Galatians 4:4 tells us that at just the right time, God sent Jesus to redeem us—and the price was high: His death on a cross. As if this wasn't testimony enough of the Father's overwhelming love, He also promised that everything He owns now belongs to us. How rich we are in Him!

Father God, Your love is utterly amazing. I'm speechless that You would think of me.

The Regenerated Generation

Put on the new self, created to be like God in true righteousness and holiness. Therefore each of you must put off falsehood and speak truthfully to your neighbor, for we are all members of one body.

Ephesians 4:24–25 NIV

Firstborn or second, oldest or baby—where you are in the birth order impacts your experience of your family. Similarly, which generation you fall in suggests what your priorities, economic status, and parenting style will be.

Followers of Jesus, on the other hand, fall under this one-size-fits-all label: "Regeneration." The word in Greek means "spiritual rebirth" and refers to becoming a new creation, to experiencing the miracle of God's life-changing power at work in one's heart and mind. *Regeneration* also means being restored to the image of God (which was His original design) so that we reflect His righteousness and holiness.

Our behavior, our activities, our language, our family life, our relationships—every aspect of our lives will now reflect God's holiness and righteousness, making us and all we do distinct from the world. So, as "new creations" with regenerated hearts and minds, we can't just pretend: we need to walk away from falsity and hypocrisy; we need to live in and live out God's holiness, righteousness, and truth as His lights in the world.

Dear God, thank You for making me a new creation. May I yield to Your Spirit so that Your righteousness shines through me as brightly as possible.

All We Could Ever Dream of

As a prisoner for the Lord, then, I urge you to live a life worthy of the calling you have received. Be completely humble and gentle; be patient, bearing with one another in love. Make every effort to keep the unity of the Spirit through the bond of peace.

Ephesians 4:1–3 NIV

It was April 1963. A man had been arrested for his part in a public protest. Now he sat alone in a prison cell in Birmingham, Alabama, where he read a letter written by some local clergymen entitled "A Call for Unity." The prisoner's lengthy and impassioned response became known as "Letter from Birmingham Jail," and in it, Martin Luther King Jr. called on "the white church and its leadership" to support the civil rights movement. As King later and often expressed, people of all colors living in true unity would be the fulfillment of his dream.

Martin Luther King Jr. wasn't the first person to write a stirring prison letter calling for unity. Two thousand years earlier an imprisoned apostle of Jesus Christ wrote to the church in Ephesus, urging its members to be humble, gentle, and patient with one another. Paul told those Christians that such a way of life would require effort and forbearance. But it would produce a social—and spiritual—reality that was far greater than anything they had ever seen.

Everything Paul longed for the church to be, and everything Dr. King longed for American society to reflect, God's Spirit enables. When we keep our eyes on Jesus, God can use us to bring unity to His body as well as to the place we call "home."

I want to be more like You, Jesus, so that You can use me to bring unity and light to the world around me.

Name above All Names

Therefore God exalted him to the highest place and gave him the name that is above every name, that at the name of Jesus every knee should bow, in heaven and on earth and under the earth, and every tongue confess that Jesus Christ is Lord, to the glory of God the Father.

PHILIPPIANS 2:9–11 NIV

Your name matters. It carries weight and meaning throughout your entire life, as Shakespeare's character Iago declares in *Othello*: "He that filches from me my good name robs me of that which not enriches him, and makes me poor indeed."

Your name is very important to God as well. Jesus told His followers to rejoice because the Father knows our names. Then He added that our names are written in the Book of Life.

Several centuries before the angel Gabriel appeared to Mary, the prophet Isaiah spoke of the child she would have: *Immanuel* would be His name, meaning "God with us." But this Messiah was to be given a more specific name, instructed Gabriel. He was to be called *Jesus*, and His kingdom would never end.

As God's representatives on this earth, we do well to keep our good name, for we wear the name *Christian*. The name that matters most, however—and will for all eternity—is the name to whom all creation past, present, and future will bow. That name? Jesus.

I bless Your name, Lord Jesus, and thank You for calling me by name.

November 22

In His Glory

When Christ who is our life appears, then you also will appear with Him in glory.

Colossians 3:4 NIV

Eternity is already happening: this very moment is part of forever. And eternity is all around us, though like the sugar maple that pulls its sap inside and drops its leaves as winter approaches, eternity isn't always apparent in the present. But when the time is right, the truth of eternity manifests itself, just as the strong branches of the tree again become filled with leaves, evidencing the life within for all to see.

Christ is ever with us and in us, always working in the world as well as in the details of our lives. One day all the now-hidden work He is doing will be illuminated by His glory. Every one of His redeemed will be revealed: the magnificent light of Christ will be our sun, and the brightness of His face will be our warmth.

How incredible that God has chosen to share eternal life with every person who believes in Him. Like the joy of spring after a long winter, our delight will be unspeakable when our Lord returns to make all things new.

What a wondrous and wonderful thought: You, my risen King, will one day return in all Your glory. I long to see You.

Perfect Execution

For God was pleased to have all his fullness dwell in him, and through him to reconcile to himself all things, whether things on earth or things in heaven, by making peace through his blood, shed on the cross.

Colossians 1:19–20 NIV

Imagine the soldier's excitement as he approached his superior with a new idea. *An ideal way to keep subjects from rebelling,* he thought to himself. "We could construct simple wooden crosses and threaten to nail people to them," he told his commander. "A nail through each wrist…and another through both feet, one on top of the other. Death by suffocation will be agonizing, humiliating. Surely this threat of crucifixion would keep peace in our kingdom."

Efforts to institute and fine-tune this new style of execution soon began. It wasn't long before Rome was crucifying rebels, putting them to death publicly as a warning to others.

Isn't it interesting, though, that this form of punishment would be the very tool of forgiveness that God would use to reconcile sinners to Himself? What Rome intended as a horrifying instrument of death, God transformed into the way to abundant life. What the Caesars thought would keep peace in Rome was what God used to bring peace between Himself and mankind. Through the merciless and cruel cross, God poured out His mercy. Through this cruel form of execution, God executed His loving plan of salvation. For you. What a wonderful Savior.

Father God, I am astounded that You redeemed Rome's instrument of death by using it to give me life.

November 24

The God Who Calls

For this I was appointed a preacher and an apostle (I am telling the truth, I am not lying) as a teacher of the Gentiles in faith and truth.

1 Timothy 2:7 NASB

Author and pastor A. W. Tozer once said this about God's call to Christian service: "A call to the ministry is not a call to be holy, as if the fact of his being a minister would sanctify a man.…God makes a man holy by blood and fire and sharp discipline. Then he calls the man to some special work, and the man being holy makes that work holy in turn."

We usually equate a call to ministry with seminary degrees and ordinations. Those are valid and important, but the call of God on a man or woman's life takes place first and last in that person's heart. The drama of a Damascus Road experience like Paul's is not commonplace. But God's call to the ministry will take over one's heart, proving just as valid and, for the one called, just as verifiable as Paul's conversion from persecutor to preacher.

The proof of the calling is in the truth the person speaks, the actions the person takes, and the faithfulness the person exhibits in the face of adversity. God calls all of His people to ministry of some kind, and He has promised—through the power of His Holy Spirit—to be with each of us whatever hardships arise.

God, what a privilege to be involved in Your kingdom work. Keep me focused on You as I serve Your people.

November 25

Eternal Realities

Therefore, since we are receiving a kingdom that cannot be shaken, let us be thankful, and so worship God acceptably with reverence and awe, for our "God is a consuming fire."

Hebrews 12:28–29 niv

Scottish minister Robert Murray McCheyne once wrote, "Live near to God, and so all things will appear to you little in comparison to eternal realities."

The things of this world—as fleeting and illusory as they are—can seem so important and feel so urgent…and be so heartbreaking. The things of this world, however, are of little value, especially in light of eternity—the *real* reality.

What are some "eternal realities"? The kingdom of God is the ultimate eternal reality: it is a kingdom that cannot be shaken, a kingdom that will never fade away in the fine print of dusty history books. God's grace is another eternal reality—one we experience best when we stay near to Him. Finally, through the prism of God's grace, we see in every aspect of this life another eternal reality: God's love.

Pray today that the consuming fire that is our God burns away the world's dross that so easily distracts us. And may this fire purify our hearts and our motives, freeing us to worship, revere, and serve our eternal God.

Dear God, help me live with my heart focused on Your values. And may I give Your consuming fire freedom to do its purifying work in me.

Perfection

Such a high priest meets our need—one who is holy, blameless, pure, set apart from sinners, exalted above the heavens. Unlike the other high priests, he does not need to offer sacrifices day after day, first for his own sins, and then for the sins of the people. He sacrificed for their sins once for all when he offered himself.

HEBREWS 7:26–27 NIV

Being designated high priest over all of Israel was an incredible honor and a huge responsibility. The high priest's job was to make sure that the sins of the nation were confessed so they could be pardoned. Consequently, the priest carefully prepared for the annual Day of Atonement—the day when he would stand before God and offer an acceptable sacrifice for the sins of his countrymen. Of course, to stand before God as Israel's mediator, the priest's sins had to be accounted for as well. He himself must be holy and pure. And what if the high priest failed in this regard? What would become of the people's sins?

Thankfully, on this side of Jesus's death and resurrection on our behalf, we don't have to worry year after year if God will accept the high priest's offering, because Jesus Himself came to earth to serve as our perfect High Priest. Take some time to come before God's throne today.

Jesus, I will be forever grateful for Your willingness to do Your Father's will and die for a sinner such as me.

The Power behind Prayer

Confess your sins to each other and pray for each other so that you may be healed. The earnest prayer of a righteous person has great power and produces wonderful results.

JAMES 5:16 NLT

There can hardly be a more humbling exercise than confession. It's hard enough to recount our sins to a holy God, but admitting our failings to our friends, our rebelliousness to our colleagues, or our insensitivity to people we've hurt can send us to our knees as well.

Ironically, that's right where God wants you. A prayer on your knees is a sacred offering that moves heaven. As Irish writer, poet, and playwright Oscar Wilde rightly observed, "It is the confession, not the priest, that gives us absolution."

The Holy Spirit can do much with a heart that's broken and tender. He shapes our entreaties, supports them, directs them to the merciful Father, and gets results in a way that our indifferent, formal words never could.

A fervent prayer on our knees for others is another gift of grace. A blessed privilege that can move mountains.

Earnest prayer can be a painful commitment, but wonderful results rain down from heaven when we open ourselves to God's tender mercies. Out of His great love, He answers heartfelt prayers and so gives the world a glimpse of His glorious love.

Merciful Father, I boldly come before You, asking You to pour Your power and Your grace into the hearts of the people I love and into the situations I care about.

Good News

For you have been born again, but not to a life that will quickly end. Your new life will last forever because it comes from the eternal, living word of God. As the Scriptures say, "People are like grass; their beauty is like a flower in the field. The grass withers and the flower fades. But the word of the Lord remains forever." And that word is the Good News that was preached to you.

1 Peter 1:23–25 NLT

While doctors have moments when the news is good—"Yes, you're going to have a baby!" or "The surgery was successful"—there are plenty of times when they find themselves reporting painful realities: "I'm sorry, but it is cancer."

Doctors see firsthand the effects of aging on the human body, how it withers like grass and fades like flowers. But the Great Physician intervenes with good news: "You have been born again!" He says to one who has heard an earthly doctor's diagnosis, "and your new life will last forever!"

The spiritual reality doesn't always strike people as good news…at first. But it is a firm and enduring comfort based on God's Word, which does not wither and die. And as the physical strength of the infirm fails, those who open their hearts will find a steadfast peace that no illness can take away, promised by a God who is as eternal as His Word and who is intent on one day making all things new.

Let me lean on You, dear Lord, when difficult news comes my way.

What Love Is

This is how we know what love is: Jesus Christ laid down his life for us.

1 John 3:16 NIV

The rock band Foreigner expressed the heartfelt plea "I Want to Know What Love Is" in one of their hit songs of the 1980s. Love "gurus" are happy to offer an explanation of what love is, but the best answer doesn't come from a twenty-first-century self-help expert. Genuine love—selfless, serving, sacrificial love—is best illustrated in a single act on a hill two thousand years ago: when God sent His Son to die on a cross, taking on Himself the consequences of our sin.

Jesus laid down His life for us. Submitting to His Father's compassionate will, Jesus did not divert His eyes from Calvary. He did not turn back from His calling. When we needed redemption, Jesus stepped forward, onto the cross—and three days later, out of the tomb.

As the old hymn says, "What wondrous love is this!" In Jesus's sacrifice and the heavenly Father's offering of His Son, we learn the answer. Do you want to know what love is? In the cross, Jesus defined love for us forever.

May I never become numb to the cross—our enduring picture of selfless, serving, sacrificial, and saving love.

Hope for the Future

I know the plans I have in mind for you, declares the Lord; they are plans for peace, not disaster, to give you a future filled with hope.

Jeremiah 29:11 CEB

When the world presses in and our lives seem to be in total chaos, remembering God's love can be difficult. The more stressed and fearful we become, the more the temptation to seek answers in other places can feel like a craving hunger. We want help and answers. But no one knows us the way God does.

He has known us—and His plans for us—from the time of our conception (Jeremiah 1:5). Even when we don't know our own minds, He does. His designs for us are never against us. He sees the big picture, and His love and mercy will bring good in our lives, no matter how rough the journey is at this moment. He wants peace for us, and hope for our future.

God does not forget about us; His mercy and kindness continually surround us, even when it feels like life is completely out of control. When we remember that, when we rely on that, we can find that a calm peace will settle on us.

Lord, when life delivers chaos into our lives, help us remember that You only desire good for us. When we trust in You, we can have hope for our future.

The Lord Will Provide

Abraham answered, "God himself will provide the lamb for the burnt offering, my son." And the two of them went on together.

GENESIS 22:8 NIV

In 1942, when he was sent on a mission to deliver a message to General MacArthur, Eddie Rickenbacker's plane went down somewhere in the South Pacific. After the crash, he and seven other crew members quickly gathered food from the aircraft and climbed into life rafts. The food supply lasted only three days, and the crew began to fear the worst.

On the eighth day adrift at sea, Rickenbacker was asleep on the raft when he felt something on his head. A seagull had shown up, right there in the middle of the South Pacific. Capturing this surprise visitor and calling it dinner, the crew rationed out the meat and then used other parts of the bird as fish bait, which connected them to a food supply and allowed them to stay alive. After twenty-four days adrift, Rickenbacker and his crew were rescued and returned home.

Spiritually speaking, humanity shares a similar story. With sin's entry into the world, we found ourselves adrift, utterly lost at sea with no ability to rescue ourselves and starving to death spiritually. Some of us were numb to our sin; others numbed by hopelessness. Then—after hundreds of years of prophecies and seemingly out of nowhere—the Lord sent His perfect Son to rescue us from the certain death of our souls. Praise to the Almighty Father, who provided what we needed to return home to Him.

God, Your compassion for my lost condition and Your willingness to rescue me compels me to bow in worship.

A Holy Promise

He has declared that he will set you in praise, fame and honor high above all the nations he has made and that you will be a people holy to the LORD your God, as he promised.

DEUTERONOMY 26:19 NIV

There's something special about the word *promise*. In Old Testament Hebrew, *promise* denotes the connection between something spoken and specific action. When we *promise* to do something, that promise adds a special weight and significance to our words. It heightens the anticipation between the parties involved and deepens their commitment to each other.

God's promises are even more significant; His holiness adds weight to His words. When God makes a promise, He is not merely striking a bargain or committing to take a certain action. He is putting all of who He is on the line. His holiness seals the covenant. By extension, when we enter into the promises of God, we are made holy in an act of miraculous power that only a supernatural God could devise.

Your promises are precious to me. Remind me of them when doubt creeps in.

Now That's Good News!

Give thanks to the LORD, call on his name; make known among the nations what he has done. Sing to him, sing praise to him; tell of all his wonderful acts.

1 CHRONICLES 16:8–9 NIV

In the late eighteenth century, when smallpox was running rampant, Edward Jenner observed that milkmaids rarely came down with the illness. That's when Jenner proposed his theory that exposure to cowpox might keep one from catching smallpox—a theory that proved to be successful. Realizing what he had discovered, Jenner shared his good news with the world and saved many lives.

The gospel of Jesus is life-saving news as well. God found us in a broken state, drowning in our own sin. And even though our sin was against God Himself, He chose to rescue us, taking upon Himself our punishment and filling us with a hope that will last for all eternity. If there was ever good news worth sharing, this is it!

To be able to personalize this news, consider your own journey with God. Where were you when He found you—and where you would be today had He not? Surely this story of yours is worth sharing! So stop for a moment and let yourself be amazed at the gospel of Jesus. Let it put a smile on your face and a song in your heart—and then pass it on!

Lord, what You have done for me seems almost too good to be true. Help me tell this great story today to someone who needs to hear it.

Above the Sky

Be exalted, O God, above the heavens, and let your glory be over all the earth. Save us and help us with your right hand, that those you love may be delivered.

Psalm 108:5–6 NIV

Perhaps the most brilliant display our galaxy has to offer is found in the Earth's higher northern latitudes. The aurora borealis, more commonly known as "the northern lights," is an explosion of color. The light bursts forth in multicolored splendor so stunning that it takes your breath away.

From stars and planets to clouds and rainbows, meteors and lightning bolts, the heavens above have always captured man's attention. The psalmist, for instance, spoke of how the glory of the sky covers all the earth. But he also recognized that the sky's glory pales in comparison to the glory of its Maker. God is exalted *above* the heavens. The most spectacular of all created space is but a dim shadow of the magnificent One who created it.

Consider for a moment the most breathtaking sight you have ever seen—and know that God is greater still. His glory far surpasses everything in His glorious creation. Stand in awe!

Almighty God, I cannot even begin to comprehend the grandeur of Your glory. I stand in awe of what I do understand, and I marvel at what I do not.

God's Will

But as for me, God will redeem my life. He will snatch me from the power of the grave.

Psalm 49:15 NLT

We human beings often talk about God's will. When life is going well, we totally support the Lord's plan for us. When the road gets bumpy or flat-out painful, we're confused at best, despairing at worst, and hardly able to believe that the Almighty's will is good *or* perfect. Especially when we hear it talked about in connection with everything from disastrous earthquakes to the birth of a child.

What does the Bible teach about God's will? Psalm 49:15 sets forth two certainties. Will God give you that job promotion? What about good health in your older years? Will God open all the doors so your children can realize their hopes and dreams? Will He bless you with a satisfying marriage? To these questions, the answer is "Maybe."

What is certain about God's will is that He *will* redeem His children, and He *will* snatch you from the power of eternal death. To be specific, our God is mighty to save you from death and gracious to redeem your life—and generous with His blessings as all of life unfolds.

Your purposes are dependable and sure, Lord. May all my other concerns pale in comparison to this certainty.

Out of Nowhere

They spoke against God, saying, "Can God spread a table in the desert? When he struck the rock, water gushed out, and streams flowed abundantly. But can he also give us food? Can he supply meat for his people?

Psalm 78:19–20 NIV

Unlike fictional tales such as *The Swiss Family Robinson* or *Castaway*, most of the miraculous survival stories reported in the headlines involve short-term experiences in adverse conditions: "3 Days Lost at Sea" or "Stranded Hiker Found after Fifteen Days in Jungle."

As remarkable as it is that civilians ever find just enough resources to survive for several days, consider an event recorded in the Old Testament. The entire nation of Israel wandered in the desert wilderness for forty years—and they never suffered from a lack of provision. God made food fall from the sky and water flow out of a rock (Exodus 16–17). Their clothes did not wear out, nor did their feet swell (Deuteronomy 8:4).

You may not know where your next job offer or mortgage payment will come from, but God does. You may sometimes feel like a wanderer lost in the forest, but don't be afraid. God will give you what you need, and He will make it appear out of nowhere if He needs to. Your heavenly Father is a wonderful, all-sufficient God who takes care of His people, even preparing a table in the wilderness.

You have been faithful to meet my every need. What would I do without You?

From Every Direction

But You, O Lord, are a shield about me. My glory, and the One who lifts my head.

Psalm 3:3 NASB

The ancient Israelites lived in a world where enemy attacks were common, so God's children often had to arm themselves for battle. Much of their weaponry was primitive: they modified household articles and farming tools for fighting. The Philistines, on the other hand, had a monopoly on iron, and they had nearly perfected the art of weapon making. Going against this far better equipped Philistine army, the Israelites had to be alert and creative in battle.

Some Israelite soldiers used a full-body shield carried by a shield-bearer. The shield-bearer's only job was to locate the incoming arrows or swords and prevent them from reaching his soldier. But sometimes a shield-bearer couldn't react in time or failed to see an attack coming from behind. These shield-bearers were, after all, only human.

The Bible says that we have the ultimate shield-bearer in God Almighty. In fact, He is both the Shield-Bearer and the Shield. And His protection is perfect, for He is a shield around us. Our Lord Almighty literally puts Himself between us and the enemy to fight our battles. No matter what Satan hurls our way or what direction he attacks from, God is aware, and He will prevail.

Glorious God, thank You for protecting and defending me every day. I'm thankful You are stronger than whatever the enemy devises.

December 8

Let the Gathering Begin

Let the redeemed of the Lord say so, whom He has redeemed from the hand of the adversary and gathered from the lands, from the east and from the west, from the north and from the south.

Psalm 107:2–3 NASB

In ancient Jewish law, the act of redemption involved a time-honored rule of kinship. If a brother died, the surviving brother would repurchase that relative's property or marry his brother's widow. At its essence, this was an act of ransom or rescue.

Similarly, all humanity needs to be ransomed from the enemy and rescued from our separation from God. Individuals who have recognized their need for forgiveness and been saved have a particular reason to declare God's goodness: after all, our redemption from sin and death was not something any of us could accomplish. Only Holy God could redeem us through His miraculous power. And He was willing to cover the cost of this divine ransom with the life of His Son, Jesus Christ.

What a blessing to be among God's redeemed! And it's a blessing we are to share with those who have yet to find their hope in Jesus. "Let the redeemed of the Lord say so," the psalmist encouraged. What are you doing to "say so"? Remember that we speak not only with words but with our actions and our attitudes. Though our actions and attitudes only go so far, hopefully they go far enough for someone to ask, "What makes you different? Where do you find hope?"

O Lord, I ask You to direct me to people who need to hear my story of redemption—and then to provide me with the words that will reach their hearts.

The Ultimate Treasure Hunt

My son, if you accept my words and store up my commands within you, turning your ear to wisdom and applying your heart to understanding, if you call out for insight and cry aloud for understanding, and if you look for it as for silver and search for it as for hidden treasure, then you will understand the fear of the Lord and find the knowledge of God.

Proverbs 2:1–5 niv

Who can forget that great scene in *Raiders of the Lost Ark* when the bad guys open the lid to the Ark of the Covenant and release the mysteries of God? And who of us has not fantasized about being an Indiana Jones, traveling the globe to exotic places on exciting treasure hunts? Well, God invites us on a treasure hunt we can do from home. He encourages us to search for Him in His Word as if He were a hidden treasure, with the passion and focus and energy and drive we would invest in a hunt for silver or gold.

If you'll accept this invitation to adventure, the wisdom and the knowledge of God you'll gain is priceless. So turn your ear and apply your heart as you pursue your Redeemer God. Keep after Him no matter the obstacles you encounter along the way. The treasure you seek is God Himself, and the hunt is truly worthwhile.

Whet my appetite for You, that I might truly pursue You with a newfound intensity.

Who?

Who has scooped up the ocean in his two hands, or measured the sky between his thumb and little finger, who has put all the earth's dirt in one of his baskets, weighed each mountain and hill?

Isaiah 40:12 msg

The world's oceans have a total volume of about 322,280,000 cubic miles. Imagine the immense hands that are able to scoop up and hold that amount of water!

Our own Milky Way Galaxy is about 100,000 light years across. To measure that distance between one's thumb and little finger would require hands far bigger than we can imagine.

Gathering all the world's dirt would require quite a basket. And hands capable of not only gathering but also measuring that amount would be far more impressive than those of any superhero.

Question: Who has hands this immense, this capable?

Answer: The Almighty God of the Bible. Creator of all, He is the One who set an expanse between the waters by speaking it into existence. The One who hung the galaxies in their places. The One who first called the dry ground "land." Only the hands that actually formed creation could take its full measure and weigh it in the balance—and those hands are the powerful hands of our God.

Who can estimate Your power, Your scope, or Your abilities, Lord? You are above and beyond all limitations and imaginings.

Unyielding Glory

For my own sake, for my own sake, I do this.
How can I let myself be defamed? I will not yield my glory to another.

Isaiah 48:11 NIV

There's a moment in the popular anthem "Praise You" where the choir begins a quiet chant—"Wisdom and majesty, power and glory be unto Your holy name now and forever more." Over and over, stronger and stronger, the choir repeats the chant until it becomes almost a shout. And then the drums kick in.

It's an inspiring, powerful moment, and a great tribute to the holy name of the Lord.

People are inclined to elevate themselves, glorify children, worship rock stars and celebrities, and find other idols to worship. But God will secure His own honor and protect His own name at any cost. He works to bring all focus back to His wisdom and majesty, power and glory.

Just as our solar system requires a steady circling around the sun for its systems to function, so our lives must be lived in obedience and submission to the Lord God. Only when we are focused on His righteousness and glory do we truly live.

Lord of all, remind me to praise You not just with my heartfelt words but with a life that holds You at the center.

December 12

Servant and King

Yet it was the will of the Lord to crush him; he has put him to grief; when his soul makes an offering for guilt, he shall see his offspring; he shall prolong his days; the will of the Lord shall prosper in his hand. Out of the anguish of his soul he shall see and be satisfied; by his knowledge shall the righteous one, my servant, make many to be accounted righteous, and he shall bear their iniquities.

Isaiah 53:10–11 ESV

In antiquity, kings were constantly trying to expand the borders of their kingdom. Doing so meant conquering people and shedding much blood. Wanting to make his name great, a king would overpower a weaker nation and claim those subjects as his own.

King Jesus stands alone, for He found satisfaction in an altogether different form of victory. Dying on a sinner's cross even though He knew no sin, Jesus shed His own blood in order to bring people into His kingdom. And He didn't bring them in as His servants. His blood cleansed them from their sin and made them righteous, so His Father God welcomed them as His children.

Truly, Jesus was like no king the world had ever seen. He looked to the interests of others, not just His own. He bore burdens of sin that were not His to bear. Jesus, the gracious Servant-King, was crushed for those He could have ruled over from the start. There is no sovereign like Him!

Jesus, I'm humbled that You descended from Your place in the heavens to shed Your blood for me. Help me to serve as You served.

Hide and Seek

"Am I only a God nearby," declares the LORD, "and not a God far away...?

JEREMIAH 23:23 NIV

What was your best-ever hiding place when you played Hide and Seek as a kid? What's your favorite hiding place when you play Hide and Seek with your own kids? However many hours you've logged hiding and seeking, it probably didn't take you long to realize there is no absolutely safe place to hide from "It." Some people in the Bible didn't know that, but others did.

When they tasted the fruit God had forbidden them to eat and realized, to their great shame, that they were naked, Adam and Eve thought they could hide from God. Not possible.

Poet-king David knew and celebrated that truth with rhetorical questions, asking where one might hide from God. Answering his own question, David stated emphatically that God could see him wherever he was, from "the depths of the sea, to the wings of the dawn." David also recognized that God looked on his heart and knew his secret thoughts.

Yes, this is our God. He is the ultimate micro-observer: seeing our hearts, knowing our thoughts, and hearing even our silent prayers. And He is the sole macro-operator: holding the universe together, ruling every nation, choreographing history, and guiding our lives. The God of the Bible, our heavenly Father, is magnificent in all that He is—and there is absolutely no hiding from Him!

You know me so well, heavenly Father. I thank You that You will never lose sight of me!

Clouds of Dust

His way is in the whirlwind and the storm, and clouds are the dust of his feet.

Nahum 1:3 NIV

White and fluffy. Black and ominous. Cottony and wispy. Clouds come in all shapes, sizes, and colors, and as part of God's heavens, they declare His glory and can teach us about Him. Recognizing this fact was the Prince of Preachers, Charles Haddon Spurgeon, who spoke to thousands of Londoners every Sunday in the late nineteenth century. He had some thoughts about clouds after gazing at the sky one evening:

> What great things clouds are to us! There we see them moving through the skies! Then they rapidly increase till the whole sky turns black and a dark shadow is cast upon the world; we foresee the coming storm, and we tremble at the mountains of cloud, for they are great. Are they truly great things? No, they are only the dust of God's feet.

A cloud of peace or an ominous mass of terrifying power—both are merely the dust of the Father's feet. There is no need to be afraid when life's challenges loom large. God is greater. Far greater.

Whatever comes, Lord, help me not to fear but to simply trust in You.

This Little Light

You are the light of the world. A town built on a hill cannot be hidden. Neither do people light a lamp and put it under a bowl. Instead they put it on its stand, and it gives light to everyone in the house. In the same way, let your light shine before others, that they may see your good deeds and glorify your Father in heaven.

Matthew 5:14–16 NIV

Around 1920, Harry Dixon Loes penned the well-known children's Sunday school song "This Little Light of Mine." It is a simple way to teach children—and to remind grown-ups—about our responsibility to be God's light in the world.

The word for "light" in Greek means "to shine and manifest with luminesence." In the prologue to his Gospel, John used this word to describe the light that had come into the world, and it is the same word Jesus used to describe Himself. Into a world dark with sin, Jesus brought the light of salvation. He promised that everyone who followed Him would never have to walk in darkness again, and that promise still holds two thousand years later.

As we followers of Christ walk in the light of His truth and grace, we reflect His goodness for others to see. To God be the glory as we take our little light and "let it shine."

Instruct me in how to reflect Your glory in all that I do and say.

Every Angle

When he had finished speaking, he said to Simon, "Put out into deep water, and let down the nets for a catch." Simon answered, "Master, we've worked hard all night and haven't caught anything. But because you say so, I will let down the nets." When they had done so, they caught such a large number of fish that their nets began to break. So they signaled their partners in the other boat to come and help them, and they came and filled both boats so full that they began to sink. When Simon Peter saw this, he fell at Jesus' knees and said, "Go away from me, Lord; I am a sinful man!"

Luke 5:4–8 niv

Don Wheeler has spent nearly seventy years reeling in all kinds of fish. In 2009, this retired insurance director from England caught a 178-pound catfish. It was his one hundredth 100-pound-plus fish! No wonder he has been dubbed Britain's best angler.

On one occasion, Jesus performed a dazzling fishing exhibition of His own. He wasn't out to set any kind of personal record; instead, He wanted to make a point. A group of professional fishermen had fished all night with no success. Then Jesus, a carpenter, told them exactly what to do, and upon reluctantly taking His advice, the fishermen snagged the catch of their lifetime. The point Jesus made? *He is Lord of all things.* He is the Lord of fish and the Lord of those who catch them.

Jesus knows everything about fish and about fishermen. And He knows everything about you and your life too. He is not just Lord, but Lord of all.

My Lord and my God! Your blessings are beyond compare.

The Pure Power of the Word

You are already clean because of the word which I have spoken to you.

JOHN 15:3 NASB

A tough workout at the gym… A day of yardwork or window washing… A summertime camping trip when the dust settled everywhere even as the temperature rose… We all know what it feels like to be sweaty, hot, and dirty. At times like these, hitting the shower is definitely one of life's sweetest pleasures.

Another great blessing is to get clean in the sense that Jesus meant it. In that context, the washing was done in order to purify—a supernatural action far beyond the scope of soap and water. Later in John's narrative, Peter resisted having Jesus wash his feet until Jesus told him, "Unless I wash you, you have no part with me" (13:9). Hearing that, Peter requested a full bath!

It is one thing to be cleansed by regular water and quite another to be purified by the living Word of God and equipped to lead a life of holiness. Only God can wash the unclean heart. And only He has the miraculous, powerful, pure living water of forgiveness and eternal life.

I praise You for Your ability to cleanse me of my sin.

December 18

The Wonderful Way

Jesus answered, "I am the way and the truth and the life. No one comes to the Father except through me. If you really know me, you will know my Father as well. From now on, you do know him and have seen him."

John 14: 6–7 niv

If someone discovered a way to cure the common cold once and for all, the world would rush to the closest pharmacy. If the medical community developed the one definitive way to kill every cancer cell a body could produce, patients in cancer wards would clamor for that life-saving drug.

When we are desperate for solutions, we gladly respond when the one sure way to what we need is made clear. Or do we?

Consider that the entire Old Testament tells of God's people seeking a way to maintain and often restore their relationship with God. In the New Testament accounts, we see that Jesus provided exactly that avenue to reconciliation with God. But He didn't just explain the way; He *is* the Way. *The* Way.

Seeing Jesus the Son, He explained, is seeing God the Father. Wonder of wonders, we can not only know the eternal God better, but we have access to Him through Jesus. Yes, by knowing Jesus, we can know the Father.

I am in awe that You have made Yourself known. Stop me when I take that for granted.

One of Us

The Word became flesh and made his dwelling among us. We have seen his glory, the glory of the one and only Son, who came from the Father, full of grace and truth.

JOHN 1:14 NIV

In 2007, Katie Davis was enjoying her life. A homecoming queen who drove a yellow convertible, Katie lived very comfortably with her family outside of Nashville. During the summer between high school and college, she decided to go on a short-term mission trip to Uganda—and that trip turned out to be anything but short-term. Working closely with orphan girls, Katie began to know and love these precious children, and she made a radical decision: she would make Uganda her home and become a mother to these kids. Leaving conveniences and comfort behind, the eighteen-year-old rented a home in the small Ugandan village where she is now the adoptive mother to thirteen girls. Her selfless example has inspired people all around the world.

Katie Davis's actions offer a compelling parallel to what Jesus did. The Prince of heaven left His royal throne and made His dwelling among us. He settled in, embraced a foreign life, and chose to love us—orphans separated from our heavenly Father. May we, like Katie and like our Lord Himself, be willing to leave our comfort zone in order to radically love with the heart of Jesus.

Enable me to live my life as a thank You for Your grace and love.

December 20

Superstition Ain't the Way

Friends, why are you doing this? We too are only human, like you. We are bringing you good news, telling you to turn from these worthless things to the living God, who made the heavens and the earth and the sea and everything in them.

Acts 14:15 NIV

"When you believe in things that you don't understand, then you suffer. Superstition ain't the way." Stevie Wonder's hit song "Superstition" dates back to the seventies, but its message is timeless: belief in the wrong things brings suffering.

Understandably, superstition arises around things we human beings can't explain. That's one of the times we are tempted to create idols. We long to worship something greater than ourselves. The people Paul was talking to in Acts 14, for instance, tried to make *him* a god and offer sacrifices in his name.

Like those people, we get sidetracked by the world's vanities and lose our focus on God. Yet hear the good news the apostle Paul proclaimed: nothing manmade can compete with the glory and wonder of God. In fact, nothing even *God*-made can compete with the glory and wonder of the Creator. He who made heaven and earth and everything in them—He alone is worthy of our worship and praise!

Lord, please work in my heart so that I may worship You and You alone.

December 21

The Center of It All

For from him and through him and to him are all things.
To him be glory forever. Amen.

Romans 11:36 ESV

We learn early on in school that all the planets in our solar system orbit the sun. The reason they do this—besides the fact that God made the solar system that way—has to do with the gravitational strength of the sun. Its pull is so strong that the planets cannot escape. What's more, if the planets were not moving through space, they would be pulled directly into the sun.

God is like the sun in this regard: everything orbits—or is supposed to orbit—around Him. As the great Creator of all things and the Sovereign over all creation, He has a gravitational pull that draws everything—living or nonliving, seen or unseen—to Him.

You are part of that *everything*. Do you feel drawn to your Creator? Do you live your life with Him at the center? Let your heart be drawn to God today as you think about His character, as you worship Him, and as you stand in awe of Him and His creation. Let Him be the center of your universe.

I long to live my life with You at the center. Keep me focused on You.

What the World Needs

Love hurts nobody: therefore love is the answer to the Law's commands.

Romans 13:10 PHILLIPS

Over and over again, Scripture presents flesh-and-blood characters essentially asking, "What's the meaning of life?" That's also the question that most of humanity has been asking since the dawn of time. To that universal question, Jesus responded by calling people to love God and to love their neighbors as they love themselves. And Romans 13:10 is another reminder of the answer to mankind's question: *love* is the meaning of life.

What may not be apparent, however, is that love involves more than being devoted to the holy but unseen God. It involves caring for our neighbors too (read: family, coworkers, church members, neighbors, other team parents, etc.)—even the ones who are hard to like. Thankfully, God's Spirit in us and with us is a transforming presence: He enables us to love with God's love, to treat people the way we want to be treated, and to extend mercy in the same way that God has been merciful to us. We fulfill all of the Old Testament law when we love the way He loves us.

Create in me the type of love that points others to You and Your life-changing love.

Helping Hands

And in their prayers for you their hearts will go out to you,
because of the surpassing grace God has given you.
Thanks be to God for his indescribable gift!

2 Corinthians 9:14–15 NIV

The first-century church in Jerusalem was poverty stricken. Never quite sure where their next meal would come from, these believers came to learn much about the way God provides for His people. Specifically, when Christians in surrounding regions heard about the hardship of the Jerusalem believers, they emptied their own pockets to send relief.

Maybe you've been blessed to experience God helping His people through His people. The Lord still works through His servants to bring relief to the suffering of others. He prompts Christians to go out into the world to provide health care and education to the less fortunate. Slave trade, sex trafficking, homelessness, and hunger are fought daily by those who claim allegiance to Jesus.

When Jesus taught His disciples to love one another, He meant for us to do so in tangible, world-changing ways. People are helped and God is glorified when we obey. So when you see hospitals, orphanages, and health-care clinics founded and operated by the people of God, remember that you are seeing God's gracious hands at work. He does wonderful things through His people.

In return for the times You have provided for me through Your people, please show me how to pay it forward.

What's in a Name?

She will give birth to a son, and you are to give him the name Jesus, because he will save his people from their sin.

Matthew 1:21 NIV

Jesus was a common name among the Jews. It was the Greek form of a Hebrew name: its original and full form is *Jehoshua*, which was usually shortened to *Joshua*. The name is derived from the verb that means "to save." And this was the name Gabriel instructed Mary to give the baby she would soon conceive by the power of the Holy Spirit (Luke 1:31).

But Jesus was not the first of God's servants to be named before birth. Among others were Isaac, Ishmael, Moses, Solomon, and Josiah. Each man held a significant place in the memory of the Jewish community as the faithful waited for the long-promised Messiah. Mary's song of praise (Luke 1:46-55) suggests that she apparently connected some of these dots as she pondered the name *Jesus*: "He will save. In my womb is the One who will save us. Messiah."

Even two thousand years later, we marvel at the way God's plan for our redemption unfolded, at the many ancient prophecies fulfilled, and at His incredible attention to detail. What a wondrous plan to save His people! That baby in the manger would one day and then throughout eternity reign as King of kings and Lord of lords. Hallelujah! Christ has come!

Jesus, from the glory of heaven to the filth of a manger, You chose to take this journey out of love. Thank You, my Savior.

Glory in the Highest

Suddenly, the angel was joined by a vast host of others—the armies of heaven—praising God and saying, "Glory to God in highest heaven, and peace on earth to those with whom God is pleased."

LUKE 2:13–14 NLT

France, Poland, Australia, New Zealand, Canada, South Africa, Britain, the Soviet Union, the United States of America, India, China, Belgium, Czechoslovakia, Brazil, the Netherlands, Ethiopia, Mexico, Yugoslavia, Norway, and Greece. Quite a list, isn't it? These countries comprised the Allies of World War II; together their armies opposed the Axis powers that threatened to control the world.

In a very real sense, the Allies were the armies of earth. Powerful, mighty, and fighting for freedom from tyranny, they prevailed. Even so, this powerful fighting force had nothing on the armies of heaven. Its soldiers are vested with power for eternity, allied with the powerful Trinity, and committed to Jesus's mission of reconciliation between God and humanity. And this immortal army gathered on that blessed night long ago to celebrate Jesus's birth. "Glory to God! Glory to God in highest heaven!" was their song of praise.

Yes! Glory to God, who lives in highest heaven, and glory to His Son, who came as a baby but would one day ascend to His heavenly throne and rule as King. Glory now and forever!

Together with all the armies of heaven, I sing, "Glory to God in highest heaven!" Glory to the newborn King!

December 26

Rewriting the Script

For the message of the cross is foolishness to those who are perishing, but to us who are being saved it is the power of God.

1 Corinthians 1:18 NIV

We know what we want in a hero, and we have definite ideas about how the script should go. Of course, heroes will struggle against insurmountable odds, but in the end we want them to overcome. A hero who dies may be a martyr or a saint, but that's not a very satisfying ending. We like heroes who *win*. And some "happily ever after" doesn't hurt!

Jesus has been a hero to generations of His followers, yet He didn't look the part on His way to Calvary. Instead, the crowd saw a failure, a fool: the man who had promised great things was dying on a cross between two criminals.

The people of Jerusalem saw in this bleeding and stumbling Jesus of Nazareth someone who had lost the fight. But that is not the end of the story. Christ's death and resurrection rewrote the script we prefer for our heroes. This divine script transcends all human expectation as it reveals the miraculous, saving power of the eternal God.

You were the One who changed the course of history—and who changed the course of my life. I praise You for the power of Your cross.

No Secret

It's in Christ that we find out who we are and what we are living for.
Long before we first heard of Christ and got our hopes up, he had his eye on us,
had designs on us for glorious living, part of the overall purpose
he is working out in everything and everyone.

Ephesians 1:11–12 MSG

Having sold over twenty million copies and now available in forty-six languages, the runaway success of the 2006 bestseller *The Secret* reveals the intensity of humanity's search for significance and happiness. Based on what the author calls "the law of attraction," the book taps into our universal longings to find meaning, purpose, and joy in life.

But the real secret—the truth—about life's purpose was shared two thousand years ago in the best-selling book ever, the Bible. *The Message* Bible reveals this truth with just two words: "In Christ."

Only in Christ can we truly find the meaning and purpose that we so desperately seek. Jesus Christ shows us both who we are (God's beloved children who have strayed) and what we are living for (to glorify and enjoy Him forever.) Only when the God of heaven is our foundation will we find meaning and purpose as well as direction. The beauty here is that God had His eyes on us long before we were even born, and His glorious love is not at all a secret. God openly loves humanity so that all can see. It just takes looking to the cross.

My relationship with You, Lord God, gives my life purpose and meaning, and I am grateful.

Solid Rock

Our prayers for you are always spilling over into thanksgivings. We can't quit thanking God our Father and Jesus our Messiah for you! We keep getting reports on your steady faith in Christ, our Jesus, and the love you continuously extend to all Christians.

Colossians 1:3–4 msg

One of the virtues that has been appreciated through the centuries is constancy, also known as steadfastness. *Steadfastness* means "dependability spread over time"; *steadfastness* means "keeping steady." And this virtue can enhance everything from the marriage covenant to parenting styles to efforts at peace and justice around the globe. But steadfastness does not come naturally.

The power of Jesus Christ is key to a believer's steadfastness in matters of faith as well as in everyday responsibilities and ongoing relationships. No matter what life brings us, what circumstances we find ourselves in, or what tomorrow holds, we can be sure-footed and confident when we are standing on the solid Rock of Jesus Christ. Standing on the Rock means trusting in His sacrificial death on the cross, relying on His truth and the Holy Spirit to guide us, and finding in Him a hope for life everlasting.

Jesus longs to be your solid Rock if He isn't already. All other ground is sinking sand.

When all around me is shifting sand, You are my solid Rock. That makes all the difference.

December 29

Knocked Out by God's Love

Behold what manner of love the Father has bestowed upon us,
that we should be called the children of God!

1 John 3:1 NKJV

In many full-contact sports, a knockout blow ends the fight. Interestingly, that kind of power is the implied meaning of the word "bestowed." In its wider application, *bestowed* means "to smite with power," but too often the meaning is watered down as if that word serves only to remind us of how expansive God's love is. God's love is indeed expansive, but it's far more.

This love comes from the Creator of the universe who wants us to know Him as a loving Father. This love is of a quantity and quality that can "smite" us. After all, God's wondrous love has no limits, no length, no breadth, depth, or height. It cannot be measured. It is indescribable.

So behold God's love for you. Take notice. Look on it with wonder. Be astonished. Meditate on this literally incomprehensible love that is beyond compare. What a wonderful blessing—to be smitten by God's lavish grace and love!

I am incredulous at the power of Your love for me.

December 30

Love above All

Above all, love each other deeply, because love covers over a multitude of sins. Offer hospitality to one another without grumbling. Each of you should use whatever gift you have received to serve others, as faithful stewards of God's grace in its various forms.

1 Peter 4:8–10 NIV

"If you judge people, you have no time to love them." Those wise words are accredited to Mother Teresa, and their implication is that when love takes over, it covers a multitude of sins—including our destructive, judgmental attitudes.

God showed us what it looks like: love takes over, love covers, love acts. Consider His works: God sent Jesus. Jesus laid down His life in fulfillment of God's design. We believers obey Jesus's admonition to love God and to love our neighbors. Yes, love acts.

But love is not comprised of just occasional efforts; it is perpetual action. It requires imagination, endurance, perseverance, commitment, and forgiveness. We often find it much easier to grumble, find fault, be inhospitable, refuse to serve, and deny using the spiritual gifts God has given us for His kingdom work. But those words "above all" in 1 Peter 4:8 should rouse us from any spiritual complacency.

So, loving Him and loving each other is God's highest priority for His people. Love motivated God to act on our behalf, and even today, love is God's amazing life-changing power in our hearts.

O God, Your bountiful love covers all my sins. Let me never forget to love You and love my neighbors with all my heart.

Undying Light

I did not see a temple in the city, because the Lord God Almighty and the Lamb are its temple. The city does not need the sun or the moon to shine on it, for the glory of God gives it light, and the Lamb is its lamp.

Revelation 21:22–23 niv

Romance, mystery, and wonder surround the moon. And why not? The moon is the only natural satellite of the earth. Once a month, it completes its orbit, its angle slightly changing, which creates the illusion of a change in shape. What's more, the gravitational pull between the moon and the earth has a huge effect on our planet: it causes the oceans to ebb and flow, creating high and low tides.

What sky-gazers might find surprising is that the apostle John pointed to a glorious future and a city that will need neither sun nor moon. The risen Savior, Jesus Christ, will be the Source of energy, a Source that will never fade or dim. The glory of God will be our everlasting light; no other source will be necessary.

On the cross, Jesus—who described Himself as the Light of the world (John 8:12)—defeated the power of darkness once and for all. By the power of His Spirit, may you walk in that light today, tomorrow, and always.

You are the light of the world, Jesus. You are all I need now and forever.

Ellie Claire
Hachette Book Group
1290 Avenue of the Americas, New York, NY 10104
ellieclaire.com

First edition: October 2018

Contributing writers: Henry O. Arnold, John Blase, Brett Burleson, Lynn Jones Green, Beverly Darnall Mansfield, Christine Schaub

Print book interior design by Bart Dawson.

ISBN: 978-1-63326-207-2 (softcover)

Printed in China
RRD-S
10 9 8 7 6 5 4 3 2